✻ The Disabled Schoolchild

THE DISABLED SCHOOLCHILD

A study of integration in primary schools

ELIZABETH M. ANDERSON

METHUEN & CO LTD
11 New Fetter Lane, London EC4P 4EE

First published 1973 by Methuen & Co Ltd
11 New Fetter Lane, London EC4
Reprinted 1975
© 1973 Elizabeth M. Anderson
Printed Offset Litho in Great Britain by
Cox & Wyman Ltd, Fakenham, Norfolk

ISBN (hardbound) 0 416 78180 2
ISBN (paperback) 0 416 78190 X

Distributed in the USA by
HARPER & ROW PUBLISHERS INC.
BARNES & NOBLE IMPORT DIVISION

Contents

Acknowledgements

The author and publishers would like to thank Her Majesty's Stationery Office for permission to reproduce statistical material from *The Health of the Schoolchild* (1972) in Figure 1.1, Tables 1.1, 1.2, 1.3, 1.4, and appendices C.1 and C.2.

Foreword

by Professor Jack Tizard

This is an excellent book. Miss Anderson is concerned with the complex educational and social problems of children who are physically disabled. She takes as her starting point the current educational doctrine, to which we all subscribe, that 'no handicapped child should be sent to a special school who can be satisfactorily educated in an ordinary school' and she examines its implications. How does it and how can it work out in practice? Is the concept of integration educationally valid, or is it something that sounds enlightened only to those who have not examined it in detail? What demands are placed upon a school which puts a severely disabled child into an ordinary class, and what extra facilities does a classroom teacher require to deal competently and sympathetically with his problems? Can the handicapped child himself cope educationally and socially in an ordinary school? What are the attitudes of his non-handicapped peers towards him? What about contacts between home, school and the medical services? What lessons for educational policy can we learn from the attempts being made by some local educational authorities in this country, and in a much more systematic way in Scandinavia, to provide special education in ordinary schools and classes?

All of us have opinions on these matters, but for the most part our knowledge is limited and our views are not well based. Moreover, as this study shows, the conventional wisdom is a pretty poor guide to the planning of services. Thus, to take only one example of the findings presented here, the severity of a child's physical handicap bears little or no relation to his educational progress in an ordinary classroom, to his social adjustment in it or to his popularity among his classmates. A much more significant factor, one which however is not represented in the current DES 'categories' of handicapped pupils, is whether or not the brain is involved in the handicap. It is children with disorders affecting the central nervous system who present the greatest educational problems in ordinary schools – and for that matter in special schools also.

Miss Anderson's data come from an intensive study of ninety-nine moderately or severely disabled children who are being educated in ordinary primary schools. Interviews with parents and teachers were also carried out, and a control group of ordinary classmates of the handicapped children was also examined to provide a check on the validity of many of the findings. The study includes a wealth of case material which adds to its richness.

The book is however, more than a research report, for Miss Anderson draws upon her wide knowledge of the field to present the *educational issues* which confront the handicapped child, his family and the educational and social services which help them to cope with education and with life. One of the great merits of the book is that it recognizes that there is no one way to achieve integration. Thus it presents in some detail many examples of different ways of solving the problems of providing adequate educational services, in different contexts and using different resources.

The type of educational provision, whether in special school, special class or ordinary class, sets the boundaries to the handicapped child's environment. It is for this reason that many parents of handicapped children and many voluntary bodies concerned with their wellbeing are pressing local authorities to do more than has been done in the past to make it possible for handicapped children to be educated alongside their ordinary peers. We see today that what appeared out of the question a decade or two ago is perfectly feasible: many severely disabled children can actually enjoy and profit from and prefer an education alongside ordinary classmates if conditions are right.

This being so, the proposals for special education in the white paper *Education: a framework for expansion* are disappointing. The government is proposing 'a rapid acceleration of the special school building programme' from £11 million to £19 million over the next four years. No mention is made however of provision in ordinary schools and nothing is said about research which might suggest alternative forms of educational provision for handicapped children. At a time when new concepts of special education are becoming more and more widely accepted, the white paper offers only old recipes.

Perhaps one reason why so little money is invested in educational research is that education is itself much concerned with the quality of life, with the realization of potential, with personal fulfilment and social adjustment. These are subjective and elusive concepts: a good education, like good health, is difficult to measure or to evaluate. However, poor educational practices, like poor health services, are easier to describe in unambiguous terms, and are often easy to remedy. And so it is here. The examples of poor educational practice and of clumsy or thoughtless handling of parents and children which Miss Anderson quotes (although she does not dwell on these) should make us all review our practice in order that we may avoid these things in future.

The pattern of research and evaluation described here is one which is relevant to special education as a whole. Most of the issues which confront the physically handicapped child also face the maladjusted, the educationally subnormal, the epileptic, the mentally handicapped, the blind, the deaf and children with speech defects. What we need if we are to improve the educational services for all handicapped children are carefully conducted evaluations of the varieties of current practice, and systematic, area-based applications, with appropriate and adequate evaluation, of different strategies of educational practice.

Author's Acknowledgements

My greatest debt is to the National Fund for Research into Crippling Diseases which provided the financial support for the entire research programme.

Next I must thank all those who participated, in particular the school health service departments and the local education authorities who cooperated so readily in giving me access to their records and in providing facilities for the study; the head teachers and class teachers who welcomed me into their schools and gave me a great deal of time and information; and above all, the parents and children without whose help this study could not have been carried out.

Among my colleagues at the Institute of Education, University of London, I should especially like to thank Professor Jack Tizard for his invaluable help and encouragement in the planning of the study and at all its stages. I am also grateful to Mrs Frances Good for advice on the statistical aspects and to Dr Simon Haskell for many informal discussions.

My warm thanks go to the many other individuals who gave me help and advice, in particular to my Swedish friends and hosts, Kerstin Janis-Brieditis and Ulf Lekemo for organizing most of my visits there, and to Dr Rosemary Begg and Michael Schlesinger for reading and commenting so helpfully on large parts of the manuscript. To Professor Vernon Mallinson of Reading University I owe an earlier debt, since it was his book, *None Can be Called Deformed* (Heinemann, 1956) which first kindled my interest in this area.

Finally I am very grateful to my secretarial assistants, Vivien Adams who helped me during the early stages of the study, especially with the testing and test scoring, and Rhonda Freeman who in the later stages gave a great deal of help with the processing and analysis of the data as well as typing the whole manuscript.

*   *   *

I am indebted to the Controller of HMSO for permission to reproduce the tables from *The Health of the School Child* (1972) and also to the College of Special Education for allowing me to base chapter 9 on my own booklet *Guide Lines for Teachers No. 10: Making Ordinary Schools Special* (1971).

I Delimiting the Problem

Chapter 1 · The Issues at Stake

*'No handicapped child should be sent to a special school
who can be satisfactorily educated in an ordinary school'*
Circular 276, Ministry of Education, 25 June 1954

This book is about the integration of physically handicapped (PH)
children in ordinary primary schools, and the statement above
which was made almost twenty years ago still summarizes official
policy. Here are two further statements, both from influential
sources:

1967: Extract from the Plowden Report (Central Advisory
Council for Education [England], 1967):

Nearly all our witnesses supported this policy [the placement of
PH children in ordinary schools where possible] and we are in
agreement with it. A handicapped child who will spend his life in
the society of normal people and often in competition with them
must learn to accept his disabilities and his differences. . . . The
unnecessary segregation of the handicapped is neither good for
them nor for those with whom they must associate. They should
be in the ordinary school wherever possible.

1970: Extract from *Living with Handicap: the report of a working
party on children with special needs* (ed. Younghusband
et al., 1970):

Ideally we should provide each child with the kinds of special
help he needs and do so with the minimum degree of separation
from his normal fellows and the minimum disturbance of normal
family life. . . . We start from the assertion that wherever possible
they should be educated in an ordinary school. But we have to
consider deeply what we mean by 'wherever possible'. . . .
There are many children in special schools who could be
educated in ordinary schools if resources were organized to cater

for them . . . some local education authorities have taken steps towards this end, at least in relation to certain handicapped groups and as a supplement to special school provision.

[Overall] . . . we welcome the move towards educating handicapped children in ordinary schools, although the question whether a child should be educated in an ordinary school rather than a special school is complex.

These statements represent the views of leading professionals from all disciplines. They comprise a consistent reiteration of laudable ideals. But are they anything more than this? How much positive action has been taken over the last twenty years in order to translate these ideals into reality? Are more opportunities in the mainstream of education available for PH children now than in 1954? Younghusband *et al.* (1970) state that some local authorities have taken steps towards organizing resources to cater for handicapped children in ordinary schools, at least in relation to certain handicapped groups and as a supplement to special school provision. But how many local authorities? Have they had any encouragement or advice from the Department of Education and Science? How carefully planned have been the 'steps' they have taken? Have they involved as substantial a financial commitment as has special school provision? Should special school provision not provide a supplement to ordinary school provision, rather than the other way round? Why are new special schools still being built in areas already well served by these? Could not the same resources be invested instead in special provision in the ordinary schools?

Undoubtedly there is a growing interest in this country in the possibility of educating more PH children in ordinary schools, and this trend shows signs of gathering momentum. Increasing numbers of authorities are experimenting with alternatives to special school placement; the Department of Education and Science has just carried out a survey of PH children in ordinary schools (DES, 1972); the question is sometimes debated in the Press and on television; smallscale research projects related to the issue are being carried out in the colleges and institutes of education. But these are still only trends and it is quite possible that at least in some areas the *status quo*, with its emphasis on provision in special schools, will be maintained. It is also conceivable that there could be a very rapid swing in the other direction, although this seems extremely unlikely.

What is more likely is that a variety of *ad hoc* provisions in ordinary schools will be made here and there, often on rather an unplanned, halfhearted basis. This could easily become true of the development of special classes for PH children. Should this happen it will not be surprising if they prove inferior to special schools. If our expressed desire to keep PH children within the normal community is a serious one we must commit ourselves actively to making available in the ordinary schools resources similar, in terms of money and expertise to those which have hitherto gone almost entirely into the special schools, and our attitude towards ordinary school placement must change from one of 'we can't do it because . . .', to one of 'we can do it if . . .'.

The size of the problem

Before discussing these issues it is important to try to establish the size of the problem. How prevalent are handicapping conditions in England and, in particular, how large is the physically handicapped group? At the beginning of 1971 there were 7,649,470 children in maintained and non-maintained schools (including nursery schools) in England (Institute of Municipal Treasurers and Accountants, 1971). The number of children who were actually receiving special educational treatment, or awaiting places was at that time 116,677, roughly 1·52 per cent of the total school population. This included children from the ten separate categories of handicapped children set out in the handicapped pupils and school health service regulations (1945), the number of children in each category being shown in the figure below.

As this shows, physically handicapped children constitute the third largest category of handicapped children. There are, however, great regional variations in the number ascertained as needing special educational treatment. In January 1968, for example, the overall incidence rate in England of PH children receiving special educational treatment or awaiting places was 1·57 per 1,000 of the school population but this varied from a figure as high as 2·04 per 1,000 in Greater London to only 1·10 per 1,000 in the eastern region (Department of Education and Science, 1969). These differences can perhaps be accounted for by such factors as the shortage of staff to do the assessments, different provision of special schools and classes, and different ascertainment rates reflecting different views on what

FIGURE I.I. *Children receiving special educational treatment or awaiting places at 31 December 1970* (From *Health of the School Child*, 1972)

Educationally subnormal : 68126

Maladjusted : 14 534

Physically handicapped : 12 057

Delicate : 8 476

Partially hearing : 4 654

Deaf : 3 938

Partially sighted : 2 422

Blind : 1 232

Epileptic : 859

Speech defects : 379

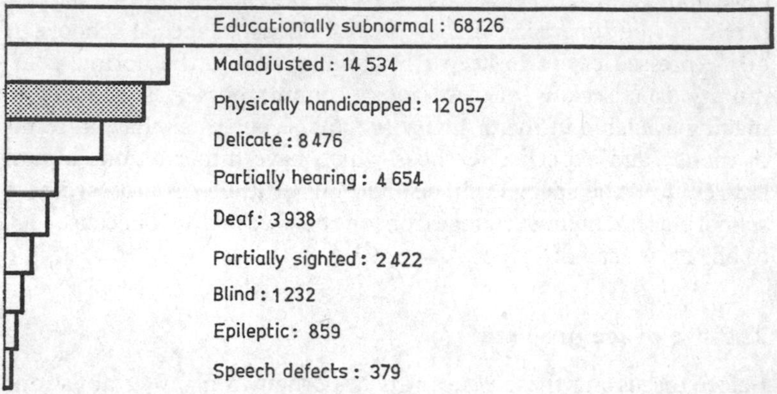

constitutes a handicap necessitating special school or special class placement.

Where were the 12,057 PH children who were receiving special educational treatment in January 1971 being educated? The main types of placement are shown in Table 1.1 below.

TABLE I.I. *Placement of PH children receiving or awaiting special educational treatment in January 1971* (From *Health of the School Child*, 1972)

Type of provision	No.	%
Requiring places in special schools	741	6·8
Day special schools (maintained and non-maintained)	6636	55·0
Boarding special schools (maintained and non-maintained)	2416	20·0
On registers of independent schools	464	3·8
In special classes or units not forming part of special schools	228	1·9
Being educated in hospitals or in homes	235	1·9
Being educated in other groups	355	2·9
Being educated at home	922	7·6
TOTAL CHILDREN	12057	100·0

Day special school placement is thus the main form of special provision in England, while boarding schools take a further one in five
PH children. Only a minute proportion (1·9 per cent) are being educated in special classes.

So far we have only been considering the number of children who
have actually been ascertained as needing special educational treatment. The overall prevalence rate of handicapping conditions is of
course very much higher. The most recent findings of the National
Child Development study (Davie *et al.*, 1972) suggest that 'by
the age of seven, almost two in every 100 children had a severe
defect, even before including defects of the special senses or the
more common handicap of moderate or mild retardation', while
the rate suggested by the 1964–5 surveys of 9–11 year olds on
the Isle of Wight (Rutter, Tizard and Whitmore, 1970) was even
higher.

Although the numbers of PH children receiving special educational treatment in special schools have been known for many years,
very little recognition has been given until recently to the fact that
there were also large numbers of PH children being educated in
ordinary schools. A recent Department of Education and Science
survey (DES, 1972) indicated that there were at least 10,200 such
children in ordinary maintained schools in England (a rate of 1·3 per
1,000 of the maintained school population). Details were obtained
about the types of schools the children attended, and the extent to
which they were visited by school doctors, nurses, therapists and
others, as well as about the nature of the defects, the presence of
incontinence, the provision of mobility and other aids, and of physiotherapy, speech therapy and transport to and from home. 'Considerable' regional variations were noted, 'depending to some extent on
the availability of day special school provision and whether it was a
rural or urban area'.

Of these 10,200 PH children, 66·10 per cent were in primary
schools, 33·42 per cent in secondary schools and only 0·48 per
cent in nursery schools. The different types of disabilities found
and their distribution in the various types of schools are shown
in Table 1.2 below. The total figure of 11,054 (rather than
10,200) which is shown reflects the fact that some children suffered
from more than one disability and so were recorded more than
once.

TABLE I.2. *Prevalence of disabilities in various types of schools, survey of physically handicapped children in ordinary schools, 1969–70, England* (From *Health of the School Child,* 1972)

	1	2	3	4
Disability	Nursery	Primary	*All secondary schools*	*All maintained schools*
Limbs: upper, lower, talipes and dislocated hips	11	1 675	702	2 388
Heart defects: rheumatic or congenital	5	1 435	671	2 111
'Others'	7	930	558	1 495
Cerebral palsy	15	1 005	442	1 462
Spina bifida	5	598	186	789
Post poliomyelitis	—	140	392	532
Perthe's disease	—	344	112	456
Muscular dystrophy and atrophy	2	189	73	264
Achondroplasia and other forms of dwarfing	3	184	66	253
Hydrocephalus: without myelomeningocele	2	210	34	246
Haemophilia and Christmas disease	—	152	92	244
Scoliosis	3	126	97	226
Amputations: upper and lower limbs	—	109	95	204
Rheumatoid arthritis	—	103	96	199
Osteomyelitis	—	52	41	93
Fragilitas ossium	—	44	22	66
Tuberculosis of bones and joints	—	11	15	26
TOTAL (DISABILITIES)	53	7 307	3 694	11 054

It is useful to ask how far this pattern reflects the situation in the special schools, and a comparison is made in Table 1.3 below.

TABLE 1.3. *Comparison of the types of physical disabilities found in ordinary and special schools at January 1971* (Figures taken from *Health of the School Child*, 1972)

Nature of disability	Total no. of children	Children in all special schools		Children in ordinary maintained schools	
		No.	%*	No.	%*
Cerebral palsy	4294	2832	66·0	1462	34·0
Spina bifida	2256	1467	65·0	789	35·0
Heart disease (congenital and rheumatic)	2805	694	24·7	2111	75·3
Muscular dystrophy	797	533	66·9	264	33·1
Congenital deformities of the limbs	2848	460	16·2	2388	83·8
Post poliomyelitis	844	312	37·0	532	63·0
Haemophilia	433	189	43·6	244	56·4
Perthe's disease	601	145	24·1	456	75·9
Miscellaneous physical handicaps	4721	1913	40·5	2808	59.5
TOTAL	19 599	8 545	43·6	11 054	56·4

* percentage of total children with each type of disability found in special school or ordinary school

(This table does not show the distribution of handicaps among a further 3,512 children awaiting special educational treatment or being provided with this in places other than special schools, but the pattern of handicaps in this group is likely to resemble that of the special school group.)

The figures show that the largest group of PH children found in special schools are the cerebral-palsied, the spina bifida children, those with heart diseases and those with muscular dystrophy, in that order, whereas in the ordinary schools the largest group comprises children with congenital abnormalities followed by those with heart diseases while the cerebral-palsied and those with spina bifida take third and fourth places.

In the case of certain handicaps, ordinary school placement is more likely. Four in five of those with congenital limb abnormalities were in ordinary schools, three in four of those with heart diseases, three in four of those with Perthe's disease and nearly two in three of those with polio. The situation is reversed in the case of cerebral-palsied children and of those with spina bifida and with muscular dystrophy, two out of three children in each of these groups being in special schools. There is, however, clearly a great deal of overlap in the actual types of handicaps found in the special and ordinary schools.

It would be most interesting to know the extent to which there is also overlap as regards severity of handicap. This could not be rated in the DES survey, but as was pointed out there, 'those in the special schools tend to be the most severely physically handicapped, many having multiple defects' (DES, 1972). This is a very reasonable assumption, but whether it is equally true for all handicaps is simply not known. Certainly it would seem to be the case for cerebral palsy where most of the children in ordinary schools have relatively mild forms of hemiplegia and where few severely handicapped athetoids or quadriplegics are found. But may it not be the case that where, for example, haemophilia or heart disease is concerned there is a great deal of overlap? Are the children with Perthe's disease, or polio, or congenital limb deformities who are in special schools much more handicapped than those in ordinary schools, or have other factors been responsible for their special school placement? In certain areas many severely handicapped spina bifida children attend ordinary schools under special arrangements and there may be more overlap in terms of severity of handicap than is recognized.

A number of clues regarding severity of handicap do come out of the DES survey. One aspect considered was whether a child suffered from multiple handicaps, that is whether he had, in addition to the physical handicap, a speech defect, a hearing defect, a visual defect or was incontinent. The results for the cerebral-palsied and spina bifida children are shown below (Table 1.4).

This table suggests that many children with these particular handicaps who are in ordinary schools do have multiple defects. Among children with other handicaps, between 10 per cent and 20 per cent generally had additional defects, incontinence and visual defects being most common.

TABLE 1.4. *PH children in ordinary schools: extent of additional defects* (From *Health of the School Child*, 1972)

Disability	Proportion of children with one or more additional defects	Most common additional defects
Cerebral palsy	29·7	Visual and/or speech
Spina bifida	43·0	Incontinence (approx. two in five children)
Myelomeningocele with Spitz-Holter valve	75·3	Incontinence (approx. two in three children)
Myelomeningocele without Spitz-Holter valve	59·3	Incontinence (approx. one in two children)
Hydrocephalus without myelomeningocele	33·0	Visual defect

Another clue to severity of handicap is given by the aids with which the children were provided. Details are given in appendix C.1, but in brief, 393 children (3·9 per cent) used wheelchairs, 14·5 per cent walking aids, 5·9 per cent prostheses and 0·7 per cent a hearing aid, while 17·1 per cent needed some personal assistance in the classroom or with meals, toileting, dressing or stairs.

In summing up, three major points can be made. The first is that the PH group is a very sizeable one. Taking the January 1971 figures for those requiring or receiving special educational treatment, and the results of the DES ordinary school survey (which only covered maintained schools) we get a total figure of 22,257, roughly half of these children being in ordinary schools. As already noted, this is likely to be a substantial underestimation of the size of the problem.

The second point which must be made is that the 'physically handicapped' category includes an enormously wide range of children in terms both of type and of severity of handicap. As is pointed out in *Living with Handicap* (Younghusband et al., 1970) one of the problems with this category is 'the wide range of capacities and needs. At one extreme are pupils who need secondary, further and even higher education. At the other . . . are pupils additionally handicapped by subnormality or sensory defects who need consideration as multi-handicapped. In between are children who can be gradually integrated into ordinary schools.'

Finally, although there are many PH children for whom ordinary school placement without much in the way of extra provision is clearly appropriate, and others for whom some form of special educational treatment (although not necessarily in a special school) is equally clearly essential, it is likely that there may be much more overlap between the PH population in the ordinary and special schools than is generally recognized.]

STOP(END)

Key issues

So much for the background figures. I should now like to return to the quotation which prefaced this chapter, that 'no handicapped child should be sent to a special school who can be satisfactorily educated in an ordinary school', to consider three important questions which it raises. Firstly, why would most of us concur with the view that ordinary school placement is desirable, wherever possible? Secondly, what do we mean by the key phrase 'satisfactorily educated' particularly in the case of physically handicapped children? Thirdly, under what kinds of special arrangements can we provide a satisfactory education for PH children?

(i) WHY SHOULD ORDINARY SCHOOL PLACEMENT BE CONSIDERED DESIRABLE?

One of the questions which this study explored was the extent to which and why the parents of PH children considered ordinary school placement desirable. Their views are discussed in chapter 2. What sort of reasoning, however, underlies the generally held assumption that handicapped children should if possible be brought up within the 'normal' community? This is surely only one rather specialized aspect of the wider question of the place of minority groups of all kinds in the community. It can be considered from two angles, one being the effect which integrated as opposed to segregated schooling has upon the members of the minority group themselves, the other its effects upon the rest of society, in this case on non-handicapped children and adults.

It is generally agreed that the adjustment of the physically handicapped person to the 'normal' world as an adult is likely to be easier
if he has had frequent interaction with it earlier in life. However this
is not an easy thing to prove or disprove and very little research has
been done in this area, partly because it is difficult to know what
criteria to use to evaluate an adult's social adjustment. It is probably
easier to measure the ability to lead an independent life or the degree
of success in finding and holding down a job. The few studies which
do exist have generally compared the vocational success of young
adults whose education had been in ordinary or special schools (or
sometimes ordinary or special classes). On the whole, studies such as
those of Cutsforth (1962) on the blind, Robertson (1963) on ESN
children and Ingram (1965) on young cerebral-palsied adults suggest
that a child who has attended an ordinary school will have a somewhat better chance of achieving occupational success than a similarly
handicapped child who attended a special school. However, the
design of studies such as these has often been weak, and the authors
are generally unable to do more than speculate about the reasons for
such findings.

Vocational success provides one way of judging the long-term
effects of a particular kind of schooling. Another way is to investigate
its effects on how a handicapped person feels about himself and his
handicap. Here again hard evidence is lacking. On the one hand it
might be argued that separation from non-handicapped children
could lead to a feeling of inferiority. Carroll (1967), for example, has
compared the effects of segregated versus partially integrated school
programmes on the self-concept of educable mentally retarded
(ESN) children in America. All the children had IQs of between 60
and 80 and they were assigned at random either to a special class or
school (where they did not mix at all with non-handicapped children
in school hours) or only part-time to a special class, spending half of
each day in the regular class. The children's self-concepts were
measured on the Illinois index of self-derogation before placement
and eight months afterwards. Those who remained part-time in the
ordinary classes showed a significant decrease in the extent to which
they devalued themselves, those who were segregated a significant
increase.

Self-derogation in this situation may be at least partially com-
municated to the child by the parents: Meyerowitz (1967), for
example, compared the attitudes of parents with ESN children in

either special or ordinary classes. Those with children in special classes 'tended to derogate and devalue their children to a greater degree'.

While evidence such as this suggests that any form of segregated schooling should be avoided, it could on the other hand be argued that placement in an ordinary class might impose social and emotional strains on children with severe physical limitations. They might feel more deprived and frustrated than if they were at school with similarly handicapped children. One of the aims of this study was to investigate this question.

The other main aspect of the integration-segregation issue concerns the attitudes of non-handicapped people to the handicapped. Although much of the research has been concerned with the attitude of the majority groups to minority groups other than the handicapped, particularly to ethnic minorities, a great deal is relevant to the integration of disabled people. The segregation of any minority group prevents the majority group from gaining intimate knowledge about and experience with individual members of that group, although interaction will not of itself necessarily lead to a favourable change in attitudes. In their comprehensive review of the studies concerned with the effects on attitudes of contacts between members of different ethnic groups, Harding and his colleagues (1969) point out that at least as regards within-school interaction, different studies have shown divergent results. Part of the explanation, they suggest, 'may lie in the characteristics of the children who were interacting in the various schools, part in the organization of classes and extra-curricular activities, part in the attitudes of teachers and school administrators and part in factors external to the school (community atmosphere, parental attitudes etc.)' Attaining more favourable attitudes seems to depend particularly on conditions of interaction 'in which the members of different groups are co-operatively engaged in the pursuit of common objectives under equal status conditions or as functional equals'.

Certainly, the segregation of any particular minority group denies members of the majority group the opportunities for social learning which are needed if they are to make changes in their own values. There is ample evidence that to a large extent the attitudes of fear and rejection which disabled people frequently face are concomitants of unfamiliarity. While familiarity alone will not ensure the acceptance of the disabled in society it is an essential first step in that direction. Acceptance includes a realistic appreciation of their abilities as well as their disabilities. Bateman (1962), for instance, found that sighted children who actually knew blind children were more positive in their appraisals of the latter's abilities than those who were personally unfamiliar with them.

Although there is general agreement that the social interaction of handicapped and non-handicapped children has important implications for the attitudes of society towards the disabled, we still do not have much detailed information about how this process operates and how it can be facilitated. Certainly integration cannot be expected to follow automatically from placement in an ordinary school. Little research has been done in this area, but in Sweden, a country fully committed to the educational integration of handicapped children, a major study of classroom integration is in progress at Lund University (Johannesson et al., 1972). Firstly the attitudes of classmates, teachers and parents towards pupils with different types of handicaps who have been placed in ordinary classes are being investigated. The second stage of the study 'will be concerned with testing methods and designing suitable material for the creation of partnership and group situations', that is with exploring the very practical ways in which integration can be furthered.

Clearly, then, one of the key issues in the debate about where PH children are best educated is the social issue. Whether social integration is actually achieved when PH children are placed in ordinary schools is something which this study explored and which chapter 4 in particular is concerned with.

(ii) WHAT DO WE MEAN BY 'SATISFACTORILY EDUCATED'?

The second issue requiring clarification was raised by the phrase 'satisfactorily educated', a phrase on which so much hangs in terms of the child's final placement. 'Education' has to be understood here in its very widest sense as including three major aspects of the child's development, firstly his intellectual needs, secondly his physical needs and thirdly his social and emotional needs.

For many physically handicapped children the requirements for academic progress are similar to those of non-handicapped children and can be provided by the normal programme in the ordinary class. For others, frequent absence and hospitalization may lead to a greater need for remedial help. A third group of children, in particular those with neurological abnormalities or sensory handicaps may have specific learning difficulties which give rise to a need for individual help from teachers with specialized training. Whether and how such help can be provided within the ordinary school was one question which this study explored.

The second main area of need lies on the physical side, particularly if the child is severely handicapped. For young children especially, physiotherapy may be exceedingly important. For incontinent children, education in how to care for themselves, to manage their appliances and to guard against infection may be vital. General training in self-help may also be an important element in the education of the majority of handicapped children. When asking whether a child can be 'satisfactorily educated' in an ordinary school these sorts of questions must all be considered.

Finally, all children have basic social and emotional needs with which the school as well as the home must be concerned. These are very clearly discussed by Kellmer Pringle and Fiddes (1970) in the introduction to their study of thalidomide children. The four basic needs these authors single out are the need for love and security, the need for new experiences, the need for recognition and achievement and the need for responsibility. The first, a sense of security, can only be given if the child is unconditionally accepted as he is. For some children, especially those whose parents find this difficult, the school will have an important part to play. In some cases children may need, at least for a period, to be placed in the more protected environment of the special school so that their self-confidence can be built up. The need for the stimulation of new experiences is one which the nature or severity of the handicap may make it difficult to meet. Wherever the child is placed he must be provided with new opportunities and experiences, both social and intellectual. The third need, for recognition and achievement, may also be difficult to meet since on the one hand expectations which are too low will lead the child to accept a poor standard of effort while those which are too high will give him a sense of defeat. It is the child's efforts in relation to his own disabilities, rather than his attainments in relation to those of his peers, which must be given full recognition and praise, and this is something which it is often difficult to assess. The last need, for responsibility, is met by encouraging the fullest possible personal independence. The more independence a child can achieve the less likely he is to devalue himself and it is very important that what a child can do is not underestimated. Occasionally, if the home is exceedingly overprotective, a period of residential placement might for this reason be desirable.

A 'satisfactory' education is, ideally, one which can meet all these needs. It is *also*, it must be emphasized, one which the parents feel is the right one for the child; older children should themselves be fully consulted. At certain periods, especially during adolescence (although there is little empirical evidence about this), a child may prefer the company of similarly handicapped classmates. Two general difficulties arise. One is that until a child has actually attended a school for some time, there will always be an element of doubt about whether that particular school can provide a 'satisfactory education'. This can be partly met by discussing the child's placement fully with the school concerned, and anticipating the more obvious problems before the final placement decision is taken. The other main problem arises where different needs conflict. The ability and personality of the child and the wishes of the parents may, for instance, point to the ordinary school as being entirely suitable socially and academically, but at a stage when intensive physio-therapy and hydrotherapy, only obtainable in a special school, may also be essential. In another case, the ordinary school may seem to provide the ideal social and physical environment but the child may have perceptual problems consequent on brain damage, which early expert training might help him to overcome. In cases such as these it will help if the areas in which specialized training or help is required are defined as precisely as possible and the goals which such help is designed to meet are specified.

A final point which must be stressed is that the child's needs must be kept constantly under review. As is stated in the Plowden Report (Central Advisory Council for Education [England], 1967), 'whether a child is sent to a special school or to a special class . . . the decision must not be regarded as final. There must be no vested interest in preserving an arrangement which is no longer necessary and teach-ers, parents, psychologists and doctors must all co-operate in ensuring this.'

(iii) HOW CAN A 'SATISFACTORY EDUCATION' BE PROVIDED FOR PH CHILDREN WITHIN AN ORDINARY SCHOOL?

In this country the main educational alternatives open to PH children are, on the one hand, placement in a day or residential special school and, on the other, placement in an ordinary class without any extra help. More often than not these are the only choices. Because they are, in a sense, extremes, it is not surprising that those concerned with the child's placement (whether they are parents, doctors, educationists or other professionals) may hold rather strong and sometimes opposing views.

There is surely no logical reason why these should be the only alternatives and in fact a number of less extreme arrangements are now being experimented with here and in other countries. In the figure below I have sketched out very simply the different sorts of arrangements which might be made. In terms of the integration/segregation issue, they can be thought of as being on a continuum. At one end is the residential special school, at the other placement in an ordinary class without extra help.

FIGURE 2.1. *Alternative forms of special educational treatment*

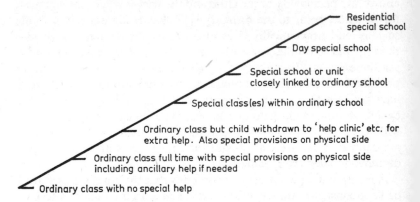

One of the aims of this study was to examine in detail how some of these kinds of special arrangements were working out in practice: this is covered in chapters 8 and 9. The most obvious 'half-way house' or 'stepping stone' between the two ends of the continuum is the special class. This type of provision has been widely developed in the United States and Scandinavia. The pace has been much slower here although recent years have seen some progress at least for certain groups of handicapped children. Dale (1967) for instance points to the growth of special classes for hearing-impaired children (from 24 in 1958 to 170 in 1968). Special classes for the partially sighted and for maladjusted children have also grown in number, but as was shown in Table 1.1 such provision is still very uncommon for PH children.

Special classes do offer a number of potential advantages. If they are kept small and staffed by well-qualified teachers they should be able to offer children the same type of individual help as can the special schools. Their location within the ordinary school should offer the child the chance of joining ordinary classes for certain activities. If transfer to an ordinary class is aimed at, there is more scope for gradually building up to this. There should also be a variety of opportunities for social interaction between the handicapped children and their peers through participation in the general activities of the school. Both the pros and cons of this system as they are being experienced in Scandinavia and in this country are discussed later in this book.

The main point which needs to be made here is that we should be thinking much more flexibly about how special educational treatment can be provided. The issue at stake is not simply whether a particular child should be placed in an ordinary class or a special school. It is whether we are willing to consider providing special educational treatment on a much wider scale within the framework of the ordinary school and to experiment with different ways of doing this.

The research study: aims and methods

To end this chapter a few words of introduction are needed about the research study which forms the main basis of this book. It was financed by the National Fund for Research into Crippling Diseases and the fieldwork was carried out by the author between September 1969 and June 1972. The overall aim of the study was to investigate the question of the integration of physically handicapped children of normal intelligence in ordinary primary schools. Five aspects of this question were singled out for attention. These were:

1 The characteristics, especially in terms of type and severity of handicap, of those PH children who are being educated in ordinary schools.

2 The process by which these children came to be placed in ordinary schools and the feelings of their parents and teachers about this.

3 The social and emotional adjustment of the children (including social relationships, social competence and the extent of emotional

B

and behavioural disorders) especially in comparison with their non-handicapped classmates.

4 The academic attainments of the children, again in relation to those of their non-handicapped peers.

5 The nature and the adequacy of the special provisions made for PH children in ordinary schools.

The three parts into which the book is divided deal with these questions. In part I the main procedure followed is described, the sample is looked at in detail and various placement problems, particularly as they are seen by parents, are discussed. Part II focuses on the children in school, and on their social, emotional and academic needs and progress, in particular on the social aspects of ordinary school placement since comparatively little research has been done in this area.

A comment is needed here about the basic design of the study. One possible approach would have been to compare the social adjustment and level of attainment of the PH children with a matched group attending special schools. This was not done partly because a study of this kind was already under way (unfortunately, the research worker concerned has been unable to continue with it) and partly because of the difficulties involved in matching two such groups. Instead the PH children were compared with their non-handicapped classmates. This, on reflection, seemed as useful an approach in many ways, since it would indicate how well the PH children were fitting into a 'normal' community, which a comparison of PH children in ordinary and special schools would not have done.

Part III of the book deals with the nature and quality of the special provisions made for the children, the position both in this country and in Scandinavia being discussed, and the book ends with a chapter summarizing the main findings and the recommendations arising from them.

Finally, it has to be pointed out that this piece of research was not intended primarily as a largescale experimental study from which statistically significant generalizations should emerge. Although the statistical significance of the results was considered, the sample was a small one (the main group consisting of 74 PH children and 148 controls) and also extremely heterogeneous in terms of the handicaps represented. The reader should therefore be cautious about making generalizations based on these results, especially where subgroups of children are concerned. The real value of a study of this kind is qualitative rather than quantitative. It lies much more in the picture in depth which it can give of the present position of physically handicapped children in ordinary schools. A great deal of use is made of case history material, and throughout the book I have tried to relate the information revealed by interviews, tests and questionnaires to previous research in education and in the social sciences, and to the major issues presented in this chapter.

REFERENCES

BATEMAN, B. (1962) 'Sighted children's perceptions of blind children's abilities', *Exceptional Children*, 29, pp. 42–6.

CARROLL, A. W. (1967) 'The effects of segregated and partially integrated school programmes on self-concept and academic achievement in educable mental retardates', *Exceptional Children*, 34 (2), pp. 93–9.

Central Advisory Council for Education (England) (1967) *Children and Their Primary Schools* (Plowden Report), HMSO, London.

CUTSFORTH, T. D. (1962) 'Personality and social adjustment among the blind', in Zahl, P. A. (ed.) *Blindness*, Hafner, New York.

DALE, D. M. C. (1967) 'Deaf education: a new approach', *Special Education* 56 (4), pp. 4–7.

DAVIE, R., BUTLER, N. R. and GOLDSTEIN, H. (1972) *From Birth to Seven: The Second Report of the National Child Development Study (1958 Cohort)*, Longmans, London.

Department of Education and Science (1969) *Health of the School Child*, HMSO, London.

Department of Education and Science (1972) *Health of the School Child*, HMSO, London.

HARDING, J., PROSHANSKY, H., KUTNER, B. and CHEIN, I. (1969) 'Prejudice and ethnic relationships', chapter 37 in Lindzey, G. and Aronson, E. (eds.) *The Handbook of Social Psychology*, V, Addison Wesley, Reading, Mass.

INGRAM, T. T. S. (1965) 'Education – for what purpose', chapter 1 in Loring, J. (ed.) *Teaching the Cerebral-Palsied Child*, Lavenham Press, Suffolk.

Institute of Municipal Treasurers and Accountants and Society of County Treasurers (1971) *Education Statistics, 1970–71*, IMTA/SCT, London.

JOHANNESSON, J., ANDREASSON, K., BERGVALL, E. and EDLING-NILSSON, E. (1972) 'The integration of handicapped pupils in the school class', *School Research Newsletter* (mimeographed), 7, National Board of Education, Stockholm.

MEYEROWITZ, J. H. (1962) 'Self-derogation in young retardates and special class placement', *Child Development*, 33, pp. 433–51.

Ministry of Education (1945) *Handicapped Pupils and School Health Regulations*, HMSO, London.

Ministry of Education (1954) *Circular 276*, 25 June 1954, HMSO, London.

PRINGLE, M. L. KELLMER and FIDDES, D. O. (1970) *The Challenge of Thalidomide*, Longmans, London.

ROBERTSON, J. S. (1963) 'Occupational success of E.S.N. school-leavers in Lindsey', *The Medical Officer*, 2864, p. 109.

RUTTER, M., TIZARD, J. and WHITMORE, K. (eds.) (1970) *Education, Health and Behaviour*, Longmans, London.

YOUNGHUSBAND, E., BIRCHALL, D., DAVIE, R. and PRINGLE, M. L. KELLMER (eds.) (1970) *Living with Handicap*, National Bureau for Co-operation in Child Care, London.

Chapter 2 · The Children and their Families

This chapter has been arranged in two main sections. In the first, a short introductory account is given of the two main handicapping conditions, cerebral palsy and spina bifida, which together affected almost half of the 99 physically handicapped children who took part in this study.

The second section focuses on the children themselves, the total sample being made up of 74 PH children in junior schools or classes, 148 of their non-handicapped classmates who formed a control group (each PH child had two controls, the two classmates of the same sex who were nearest in age) and 25 PH children in infant classes or schools. In addition, 241 families and 91 schools participated. The procedures followed in selecting the sample, the nature and extent of the children's disabilities and the main characteristics of their families and schools are each discussed in turn.

1 Major handicapping conditions

(i) CEREBRAL PALSY

As was pointed out in chapter 1, cerebral palsy affects a substantial proportion of children in both special and ordinary schools. Survey findings of the incidence and prevalence rates vary, but a reliable study of 11,865 5–14 year olds on the Isle of Wight (Rutter *et al.*, 1970a) gave a prevalence rate of 2·9 per 1,000. Various surveys of cerebral-palsied children suggest that roughly half have an IQ of 70 or below. This still leaves a substantial proportion whose intellectual handicaps are not marked; Hewett (1970) in her east Midlands study found that 26 per cent of the 125 school-age CP children in her sample were attending ordinary schools.

Of the three major types of cerebral palsy, spasticity, athetosis and ataxia, it is the first which is most often seen in ordinary schools. Most of the juniors in the study suffered from the form of spasticity called hemiplegia. Here the motor area of one cerebral hemisphere has been damaged with resultant spasticity on the contralateral side of the body. A few children were diplegics (with spasticity on both sides of the body, the legs being more affected than the arms), and among the infants were two quadriplegics, a form of cerebral palsy where all four limbs are affected by weakness or paralysis. Only one of the children in the study had some degree of ataxia. Here damage to the cerebellum is involved with resultant incoordination of movement and unsteadiness of gait. Finally two of the infants were partly athetoid, athetosis being a common form of cerebral palsy springing from damage to the basal ganglia and resulting generally in abnormal posture and involuntary movements which seriously interfere with normal control.

Cerebral-palsied children frequently suffer from a wide range of additional disorders: sensory deficits, especially of hearing and vision, are common, probably almost 50 per cent of cerebral-palsied children have associated speech disorders and epilepsy is not infrequent. Other problems which may be difficult to detect such as perceptual and visuo-motor disorders are often also found. The former can be detected, for instance, by asking the subject to match shapes, a purely perceptual task, whereas visuo-motor ability relates to eye–hand coordination and can be detected only when the child is required to carry out constructive tasks such as drawing or block-building. Such disorders have been reviewed by Wedell (1960, 1961) and Abercrombie (1964) while Tyson (1964) has shown that many cerebral-palsied children show weaknesses in tactile shape recognition. As Abercrombie (1968) points out, the specific difficulties of some cerebral-palsied children in perceiving and manipulating spatial relationships reflect very basic disorders of cerebral processes. An important factor contributing to a 'space perception' disorder is likely to be the deprivation of normal spatial experience which results from defective or disordered movement. In Abercrombie's words (1968), 'the various disordered motor activities of the cerebral-palsied should profoundly affect mental development. . . . This will be shown in weaker development of perceptual skills and consequently in generalized lowering of the IQ.' Visuo-motor disorders however, cannot be explained by this lack of experience since 'they are present in spastic children but not in children similarly handicapped as to movement in space by athetosis or by congenital disorders other than brain damage which limit locomotion'. Visuomotor disorders may also appear in children who have had minimal deprivation of spatial experience, for instance in 'clumsy' children. One factor which may be playing a part is a conflict between attentiveness to different stimuli, reflecting a basic disorder of cerebral functioning.

In summary, a cerebral-palsied child is quite likely to suffer from a constellation of handicaps (see appendix B.2) which, although when they are taken separately may be of minor importance, together may give rise to considerable learning difficulties for even the 'mildly handicapped' cerebral-palsied child.

(ii) SPINA BIFIDA AND HYDROCEPHALUS

As in the case of cerebral palsy a series of epidemiological surveys have shown considerable variations in the incidence of the disorder. Laurence (1966) gave a figure of 4 per 1,000 for the mining area of Glamorgan and estimated the national average to be about half of this, while Spain (1970) suggests about 1·5 per 1,000 for the GLC area. There is general agreement that about half the children will survive to school age, and there can be no doubt that this group will soon comprise a very significant proportion of all PH children. In the study reported here twelve of the infants had spina bifida and hydrocephalus and two spina bifida alone, while in the junior group there were eight spina bifida children with hydrocephalus and four without.

Since spina bifida children form a very diverse group as regards severity of handicap and intelligence, generalizations cannot be easily made about the type of school placement which will be appropriate. Lorber (1971) looking at spina bifida children born between 1959 and 1963 found that 3 per cent of the survivors had no physical handicap, 15 per cent a moderate handicap, 49 per cent a severe handicap combined with an IQ of 80+, 21 per cent a severe handicap and an IQ in the range 61–79 and 12 per cent 'extreme' handicaps and IQs below 60.

Spina bifida (due to a congenital malformation of the spinal cord, of the immediate coverings of the cord and of the backbone) is of two main types, spina bifida meningocele which generally has few serious *sequelae* and spina bifida myelomeningocele. Here the imperfectly formed spinal cord reaches the surface, and is exposed to injury, drying out and infection; the nerve centres controlling the leg muscles and the lower bowel and bladder may be damaged with resultant paralysis and incontinence.

Studies such as those of Lorber (1971) suggest that approximately 75 per cent of spina bifida children also suffer from hydrocephalus, that is, a blockage of the free flow of fluid around the brain. In spina bifida children hydrocephalus is usually associated with a malformation of the cerebellum, the Arnold–Chiari malformation. The build-up of fluid results in enlargement of the head or, when the bony structure cannot extend at a sufficient rate, pressure on and damage to the brain itself. Since 1958 it has become increasingly common practice (where hydrocephalus is present or suspected and does not show early spontaneous arrest) to insert a valve mechanism (usually the Spitz–Holter or Pudenz–Heyer valve) into the head. This drains the excess fluid from the lateral ventricles into a silicone pump, from where it drains through a catheter into the venous system and is ultimately reabsorbed by the body. All the spina bifida children with hydrocephalus in the study had such valves.

The actual physical handicaps of the children, particularly impaired mobility or complete paralysis of the legs, and bladder and/or bowel incontinence, were in many cases considerable. What is of greater interest here, however, is that evidence is steadily accumulating that the neurological abnormalities of such children are likely to give rise to specific learning difficulties. A detailed account of such problems is given in my own recent review of the literature (Anderson, 1973) and only a few of the main findings can be mentioned here.

Spain (1970), for example, who has been carrying out a follow-up study of about 160 spina bifida children born in the GLC area between April 1967 and March 1969 found when testing the children at 2–3 years old that those with valves (that is, those who had hydrocephalus, or in whom hydrocephalus was suspected) did poorly on the subscale of the Griffiths test involving eye–hand coordination. She suggests that this result may imply 'some kind of cortical or brainstem damage, specifically affecting the finer hand movements or perception of shape'. Her later work has entirely confirmed these findings (Spain, personal communication, 1972).

Also of interest are a series of experimental studies which were carried out in Hull by Miller and Sethi (1971a, 1971b), designed to look at spatial and motor deficits in children with infantile hydrocephalus. Their subjects were sixteen hydrocephalics (with or without spina bifida) matched to sixteen children without neurological abnormalities. Using the Bender Gestalt and Frostig tests to study the perception of visuo-spatial relationships they found that the experimental group had extremely poor visuo-spatial perception and that there was also a special difficulty in figure-ground discrimination (Miller and Sethi, 1971a). When they extended their work to the tactile modality they found that hydrocephalics appeared to be specifically impaired in the perception of tactile stimuli (Miller and Sethi, 1971b).

So far there have been comparatively few studies of this kind, and much more research is needed before a clear picture emerges of the specific learning difficulties of children with spina bifida and hydrocephalus, and of the extent to which special teaching techniques are required to help them. A start will at least have been made when a greater awareness has been created among ordinary schoolteachers (and this is the responsibility of the colleges of education) that both cerebral-palsied children and those with spina bifida and hydrocephalus may have hidden learning difficulties in addition to the more obvious problems which spring directly from the physical handicap. As Henderson (1968) and others have pointed out, the pattern of disabilities in children in England and Wales has changed markedly during the last two decades and 'simple' acquired handicaps such as poliomyelitis and tuberculosis have been replaced in importance by those such as spina bifida and cerebral palsy, with their much more diffuse and complex effects.

2 The sample

(i) SELECTION OF THE SAMPLE AND GENERAL PROCEDURE

The physically handicapped children taking part in this study fell into two main groups, a large group of seventy-four juniors (the 'junior group') aged from 7 years 5 months (7.5) to 10 years 11 months, (10.11) attending junior I to junior III classes of ordinary primary schools, and a small group of twenty-five children aged from 5.4 to 7.11 years (the 'infant group') in ordinary infant schools or classes. For each handicapped junior there were two controls, these being the two classmates of the same sex who were nearest in age. Details of the age of the juniors in the different groups and of their distribution by school class are shown in appendices D.1 and D.2.

Altogether ninety-one schools in seven different local education authorities were involved. The parents of all the PH children also participated and the parents of all but six of the controls. As is the usual practice, the anonymity of the local authorities, schools and children has been retained and where case history material is presented the names of the children are fictitious. All the participants were extremely cooperative. As a result there were few delays and (with the exception of a test given on follow-up visits to fifteen schools) all the interviewing of the parents and teachers and the testing of the children was carried out by the author.

The first thing that has to be stressed about the sample is that it was not a randomly drawn one but at least in some ways (and particularly in the case of the 'infant group') highly selective. Firstly, it was selective in the sense that the local authority areas included were not randomly drawn. Largely because of the resources available it was decided to confine the study to the south of England. Initially it was planned for London alone, but it became clear that because of the large number of special schools in London, this would have limited its value, since severely or even moderately handicapped children are unlikely to be placed in ordinary schools as frequently as in certain other areas. The study was therefore extended to a number of local authority areas outside London, the aim being to select areas which would provide a good cross-section of socio-economic groups in urban industrialized areas, in old and 'new' country towns and in rural areas.

Secondly, even within these areas, true random sampling of the physically handicapped population of a particular age group was not carried out. For a start, the children selected included only those whose names appeared on the handicapped registers kept by the local authority health departments. These registers are meant to be completely comprehensive but this ideal is probably never fully realized and there are great variations from one area to another regarding the completeness of the register.

The category 'physically handicapped' refers in Britain to children 'not suffering solely from a defect of sight or hearing who by reason of disease or other crippling defect cannot be satisfactorily educated under the normal regime of ordinary schools' (Ministry of Education, 1959). As regards the junior group, all those appearing on the register as 'PH' and in their first three years of junior school were included with the exception of (a) those with heart disorders

(b) those with disorders of the blood other than haemophilia (c) those with metabolic disorders (d) those with disorders of the chest and lungs (e) very lightly handicapped children and (f) children who were registered as educationally subnormal as well as physically handicapped.

A major reason for the exclusion of children in groups (a) to (d) was that they are generally classified as 'delicate' rather than 'physically handicapped' children. Certainly a substantial number of children with heart disorders are still found in PH schools, but these children when placed in ordinary schools generally require little special treatment other than extra supervision; for this reason, and because it would have been difficult to have assessed the severity of the disorder, they were excluded. Haemophiliac children were included, since they are often classified as physically handicapped. One exception to the exclusion of children with metabolic disorders was made: this was a girl with maple syrup urine disease who had previously attended a special PH school.

Group (e), the minimally handicapped children, were excluded since ordinary school placement poses few problems for them. They included children with handicaps such as mild talipes or non-chronic conditions such as Perthe's disease, who in fact are often not placed on handicapped registers. Generally their medical records provided sufficient information to enable a decision to be made about their inclusion in the study, but in a few cases a visit to the home was necessary first.

Finally, group (f), children registered as ESN, were excluded since it was intended from the start that the study should include only children within the 'normal' range of intelligence.

In the infant group the method of selection was rather different. Here the aim was to obtain a small group of rather severely handicapped children who had been placed in ordinary infant classes, and for whom some sort of 'special' provision was likely to be required. The findings about how these children were functioning and about the adequacy of the provisions made for them would, it was hoped, give some idea of the feasibility of placing quite handicapped children in ordinary schools, and of the main problems involved.

Thus the main criterion for inclusion for the infants was severity of handicap, but it was also felt desirable to look at both rural and urban schools. Six local authority areas were therefore chosen which were already participating in the junior study. Two (where most of the children were in town schools) were known to have considerable interest and experience in placing handicapped children in ordinary schools, and together provided sixteen out of the twenty-five infants. Of the others, two were chosen as they were predominantly rural, and two were highly urbanized. In each of these areas the handicapped registers were again used, and the children with disabilities whose effects were likely to pose serious problems in an ordinary school (owing for example, to incontinence, severely restricted mobility, severe haemophila or specific learning disabilities) were selected. This small group was thus a highly selected sample.

For both infant and junior groups the procedure followed was similar. After the local authority areas had been chosen, the medical officer of health and the local education authority officials concerned were contacted, and the study discussed with them. Once their permission to go ahead (subject to the parents' agreement, a most important proviso) had been obtained, the names and addresses of those PH children in ordinary schools were obtained from the handicapped register of each school health service. An introductory letter was then sent to the parents, and a preliminary meeting to discuss the study suggested. It was emphasized that it was the National Fund for Research into Crippling Diseases study rather than any local authority or government body. In many cases parents needed direct reassurance that the aim behind the study was not that their children should be moved into special schools but rather that the question of the placement of PH children in ordinary schools should be explored in as objective a way as possible.

The response of the parents was very good indeed. Although 28 of the 127 contacted did not ultimately take part, this was generally for reasons other than an unwillingness to participate and in fact only four of those suitable for the study were unwilling to take part (below 4 per cent). Possibly the very low refusal rate reflects the interest parents feel in the question of the integration of handicapped children. Several parents confessed that initially they had felt uneasy about participating (mainly in case their child was in any way 'singled out' in an ordinary class), but had agreed as they thought the study 'might help other PH children to go to ordinary schools'.

Once the parents had agreed to take part, contact was made with the schools concerned either directly or through the LEA. Again the response was good; only four schools out of the ninety-five approached were unwilling to take part (4·2 per cent). One gave the reason as 'too busy', another 'family reasons' in the child's home, the third that it would interrupt the child's schooling (the child had recently returned from hospital) while the fourth gave no reason. During the visit to the school, the heads and class teachers were interviewed, the controls selected and the children were tested, a whole day usually being spent in each school, and in a few cases a second visit being required. In addition to this, class teachers were left with a number of forms to fill in and return. In the infant group these were returned in all cases. In the junior group four teachers failed to return the behaviour rating scales and a record of school absences, while seven teachers (including the four above) failed to return forms giving reading and arithmetic ratings.

After schools had been visited, the mothers of the controls and the handicapped children were interviewed for from one to two hours in their homes. In the rural areas the interview usually took place in the late afternoon or early evening of the same day as the school visit: otherwise they were held on a different day but not more than a fortnight afterwards.

Interviews were held with 241 families, that is, all except 6 (2·3 per cent) of the total sample, these 6 all being in the control group. Only one mother refused to take part: of the others, one was never found at home, and four were not visited because they lived in villages to which transport was not at the time available. After the interview (which was occasionally with both parents) a behaviour rating scale was left with the parents to fill in and return: a total of twenty-three parents (9 per cent) failed to return these forms after two reminders.

The interviews themselves were fairly structured, but 'probe' questions were often used to elicit further information. Spontaneous expression of views was encouraged, these being recorded verbatim where possible. Slightly different interview schedules were used for children in the infant and junior groups, both for the parent and the teacher interviews.

(ii) THE HANDICAPPED GROUP: NATURE AND EXTENT OF DISABILITIES

(a) Assessing the severity of handicap

It was felt to be very important that in a study of this kind an attempt should be made to assess the severity of handicap, and that this should be done in a way which was as objective and as easily replic-able as possible. Clearly severity of handicap is a potentially import-ant factor in determining the success or failure of a child in various aspects of school life, and indeed in determining whether that child is placed in an ordinary school at all.

For the purpose of this study the system of assessment used had to fulfil several functions: (a) it had to be such that a non-medical person could rate the child, on the basis of medical and other records where available, and on the questions put to the mother about the ways in which the disability affected the day-to-day functioning of the child; (b) it had to provide a practical method of distinguishing between at least three grades of children, those who are mildly, moderately and severely handicapped; (c) it had to be a system of assessment which would enable a comparison (as regards severity of handicap) to be made both between children with the same diag-nostic label and between children with quite different disabilities; (d) it had to provide a means of comparing not only the overall severity of the handicap but also the distribution of functional impairments within and between individuals (for example to show whether hand control was more impaired than mobility).

The system finally chosen was a modified form of the Pultibec system proposed by Lindon (1963), his ratings for severity of handi-cap, however, being compressed to four for the purpose of this study, that is from grade 1 (complete normality) to grade 4 (denoting a severe handicap).

As Lindon suggested, each child's functional capacities are rated on a 1–4 scale under eight main headings, the code letters of which form the word 'Pultibec'. The first four (group A) deal mainly with physical and motor capacities and include physical capacity (general) upper limbs (subdivided into right and left), locomotor (subdivided into right and left) and toileting. The next four (group B) are qualities related to behaviour and communication and include intelli-gence, behaviour, eyesight (right and left eye) and communication (subdivided into speech and hearing).

Once each of the eight 'functions' listed above has been rated on the basis of all the available information, a 'profile' can be drawn up for each child (for examples see appendices B.2 and B.3). These profiles are very useful in showing the child's main areas of strength and weakness, and in allowing children handicapped in different ways to be directly compared.

The final stage of the assessment involves the assignment of each child to the mildly, moderately or severely handicapped group on the basis of the profile, using strict criteria which take into account:

1 The total number of problems.
2 Whether these are concerned mainly with physical/motor capacities (i.e. the A [PULT] side of the profile) or with behaviour/communication (the B [IBEC] side of the profile).
3 The severity of the problem, a grade of 1 indicating no problem, of 2 a 'minor' problem and of 3 or 4 a 'major' problem.

The criteria used to rate the children were chosen specifically for this study and were as follows:

1 Mildly handicapped children were those who had, on the physical/motor (A) side, no major problems and not more than four minor problems, and on the behavioural/communication side (B) not more than three major problems. The total number of problems of a child in this group could not exceed eight: i.e. a child with over eight minor problems would be classified as moderately rather than mildly handicapped.

2 Moderately handicapped children were those with at least one but not more than three major problems in A, or children with a total of not more than six major problems in A and B together, or children with more than four minor problems in A or more than eight minor problems overall.

3 Severely handicapped children were those with more than three major problems in A or more than six major problems overall.

The system may sound a little cumbersome but in fact it proved exceedingly workable. To examine its reliability, the first fifty children in the study were rated by two examiners, the author and an educational psychologist with considerable experience of PH children, who completed a separate Pultibec profile for each child based on a summary of all the relevant information. The overall level of agreement between the two raters was 94 per cent. There was perfect agreement in the rating of the severely handicapped children and only a very minor degree of disagreement about the mildly and moderately handicapped groups. Further details of the system are given in appendix B.1.

The composition of the infant group as regards severity of handicap was that one-third of the children were moderately and two-thirds severely handicapped. The large proportion of severely handicapped children was of course entirely due to the selection procedure which has already been described. The junior group was rather different, and findings are summarized below in Table 2.1.

TABLE 2.1. *Severity of handicap: junior group*

Severity	Boys	Girls	Total	% of overall total
Mild	7	6	13	17·5
Moderate	27	18	45	60·8
Severe	8	8	16	21·6
TOTALS	42	32	74	100·0

The bulk of the children fell into the moderate group. This was to be expected since, as has already been mentioned, children with minimal handicaps were excluded and children with severe handicaps tend to be in special schools. It is very important to note, however, that there is considerable overlap between children in special and ordinary schools (see also chapter 3). The report of the chief medical officer of the Department of Education and Science (1963 and 1964) includes, for example, this statement: 'What is beyond doubt is that some severely physically handicapped children – as seriously disabled as any in special schools – do as well in ordinary schools provided that adequate support is given them.'

The other point to notice concerns the sex ratio of the children. In the junior group the male/female ratio was 1.3 to 1 [very similar to the 1.2 to 1 ratio in the Isle of Wight survey physical disorder group (Rutter, Tizard and Whitmore 1970b)]. In the infant group the male/female ratio was 2.6 to 1 and even higher (3.7 to 1) among the spina bifida children.

(b) *Nature of the disabilities*

A summary of the major types of disabilities involved in the junior group, together with the severity of handicap, is given in Table 2.2. Something has already been said about cerebral palsy and spina bifida; a useful concise account of most of the other disabilities mentioned in this section exists in Dr White Franklin's book, *The Care of Invalid and Crippled Children* (1960) and uncommon terms are also explained in appendix N.

TABLE 2.2. *Nature of disabilities with severity of handicap: junior group*

Type of disability	Extent of disability				
	Mild	Moderate	Severe	Total No.	%
Cerebral palsy	6	9	1	16	21·6
Spina bifida:					
with hydrocephalus	0	2	6	8	
without hydrocephalus	0	4	0	4	16·2
Congenital abnormalities					
(excluding thalidomide)	4	14	0	18	24·3
Thalidomide deformities	1	0	3	4	5·4
Haemophilia	0	4	0	4	5·4
Other	2	12	6	20	27·0
TOTALS	13	45	16	74	
(percentages)	17·5	60·8	21.6		100·0

The pattern of disabilities is very similar to that discussed in chapter 1 with the cerebral-palsied and spina bifida children comprising the largest single groups. Further details are given about these children in section (iii) of this chapter.

Of the eighteen children with congenital abnormalities, ten were congenital amputees, three had bilateral talipes, two had deformities of the hands and feet and one had vestigial upper limbs. The 'other' group included children with a great variety of handicaps. Four children had deformities of the genito-urinary system, two children had rheumatoid arthritis and there was one case of each of the following: diastrophic dwarfism, achondroplasia, amyotonia congenita, arthrogryposis, fragilitas ossium, kyphoscoliosis, congenital dislocation of the right hip, polio, post-accident amputation of the right thumb, post-tumour amputation of the left leg, maple syrup urine disease, paraplegia following a spinal injury, right hemiparesis following a fractured skull and minimal cerebral dysfunction. The composition of the severely handicapped group is of particular interest and is shown in appendix D.5.

One way in which the data can be looked at is in terms of the major functions which are impaired. These are shown in Table 2.3.

TABLE 2.3. *Major functional effect of handicap: junior group*

Type of problem	No.	%
Impaired mobility	30	40·5
Impaired hand control	27	36·4
Incontinence	12	16·2
Bruising and swelling of joints with temporary impaired mobility	4	5·4
Restricted diet	1	1·5
TOTAL	74	100·0

This table shows the most serious area of impairment for each child. In the case of several of the children many functions were impaired. Half of the incontinent children had impaired mobility, with three being confined to wheelchairs, while most of the cerebral-palsied children were hemiplegics with impairment of mobility and manipulative skills and often of speech as well; in three cases they also suffered from epilepsy.

Four of the children had two distinct handicaps. These included congenital dislocation of the hips with mild congenital heart disease, congenital abnormalities of the hands and feet with a mild bilateral hearing loss, congenital absence of the left arm with bilateral ptosis, and bilateral talipes with kidney duplex.

Toileting problems may lead to difficulties in school placement: a total of fifteen children in the junior group were handicapped in this way (appendix D.4), while over half of the infant group were incontinent. The number of incontinent children attending ordinary schools is likely to increase rapidly, as appendix C.2 suggests. Throughout the book the term 'incontinent' refers to the child's 'natural' way of functioning. This was controlled to a greater or lesser extent either by a daily management routine or by the use of a variety of appliances, while in some cases surgery had been carried out.

Within the infant group the pattern of disabilities was less varied. Details are shown in Table 2.4 below.

TABLE 2.4. *Nature of disabilities with severity of handicap: infant group*

Type of disability	Extent of disability		
	Moderate	*Severe*	*Total*
Cerebral palsy	1	2	3
Hydrocephalus with secondary			
spastic paraplegia	1	0	1
Relapsing peripheral neuritis	0	1	1
Spina bifida:			
with hydrocephalus	0	12	12 ⎱ 14
without hydrocephalus	1	1	2 ⎰
Genito/urinary abnormalities	4	0	4
Haemophilia	1	1	2
TOTALS	8	17	25

Spina bifida children, most of whom had hydrocephalus, comprised over half of the group. A total of fifteen children (eleven with spina bifida and four others) were incontinent and seven of the children were confined to a wheelchair for most of the time, while the mobility of all the children but two was to some extent impaired.

(c) *Hospitalization*

Many of the children in the study had experienced long periods of hospitalization, as the comparison with the control group in Table 2.5 below illustrates.

Only 14 per cent of the handicapped children had never been hospitalized, as compared to 74 per cent of the controls. With two exceptions, none of the controls had been hospitalized for more than a total of four weeks, while 56 per cent of the handicapped group had spent over a month in hospital and 49 per cent over ten weeks. The five handicapped children who had been hospitalized for over fifty weeks included one child (absence of lower bowel) who had been brought up in hospital until the age of five, one with rheumatoid arthritis, one with spina bifida and hydrocephalus, one with diastrophic dwarfism and one with congenital dislocation of the hip

TABLE 2.5. *Total hospitalization of handicapped children and controls*

Total hospitalization in weeks	Handicapped group No. = 74		Controls No. = 148	
	No.	%	No.	%
None	11	14	110	74
1–4	22	29	30	21
5–10	5	7	2	1
11–50	31	42	—	—
Over 50	5	7	—	—
Not known	—	—	6	4

The amount of hospitalization after the age of five (i.e. when the child was likely to have started school) was also examined (see appendix K.2). Here the differences were not as marked, although 29 per cent of the PH children, compared to only 1 per cent of the controls, had spent a month or more in hospital. The effects of hospitalization and of school absence are looked at in more detail in chapter 7.

(iii) CHILDREN WITH NEUROLOGICAL ABNORMALITIES

(a) *Composition of the group*

The PH group was extremely diverse in terms of the range of handicaps included and it was felt essential that one major subdivision should be made. This was the division of the group into children with and without neurological abnormalities, the term being used here to refer to upper central nervous system (above the brainstem) abnormalities. Such a division tends to be concealed by the blanket category 'physically handicapped'. This term, by focusing attention on the motor handicap, may obscure the fact that for certain children neurological defects leading to specific learning difficulties may exist and may be of more significance than the physical aspect of the handicap.

Reynell (1970) makes the distinction quite clearly when she points out that 'children who have abnormal brain function must be considered to have complex handicaps. In addition to their physical handicap there is often some general or specific intellectual impairment; there may be perceptual disorders, there may be sensory handicap, there may be speech or language disorder.' If the neurologically impaired group do tend to have such disorders they can as a consequence be expected to have many more learning difficulties than those who are purely motor handicapped. Poorer performance can be anticipated unless (and sometimes even if) special teaching methods are used to combat these difficulties. Although it was not possible to test the children in the study for spatial or visuomotor difficulties, it was likely that these were operating in a number of cases.

For these reasons it was felt to be important to distinguish in the study between children with and without neurological abnormalities. In doing so the difficult problem immediately arose of the criteria which were to be used in assigning children to either group. In the case of the cerebral-palsied children no real problem existed since, by definition (Bax, 1964), cerebral palsy is 'a disorder of movement and posture due to a defect or lesion of the immature brain'. In two other cases the decision to assign children to this group was straightforward, one being a child with unequivocal brain damage consequent on a fractured skull and the other a child with 'minimal cerebral dysfunction' in whom certain abnormal neurological signs had been found on physical examination.

Where the spina bifida children were concerned the problem was more difficult, but it was decided that where there had been a diagnosis of hydrocephalus (arrested in every case by the insertion of either a Spitz–Holter or Pudenz valve) the child should be placed in the neurologically abnormal group. In the minority of cases where there had been no apparent hydrocephalus, the spina bifida children were placed in the 'without neurological abnormalities' group. It is often impossible to be sure whether upper central nervous system lesions do exist. As Spain (1970) points out, a diagnosis of hydrocephalus may be made and a valve inserted when the symptoms are very mild or doubtful, while on the other hand a few children in whom hydrocephalus is not diagnosed may in fact have suffered from minor neurological impairment. For the purposes of this study all that can be said with certainty is that there was good evidence that all the children in the neurologically abnormal group had suffered from some kind of upper central nervous system impairment. There may on the other hand have been a number of children in the 'without neurological abnormalities' group (and indeed among the controls) in whom minor undetected neurological abnormalities did exist.

In the infant group sixteen of the twenty-five children had neurological abnormalities. Three had cerebral palsy and one had hydrocephalus with secondary spastic paralysis while twelve had spina bifida and hydrocephalus (Table 2.6).

TABLE 2.6. *Children with upper central nervous system abnormalities: infant group*

Nature of damage	Boys	Girls	Total	
Cerebral palsy:				
quadriplegia	I		I ⎫	
quadriplegia and athetosis		I	I ⎬ 3	
diplegia and athetosis		I	I ⎭	
Hydrocephalus with secondary				
spastic paraplegia		I	I	
Spina bifida and hydrocephalus	10	2	12	
TOTAL	11	5	16	

In the junior group there were twenty-six children (one-third of the sample) with neurological abnormalities. The composition of this group is shown in Table 2.7 below, and short casenotes for the children are available in appendix E.

TABLE 2.7. *Children with upper central nervous system abnormalities: junior group*

Nature of damage	Boys	Girls	Total	
Cerebral palsy:				
a. right hemiplegia	5	4	9 ⎫	
b. left hemiplegia	2	2	4 ⎪	
c. mild diplegia	2	0	2 ⎬ 16	
d. mild ataxic diplegia	I	0	I ⎭	
Spina bifida and hydrocephalus	4	4	8	
Miscellaneous:				
minimal cerebral dysfunction	I	0	I ⎫	
right hemiparesis after fractured			⎬ 2	
skull	I	0	I ⎭	
TOTAL	16	10	26	

Severity of handicap in the children with and without neuro-logical abnormalities was also looked at. The two groups were roughly comparable, although the neurologically abnormal group contained a smaller proportion of moderately handicapped children and a larger proportion who were either mildly handicapped (usually the cerebral-palsied) or severely handicapped (the spina bifida and hydrocephalus group).

(iv) THE HOME BACKGROUND OF THE CHILDREN

So far the sample has been looked at in terms of the physical characteristics of the children. Their home background had also to be taken into account and a little is said in this section about certain features of the families of the handicapped and control group children.

(a) Social class

To have matched the PH children and controls on social class would have been difficult since the parents were not interviewed until after the visit to the school. As the controls and handicapped children attended the same schools, each school tending to draw its pupils from similar socio-economic backgrounds, it was felt unnecessary to attempt such a match. The Registrar General's classification of occupations (1960) was used to classify families, classes I and II being combined and also classes IV and V. The composition of the sample is shown in Table 2.8 below.

TABLE 2.8. *Social class in handicapped and control groups and in fathers of primary school children in England and Wales as a whole*

Social class	Handicapped group		Controls		Total group		1964 national survey *
	No.	%	No.	%	No.	%	(%)
I and II	15	20·2	40	27·0	55	24·7	18
III (non-manual)	8	10·8	15	10·1	23	10·3	11
III (manual)	31	41·8	50	33·7	81	36·4	48
IV and V	20	27·2	43	29·0	63	28·3	22
TOTAL NO. OF CHILDREN	74		148		222		

* Taken from the Plowden Report, II, p. 100

For the handicapped group, the social class distribution is very similar to the national distribution. In the case of the controls, families in social classes I and II are somewhat overrepresented and those in social class III (manual) correspondingly underrepresented. Although these differences between the groups are not statistically significant, it is still worth bearing in mind, particularly when academic attainment is considered, that a slightly higher proportion of the controls came from professional families, while a slightly higher proportion of the handicapped group were the children of manual workers. As the incidence of handicapping conditions tends to be higher in social classes III–V, a difference between the groups in this direction could have been expected.

Comparisons as regards social class were also made between children with and without neurological abnormalities (appendix D.6). While the social class distribution in the group without such abnormalities closely resembled the national distribution, professional families were presented in the neurologically abnormal group.

The relationship between social class and severity of handicap was also investigated. Over one-third of the severely handicapped children (but only 16 per cent of the mildly or moderately handicapped group) came from professional families, possibly because such parents are in a better position to resist the pressures to place severely handicapped children in special schools.

The social class distribution of the infant group was very similar to that of the juniors. 20 per cent belonged to social classes I and II, 20 per cent to III (non-manual), 36 per cent to III (manual) and 24 per cent to IV and V. The only deviation from the national figures is a slight overrepresentation in III (non-manual) and a corresponding underrepresentation in III (manual).

(b) Family factors

In addition to socio-economic status there are a larger number of what can loosely be termed 'family factors' whose effects might usefully be considered. Studies such as those of Douglas (1964), Kellmer Pringle, Butler and Davie (1966) and Davie, Butler and Goldstein (1972) have shown the influence of these factors upon educational achievement and progress. In a study of this kind, however, only a small number of such factors could be considered. In the case of one of these, the existence of a broken or incomplete home, the total number of children with such a background was so small that no statistical analysis was possible.

Another factor which may be important is family size. Douglas (1964), for example, has established that there is a relationship between this and measured ability, children from larger families tending to perform less well. When the size of family in the handicapped and control group was compared (appendix D.7) no significant differences were found. There was a slight tendency for a greater proportion of the controls (38 per cent) than the PH children (28 per cent) to come from families with over three children. In the infant group the pattern was similar: 12 per cent were only children, 64 per cent came from two- or three-child families and 24 per cent from families with four or five children.

The birth order of the children was also looked at (appendix D.8) but once again there were no major differences between the groups, although the neurologically abnormal group had a slightly higher proportion of eldest children and of twins. The pattern in the infant group closely resembled that of the neurologically abnormal children.

Another factor which can have a strong adverse influence is that of overcrowding (which is officially judged to be present when there are more than 1·5 persons to a room). Only 13 children of the 222 in the junior sample were living in overcrowded conditions and there were no differences between the control and handicapped groups. Families with handicapped children often experience other problems in connection with housing, and all the mothers were asked whether and to what extent they felt dissatisfied with their housing. Surprisingly, no differences were found in the proportions of mothers (about one-quarter) in the two groups who expressed dissatisfaction; although in a few cases the reason for dissatisfaction was directly related to the specific needs of the handicapped child, this was not generally the case.

There was a difference in the amount of dissatisfaction expressed when the families' experiences with the medical services were discussed. 16·2 per cent of the parents of the PH children were slightly dissatisfied and 10·8 per cent moderately or very dissatisfied, compared to only 5·0 per cent and 1·4 per cent in the controls. This difference is not unexpected in view of the much greater contact with the medical services which families with handicapped children have.

Another family characteristic which was looked at was the proportion of mothers in the different groups who went out to work. It now seems fairly certain (for example, Davie *et al.*, 1972) that for a mother to go out to work does not in itself have an adverse influence on a school-age child. Were mothers with handicapped children in fact more confined to the home? The findings (appendix D.9) suggest that this was to a slight extent the case: whereas half the mothers of the control group children went out to work, only just over one-third of those with handicapped children did so. Almost the same proportion had full-time jobs, but a smaller number did part-time work.

(c) The schools

Finally, what sort of areas did the children in the study come from and what were their schools like? Seven different local education authorities participated in the study and the numbers of children provided by each are shown in Table 2.9 below.

TABLE 2.9. *Distribution of sample by type of LEA*

Nature of LEA	No. of children: junior study	No. of children: infant study
ILEA (7 inner boroughs only)	32	2 (1 inner borough)
Outer London borough	7	1
Suburban county (education division)	9	5
Suburban county (education division)	4	10
Suburban county (selected areas)	11	not included
Rural county	7	5
Rural county	4	2
TOTAL CHILDREN	74	25

The highly selective nature of the infant group has already been discussed. In the case of the juniors, just over half came from selected London boroughs, each borough providing from two to eight children. One other inner borough was in fact approached and agreed to take part, but on its handicapped register there were no children in ordinary schools who met the criteria (in terms of age, type and severity of handicap) for inclusion in the study. In the county areas either all the suitable children in an education division were included, or, for the rural counties, all the children in the county as a whole. The only exception was a 'suburban' county where the list of children was compiled by a senior school medical officer after a full discussion of the criteria to be used, the children being drawn from all over the county.

An attempt was made to select areas which would provide schools in as many different settings as possible. The result was that forty-one (55·4 per cent) of the juniors came from London schools, nine- teen (25·6 per cent) from schools in towns outside London (includ- ing two industrial areas and several smaller old or 'new' towns) and fourteen (19·0 per cent) from village schools. Of the infants, only two were in London schools, five in village schools and eighteen in town schools.

The bulk of the children (66·2 per cent of the juniors and 52·0 per cent of the infants) were in schools with from 200–400 pupils. 8·1 per cent and 16·0 per cent respectively were in schools of under 100 pupils and 8·1 per cent and 4·0 per cent in schools of over 500. Size of class is of greater importance than size of school. Details are given in appendix D.3, but the main feature was that approximately 39 per cent of the juniors were in classes of thirty or below, 34 per cent in classes of thirty-one to thirty-five and 27 per cent in classes of thirty-six or over, the pattern being very similar for the infants.

To sum up, the salient features of the 'junior' group were as follows. The pattern of the children's handicaps closely resembled that found in the national survey of P H children in ordinary schools, except that children with heart defects were not included. The handicaps ranged from mild to very severe and one-third of the group had, in addition, above brainstem neurological abnormalities. The social class distribution of the P H group closely resembled the national distribution, whereas in the controls there was a slight over- representation of professional families. The children's placements varied from large multistoried city schools to one-class village schools, with three in five of them in classes of over thirty pupils. In all these ways the sample, although a fairly small selected one, did seem to be representative of P H children in ordinary primary schools in England.

REFERENCES

ABERCROMBIE, M. L. T. (1964) *Perceptual and visuo-motor disorders in cerebral palsy*, Little Club Clinics in Developmental Medicine, II.

ABERCROMBIE, M. L. T. (1968) 'Notes on spatial disability, movement, intelligence quotient and attentiveness', *Developmental Medicine and Child Neurology*, 10, pp. 206–13.

ANDERSON, E. M. (1973) 'Cognitive deficits and behavioural disorders in children with spina bifida and hydrocephalus', *British Journal of Educational Psychology* (in press).

BAX, M. C. (1964) 'Terminology and classification of cerebral palsy', *Developmental Medicine and Child Neurology*, 6, pp. 295–7.

Central Advisory Council for Education (England) (1967) *Children and Their Primary Schools* (Plowden Report), HMSO, London.

DAVIE, R., BUTLER, N. R. and GOLDSTEIN, H. (1972) *From Birth to Seven, The Second Report of the National Child Development Study (1958 Cohort)*, Longmans, London.

DOUGLAS, J. W. B. (1964) *The Home and the School*, MacGibbon and Kee, London.

FRANKLIN, A. WHITE (ed.) (1960) *The Care of Invalid and Crippled Children*, Oxford University Press, London.

HENDERSON, P. (1968) 'Changing patterns of disease and disability in school children in England and Wales', *British Medical Journal*, 2, pp. 329–34.

HEWETT, S. (1970) *The Family and the Handicapped Child*, Allen and Unwin, London.

LAURENCE, K. M. (1966) 'The survival of untreated spina bifida cystica', *Developmental Medicine and Child Neurology*, 8, Supplement 11, pp. 10–19.

LINDON, R. L. (1963) 'The Pultibec system for the medical assessment of physically handicapped children', *Developmental Medicine and Child Neurology*, 5, pp. 125–45.

LORBER, J. (1971) 'Results of myelomeningocele', *Developmental Medicine and Child Neurology*, 13 (3), pp. 279–303.

MILLER, E. and SETHI, L. (1971a) 'The effects of hydrocephalus on perception', *Developmental Medicine and Child Neurology*, Supplement 25, pp. 77–81.

MILLER, E. and SETHI, L. (1971b) 'Tactile matching in children with hydrocephalus', *Neuropaediatrie*, 3, pp. 191–4.

Ministry of Education (1959) *The Handicapped Pupils and Special Schools Regulations 1959*, Statutory Instrument No. 365, HMSO, London.

Ministry of Education (1964) *The Health of the School Child*, HMSO, London.

PRINGLE, M. L. KELLMER, BUTLER, N. R. and DAVIE, R. (1966) *11,000 Seven Year Olds*, Longmans, London.

PRINGLE, M. L. KELLMER and FIDDES, D. O. (1970) *The Challenge of Thalidomide*, Longmans, London.

Registrar General (1960) *Classification of Occupations*, HMSO, London.

REYNELL, J. (1970) 'Children with physical handicaps', chapter 15 in Mittler, P. (ed.), *The Psychological Assessment of Mental and Physical Handicaps*, Methuen, London.

RUTTER, M., GRAHAM, P., YULE, W. (1970a) *A Neuropsychiatric Study in Childhood*, Clinics in Developmental Medicine, 35/6, Spastics Society/Heinemann, London.

RUTTER, M., TIZARD, J. and WHITMORE, K. (ed.) (1970b) *Education, Health and Behaviour*, Longmans, London.

SPAIN, B. (1970) 'Spina bifida survey', GLC Research and Intelligence Unit, *Quarterly Bulletin*, 12, pp. 5–12.

SPAIN, B. (1972) Personal communication.

TYSON, M. (1964) 'Shape matching test', chapter 7 in Abercrombie, M. L. et al. (ed.), *Visual, Perceptual and Visuo Motor Impairment in Physically Handicapped Children, Perceptual and Motor Skills*, Supplement 3, 18, pp. 561–625.

WEDELL, K. (1960) 'The visual perception of cerebral-palsied children', *Journal of Child Psychology and Psychiatry*, 1, pp. 215–27.

WEDELL, K. (1961) 'Follow-up study of perceptual ability in children with hemiplegia', in *Hemiplegic Cerebral Palsy in Children and Adults*, the report of an international study group held in Bristol, Spastics Society/Heinemann, London.

Chapter 3 · Placement Problems

This chapter is especially concerned with the practical problems faced by parents in obtaining suitable placement for their children in ordinary schools. As Hewett (1970) has pointed out in her study of cerebral-palsied children, this is often a major source of anxiety. The question of assessment which is closely related to that of placement will not be dealt with in any detail here. A very comprehensive recent account is given in the book edited by Peter Mittler (1970), *The Assessment of Mental and Physical Handicap*, while administrative problems are covered in chapter 6 of *Living With Handicap*, (Younghusband *et al.*, 1970).

In the opening section of this chapter a brief account is given of 'normal' placement procedures and of some of the ways in which ideals and reality fail to match up. Next the placement history of the children in the study is examined, the results supporting the point made in the previous chapter about the degree of overlap between children in special and ordinary schools. The main part of the chapter deals with the specific problems encountered by the parents, all these being illustrated by case history material. Finally, detailed consideration is given to parental attitudes regarding special versus ordinary school placement, and the reasons underlying these.

The material used in the chapter has been drawn from a number of sources: firstly and most important, from interviews of one to two hours which I had in their homes with the ninety-nine mothers concerned (or occasionally with both parents), secondly from interviews with heads and class teachers in the schools and thirdly from the children's medical, educational and other relevant records, where these were made available.

An outline of 'normal' placement procedure

The 1944 Education Act, recognizing the importance of early education for the handicapped child, gave the right to parents and local authorities to request that a child's needs for special educational provision be formally ascertained at any time after he is 2 years old. The essentials of the assessment procedure are summarized by Mary Sheridan (1965). They include 'careful preliminary observation with full medical examination and psychological assessment, carried out by specially experienced medical officers and educational psychologists who are authorized by the Department of Education and Science for the purpose'. Several assessments may be necessary before a final decision about placement can be taken.

In *Living with Handicap*, Younghusband *et al.* (1970) suggest that:

ideally, placement should be made as the result of a team decision with the parents, in which due weight has been given to medical, psychological, social and educational information. . . . The head-teacher of the receiving school should certainly be involved in the decision rather than being simply informed of a new entrant. . . . Not the least important of the persons to be fully involved in the decision are the parents. They should be clearly informed of the reasons for the recommendations and their agreement and co-operation sought. It has been suggested that all admissions to special schools should be voluntary, the end of a process of educational guidance rather than of formal ascertainment. . . . One likely consequence is that medical officers, psychologists, teachers, social workers and administrators will have to spend more time on discussion and explanation.

Unfortunately, what in fact happens is often very far from this ideal. As Hewett (1970) points out, if the child is ascertained at all, 'this happens most often when the child's fifth birthday is imminent. The decision will then be taken either to include the child in the ordinary school system or to offer special education in a special school or class.' In my own study, as in Sheila Hewett's, the majority of children had been examined or ascertained (if at all) by local authority medical officers. Only in a minority of cases was a psychological assessment given before the child started school although this may not, of course, always be necessary. As Hewett found, the placement of many children was not seriously thought about until they were well into their fourth year, and the decision taken often appeared to be made on the basis of a rather brief visit by the medical officer to the child at home or on an interview in a clinic, or it might be made on the basis of the recommendations of a hospital consultant who had probably never seen the home or the school. Rarely did there seem to be full consultation between all those with useful knowledge about the child, and school heads were often 'informed' rather than 'consulted' about the placement of a handicapped child in their school.

Very few studies have been made in which a systematic attempt is actually made to analyse the reason for the type of special provision recommended. This was done, however, by Pless, Rackham and Kellock (1967) who looked at the reasons for the admissions of handicapped pupils (diabetics or asthmatics) to residential institutions. Although the handicaps in question differ from those of the children in the study, their conclusions are worth considering. In the case of 'a minority of authorities' they found that 'a great deal of thought had been given to the problem of the individual child; that all local resources had been exhausted; and that residential care was the best solution under the circumstances'. On the other hand, an equally strong subjective impression was formed that other authorities had 'found the disease a convenient excuse in which to pigeon-hole a difficult social problem'. Generally the authors found it was the psychosocial rather than physical factor which was the major determinant in the placement decision.

A second relevant conclusion was that there were

wide differences in the standard of selection (i.e. for residential school placement) between different local authorities. . . . In the case of physical conditions, these differences may be explicable through variations in the provision of medical facilities or the use of these services. A number of children are undoubtedly in residential homes only because too little support, whether medical or social, had been given in the home, when such support in another area would have been readily mobilized.

This statement could well be applied to the enormous variations between local authorities as regards the amount of special provision they are able or prepared to make in ordinary schools. Certainly, general trends are becoming clear. As Younghusband *et al.* (1970) point out,

> Educational provision for handicapped children was once thought of largely in terms of special school provision. It was never really valid to think in this way . . . but it is even less valid at the present time, owing to the trend towards the provision of special classes and units in ordinary schools and the inclusion, where appropriate, of fairly severely handicapped children in ordinary schools and classes.

While this is true, it is still the case that for many parents of handicapped children the possibility of suitable provision being made in an ordinary school depends very much on chance, that is, on where they happen to live.

Placement history of the children in the study

Detailed instances of the sorts of problems outlined above will be considered later. What recommendations and decisions, however, were actually made about the children in this study? In the case of the infant group, seventeen of the twenty-five children had been considered for special school placement although, owing largely to parental insistence, all had ultimately been placed at least for a trial period in an ordinary school. For the group of juniors, details are given in Table 3.1 below.

TABLE 3.1. *Placement history of children in the junior group*

Type of initial placement	No.	%
a Ordinary school: special school never suggested	30	40·4
b Ordinary school: special school initially suggested	28	38·1
c Ordinary school: transfer to special school suggested	9	12·1
d Special unit: transferred to ordinary school	2	2·7
e Special school: transferred to ordinary school	4	5·4
f Part-time ordinary class, part-time partially-hearing class	1	1·3
TOTAL CHILDREN	74	100·0

c

These findings suggest that there may be a considerable degree of overlap between the present ordinary and special school populations of PH children. Ordinary school placement had been the 'obvious' choice for fewer than half the children in the study. In the case of group (b), the suggestion of special school placement had been made by a great variety of people including local authority medical officers, hospital consultants, GPs, health visitors, social workers and others, and both the strength with which the recommendation had been made and the persistence which the parents had had to display in order to obtain ordinary school placement also varied greatly.

In some cases [group (c)] children had been considered for transfer to special schools or units. Without exception, these were children who had neurological abnormalities in addition to the physical handicap. In two cases a transfer had been suggested while the child was in an infant class. In one, the class teacher had opposed the move, and in the other case, the head. For the other seven children transfer had been suggested when it was time to move into junior school. Three of these children were cerebral-palsied, three had spina bifida and hydrocephalus and one had brain damage after a fall. Five of the children were sent to junior schools initially for a trial period. Of the other two, one is probably being transferred to a special school after only a year in an ordinary school in order to obtain more individual help. The other, a girl severely handicapped by spina bifida and hydrocephalus, has many difficulties, both physical and intellectual, and it has been recognized that an ordinary school can only 'contain' her until her parents feel able to accept special school placement.

In the cases of groups (d) and (e), the children had had some form of special education before being moved to an ordinary school. Details are shown in Table 3.2 below.

Two of the children had attended special units: the spina bifida child had been transferred at the end of the infant stage. The child with amyotonia congenita had been placed in a diagnostic unit as his mobility was very limited; he fell over easily if he was only 'brushed against', the village infant classroom was crowded and there was a long walk across the playground to the lavatories. However, his mother became anxious when she noticed he had 'begun to copy the mongol and mentally handicapped children in the unit' and at her request he was transferred at once to the village school, a placement which has proved most successful.

TABLE 3.2. *Children transferred from special schools or units*

Handicap	Type of special provision	Age when started (yrs)	Age at transfer (yrs)
Left hemiplegia	Day hospital school	4·0	5·4
Amyotonia congenita	'Diagnostic' unit	4·5	5·11
Spina bifida and hydrocephalus	Day PH school	4·7	7·1
Maple syrup urine disease	Day PH school	4·11	8·3
Absence of lower bowel	Residential PH school	5·1	8·1
Spina bifida and hydrocephalus	Day PH unit	6·2	7·11

Of the children moved from special schools, transfer was requested in two cases by parents who also felt their children needed the intellectual stimulus of an ordinary school; in another case the family moved out of London and the mother requested ordinary school placement. In the last case the child had been in care and when she was finally fostered the head of the local school approached the foster mother and offered to take her.

One question worth considering is whether the fact that a child has been considered for or placed in a special school is any indication of the likelihood that that child will succeed academically and/or socially in an ordinary school. It seems reasonable to suppose that those children whose ordinary school placement was at some stage in doubt would as a group have done less well. Table 3.3 shows that this is not the case.

There is in fact no difference whatsoever, either as regards academic success (where children were rated as 'high' as opposed to 'low' achievers, see chapter 7), or social adjustment (where 'high' and 'low' ratings were also given, see chapter 6) between these two groups. There are of course many ways of interpreting this finding. One is that consideration for special school was not made primarily on educational grounds but for physical reasons and therefore is unlikely to give any indication of educational success. Another is that those parents who successfully opposed special school placement may on the whole be a group who take a particularly keen interest in their children's education, and who also encourage the

TABLE 3.3. 'Outcomes' in relation to placement history of handicapped children

| | SS at some time | | | | | |
| Type of outcome | No question of SS* suggested or attended. No. = 30 | | No. = 44 | | Total No. = 74 | |
	High	Low	High	Low	High	Low
Academic success	53·3%	46·7%	52·2%	47·7%	52·7%	47·3%
Social adjustment	46·7%	53·3%	45·4%	54·5%	45·9%	54·0%

* SS = special school

children to mix in the normal community, with beneficial results for both their educational and social development. However they are interpreted, the results do offer some evidence that the parents' decisions to insist on ordinary school placement were in the majority of cases sensible and well founded, at least to the extent that their children are doing as well as those for whom special school was never suggested.

Placement problems

The problems which arise when the school placement of a physically handicapped child is being considered are likely to be seen slightly differently by the different professions involved. A hospital consultant, a head teacher, a physiotherapist, a social worker, an educational psychologist and a local authority education officer are likely to emphasize different needs and to envisage different kinds of practical problems. In this section, however, it is the problems which cause the parents most anxiety which I have deliberately chosen to discuss, since their viewpoint has not always been well represented. The problems which were most often mentioned to me included lack of advice or contradictory advice about placement, often coupled with delays in placement which were detrimental to the child; the refusal of ordinary schools to accept a PH child; the frequent need for parents to show considerable persistence in order to obtain ordinary school rather than special school placement and finally difficulties relating to placement at each educational transition point, that is from infants to juniors and juniors to secondary school.

These problems will be considered in turn, but first three case histories will be outlined which, taken together, illustrate in a vivid form all the problems mentioned above. All three concern severely handicapped children living in rural areas, a group for whom difficulties are most likely to occur. My purpose in relating these is not to level criticism at any particular local authority or individual but rather to give a realistic account of the kind of difficulties which do occur and of the multiplicity of factors which may influence the final placement. They also show how a series of setbacks in obtaining suitable placement for a child may, when taken individually, appear to be of minor importance: only when pieced together into a 'history' extending perhaps over several years can their full impact on the child's development be seen, and the prolonged anxiety caused to parents appreciated.

Three case histories

CASE I JOHN, A CHILD HANDICAPPED BY SPINA BIFIDA AND HYDROCEPHALUS

John was born with a myelomeningocele which resulted in flaccid paralysis of the lower limbs and double incontinence. His hydrocephalus was controlled by a Pudenz valve inserted when he was 8 months old. When he was assessed at 4 years old the severity of his handicap was apparent. He had bilateral dilation of the ureters and constantly recurring urinary infections; his bladder was expressed several times daily and he had no bowel control. A skull defect had resulted in a large cystic swelling above the valve and slight dysarthria was also present. Bilateral dislocation of the hips and bilateral talipes were noted, and he was virtually confined to a wheelchair. To the paediatrician it was 'evident that he will be unable to go to an ordinary school'.

Until John was almost 9 years old, the educational provision arranged for him can only be described as patchy and makeshift. The first possibility discussed (when John was four and a half) was that of placement as a weekly boarder at a PH school, but as the school was unwilling to take incontinent pupils and his parents were opposed to special schooling a decision was deferred until John was 5·3 years old. At this stage, the local GP tried to arrange morning placement in a local school on a trial basis, but the school refused. When he was nearly six, John was admitted to another local school for afternoons only. Unfortunately the class teacher was exceptionally unsympathetic: she complained the child was 'smelly' and did nothing to include him in the afternoon's activities and after two weeks told his mother, 'his fortnight is up and he must go'. Shortly after this, he was admitted for mornings only to a nearby village school. When he was 6 years 4 months old the head offered to take him full-time since his concentration and maturity had increased so much.

At 7 years 2 months the head said he must leave as he was by then over age and his sympathetic class teacher was leaving. A place was offered him at a boarding school for spina bifida children but his parents refused this. Instead they contacted all the local junior schools; all refused him. After a two-month gap they obtained six hours a week of voluntary tuition for him from a retired teacher. A year later when John was nearly eight and a half home tuition was provided by the LEA.

The reluctance of his parents to having the ileal loop operation done (to ease the problem of incontinence management) was overcome at this stage, and after a successful operation John, at nearly 9 years old, was admitted to a local junior school, where, despite a medical and educational history which might have proved traumatic for many children, he has settled in remarkably quickly and well, although he is clearly a long way behind his peers. Admittedly his case was a particularly difficult one, but it does show how lack of early advance planning and liaison among those concerned with his educational future contributed to a situation where, apart from a brief spell between the age of 6·4 and 7·2, this clearly educable and sociable child was denied full-time education and the company of his peers until he was nearly 9 years old.

CASE 2 MARK, ANOTHER CHILD WITH SPINA BIFIDA AND HYDROCEPHALUS

Mark's case is comparable in many ways with the previous one since he is similarly handicapped and also lives in a rural area. His parents, however, were willing to accept a special school from the start and when he was 4 years old the hospital consultant and the local authority medical officer decided to approach a PH school which accepted weekly boarders. After the parents had been taken to visit the school and were impressed by it, the psychologist wrote recommending early admission as the child was homebound. When Mark was four and a half the head wrote to say they could not accept an incontinent child. The next move was made when he was 5·2 years old, when the local authorities asked the school to try the child with a urinal. The reply was that there were no vacancies.

By the time Mark was five and a half, his mother began to 'feel desperate'. Encouraged by the local authority officials, she visited the local infant school to discuss whether the child could be admitted on a temporary basis. The head's reply was predictable and probably fairly typical: 'When I saw how limited he was in his movements, I felt it would be extremely difficult to place him in such a large school, because of the probability of his being knocked down . . . I felt I could not take the responsibility for his welfare.' She also thought that it would be unfair to the class teacher who would have him. The mother ended her account to the local authority of this visit: 'we had a very long talk and I asked her if it would be all right for mornings only, but she still said no, so what will happen now?'

By now everyone was concerned. The PH school had no place for the next eighteen months and the upshot was that the director of education himself approached a village school several miles away and asked whether the child could be admitted on a temporary basis pending admission to the PH school. The head agreed, although she told me that she would like to have been given much more information about the child especially as she knew nothing about spina bifida. Mark's mother was informed that he had been accepted and that she would hear about arrangements: owing to a lack of liaison between health and education, nothing was done. Term began and the head, who had also heard nothing, 'assumed the matter had fallen through when the child did not turn up'. Eventually the now 'desperately worried' mother contacted the health visitor and the matter was sorted out.

Once more, a combination of circumstances at least some of which were avoidable resulted in a child being deprived of schooling until the age of 5 years 8 months. In this case the delay was particularly unfortunate in that, although the home was in many ways an excellent one, the child was so 'good' that his mother had not felt the need to provide him with stimulating play material nor had he ever painted or drawn before he started school.

CASE 3 DAVID, A CHILD WITH SEVERE HAEMOPHILIA

Like the other two children, David is also severely handicapped and lives in a rural area. His placement history is discussed since it illustrates how sometimes, even when the school staff and local authorities do all they can, the needs of a handicapped child cannot be met in an ordinary school.

David's haemophilia is more severe than that of any other children in the study: he has 'easy ability to bleed when minimal disturbance occurs' and has been hospitalized many times since his first admission at fourteen months. One hospital report states that 'even on the most minor movements in bed his ankle has blown up' and he bleeds particularly easily into the left knee. As a result he spends much time in a wheelchair.

The parents requested early admission to school and when he was 4 years 10 months old the school medical officer arranged placement in a small village primary school where he could remain until he was 11 years old, since the parents were strongly opposed to special school placement. The school was two miles from his home, and he first travelled by school bus. A request from the parents and welfare officer that, since this was too dangerous, he should be provided with taxi transport provoked a long series of letters with the local authority who were worried about the expense involved. At that stage their attitude was that if handicapped children were admitted to ordinary schools 'they must be capable of being treated more or less as ordinary children since if they need special or exceptional treatment which ordinary schools can't provide they really need special education with all its implications.' (This attitude, in which special provision is by inference equated with special school placement, is of course changing and in fact this local authority did eventually make a number of special provisions for David in the village school.)

The transport problem was solved by a petrol allowance being paid to the parents by the LEA. However, other problems followed. Most serious was the child's frequent absence from school with bleeding episodes. In the autumn term (when he was 5½ years old) he attended school for only nine full days, in the spring term for only thirty days and in the summer term the pattern was similar. Although there was a day special school in the county, the consultant thought the long journey there 'would give more than adequate opportunities for traumas to occur', and as a result the local authority wrote to the Department of Education and Science requesting information about residential schools for haemophiliacs.

By the time David was 6 years 3 months old the school head was becoming anxious and her reasons are worth quoting:

> We are becoming increasingly worried about his future. His attendance is spasmodic. His legs seem unable to support his weight and he is frequently having fresh plaster casts applied. He has to be lifted from his wheelchair each time he wants to go to the lavatory and the class teacher has to leave the rest of the children while attending to his needs. Although we do our best to accommodate him in the classroom I am wondering if he is frustrated by watching the other children at their play, and I fear he is becoming more than we can handle physically. As much as we love him I think we must face the possibility that shortly we shall no longer be able to give him all the help and attention he needs.

The local authority responded immediately to this letter: a senior medical officer visited the school and recommended the appointment of a 'lay assistant', modifications to the toilet and the provision of ramps, and future placement in a special school. The first two recommendations were carried out rapidly, but the last has proved more difficult. After considerable delay the local authority received a list of four residential schools for PH children near haematology units. By now, the child's consultant was also strongly urging residential placement where the child could receive 'continuous education and easy treatment'.

When I visited the school David was 8 years 4 months old. He had been kept for an extra year in an infant class and everyone concerned, including the parents, was now anxious that he should start the following term, at eight and a half, in a special school. However the summer term was due to end in three weeks and no definite arrangement had yet been made. As his mother put it, 'time is running out . . . there will be hardly time to visit the [new] school now before term is over.' This case illustrates the need for early assessment and planning rather than *ad hoc* attempts, however commendable, to meet difficulties after they have arisen. It also shows the need for regular reconsideration of the initial placement decision since sometimes, as here, an ordinary school will not be able to meet a severely handicapped child's needs.

Specific problems

(i) INADEQUATE ADVICE OR CONSULTATION

While it is sometimes the case that problems arise because too many different people are concerned with a handicapped child, it is also true that many parents feel that they receive inadequate help and support in finding the right placement.

The mothers of the twenty-five handicapped children in infant classes were asked how satisfied they had been with the advice they received about the child's education and their replies are shown in Table 3.4 below.

TABLE 3.4. *Mother's satisfaction with advice on educational place-ment: infant group*

Satisfaction rating	No.	%
Satisfied	6	24
Fairly satisfied	6	24
Dissatisfied	9	36
Other	4	16
TOTAL	25	100·0

Of the parents who were satisfied, four came from the same area and were full of praise for the local authority medical officer, as remarks like these indicate: 'She was very good and came round frequently'; 'They've been very helpful. . . . She asked me what sort of schooling I'd like'; 'They've been very good indeed.' One mother who had received constant support from a spastics centre since the child was a baby was also very satisfied.

The main complaint of the six parents who were only 'fairly satisfied' was either that the advice they received was given simply during one rather short talk with a medical officer, or because it had come very late. The 'dissatisfied' group had received virtually no advice: the four 'other' cases were all from professional families who had, as one mother put it, 'got ourselves organized'. One had raised the question with a local head at a parent-teacher meeting when her child was only two; another asked the local education committee to come and discuss the matter with her; the others had been new-comers to the district and had themselves contacted the LEAs.

Over half the children in the infant group came from two local authority areas which are well geared to making special provision in ordinary schools. This and the fact that the children tended to be severely handicapped meant that they were more likely to come to the attention of the LEA at an early age, and that the parents were more likely to have been given adequate help than were many of the parents in the 'junior' group. Some examples are given below of the lack of help which parents of children in the latter group received.

A particular unfortunate case was that of Mary, who was quite severely handicapped by spina bifida and hydrocephalus. When Mary (a city child) was four and a half her mother approached the local infant school (since no one had offered her advice on placement) and Mary was accepted there provided that her mother came in to change her nappies. In this case the parents were adamantly opposed to special schooling and their consultant agreed that the child could 'manage' an ordinary school and could attain a 'dull average performance'. Schooling was then interrupted by extensive surgery. At nearly five the child had a Spitz–Holter valve inserted and the following year the ileal loop operation with diversion of the ureters was carried out to relieve severe and chronic urinary infections.

Shortly before the child was seven the school reported that they were finding the situation too much as the child was still soiling, and that they considered her unsuitable for ordinary junior school. At this stage the family were rehoused. The new local school would not accept Mary and the parents were asked by the local authority to consider a PH school. They again refused and, as their home was on the boundary of two LEAs, tried another primary school in local authority B. In the mother's words, 'I was knocked over and cried my eyes out when the head said to my husband and I, "we'd love to have you": no one had ever taken Mary as she stands.' A few days later someone from local authority A came around and informed the mother that arrangements had been made for the child to go to a special school. The mother in turn informed them of the arrangements she had made and these were allowed to stand. To the mother, local authority A had seemed 'cruel, they treated us as outcasts, as if we were dirty', whereas local authority B 'have been marvellous'. The child's placement in a special class in an ordinary school has not been entirely satisfactory, but the case illustrates very clearly the effect on the parents which lack of support may have.

Another parent who felt very strongly that she had received

inadequate advice, at least at the early stages when she was most in need of support, was the mother of a child who suffered from bowel incontinence owing to a congenital deformity. When the child was four she had asked a social worker what to do about schooling and had been advised to write to what was then the Ministry of Education. Four months later, having received no reply, she approached the local educational authority who could only offer a home tutor. They thought that 'with luck' a special school might accept the child at 7 years old. With the consultant's support the mother then approached a local infant school, who agreed to take the child, and an extra welfare assistant was appointed. Two years later the head of the junior department refused to take the child. Another head was approached by the local authority and also refused, whereupon the mother took the child around to the school; when the head 'saw how normal he was' he changed his mind and two days before term began the parents were offered a place. In fact this child now is thoroughly integrated socially and making excellent academic progress.

In some cases parents had received advice but the timing had been inappropriate. One mother with a spina bifida child was approached by a social worker who wanted to discuss schooling when the child was a year old; she then heard nothing until the child was four. Home tuition was arranged when he was 5 years 3 months old and not until he was six and a half was he admitted to an ordinary infant school with a special assistant. In another case a hemiplegic child had been assessed and ascertained as physically handicapped when he was 1 year 10 months old. At four, admission to a day hospital school was recommended but the mother was not told about this until the day before the ambulance arrived and had no time to 'prepare' him.

In several cases parents heard about appropriate provision by chance. One spina bifida child was receiving home tuition since the parents did not want residential schooling. Through friends the parents heard about a local unit for PH children in an ordinary school; they contacted the local education authority and the child was admitted at 6 years 2 months old. One parent of a spina bifida child was becoming increasingly anxious as she was not keen on residential schooling for a 5 year old: another mother at the pre-school playgroup suggested home tuition. This was arranged (and the child later transferred to an ordinary school) but as the mother said, 'If this hadn't been mentioned casually I wouldn't even have known the possibility existed.'

Sometimes it is not the lack of advice which is a problem, but the fact that contradictory advice is given. One mother with a spina bifida child had maintained close contact with her health visitor, who wrote to the local health department 'I strongly recommend Anthony goes to an ordinary school; he appears alert and intelligent, his speech is good and he is friendly.' She went on to arrange placement in the local infant school. In the meantime, the school medical officer had told the mother the child (whose IQ on the Stanford–Binet was 152) would 'definitely' have to go to a special school. Eventually he changed his mind and the child (whose nickname is 'brains') is making excellent progress.

Other examples concern incontinent children. In one case the child's multiple congenital defects had necessitated a ureterostomy; he also had a severe respiratory complaint. The consultant suggested an 'open-air school' and the medical social worker thought 'there was little likelihood a normal school could cope with his ureterostomy', but the parents on contacting their general practitioner were told there was 'no need' for a special school and the local head agreed to take the child provided that an extra welfare assistant was appointed. The other case was somewhat similar. The child in question had bilateral hydronephrosis and hydroureters, and was constantly wet. The health visitor thought him 'quite unsuitable' for ordinary school and the local welfare centre recommended special school placement. The child's consultant on the other hand said there was 'absolutely no need' for special school placement and although 'confused' by this contradictory advice the parents decided to trust his judgement.

Certainly, of all the placement problems raised by parents, the lack of adequate advice was one of the most frequently mentioned. Bitterness may often result even in the most sensible of parents, as in the couple who when I asked whether anyone had even come to discuss their child's schooling with them simply burst out laughing.

(ii) REFUSAL OF ORDINARY SCHOOLS TO ACCEPT
  PH CHILDREN

In the junior group ten children (13 per cent) who had been assessed as suitable for ordinary schools had been refused a place on one or more occasions. In the case of four the head had initially refused but had later changed his mind; in four more cases, the first school approached had refused but the next had accepted the child; while in two cases more than two schools had refused to accept the child.

There seemed to be no pattern in the characteristics of the children refused places. Five were severely handicapped and five only moderately so. In the case of two haemophiliacs the schools 'did not want the responsibility' but eventually agreed to take the children for trial periods. Three of those refused places had congenital abnormalities. One had a congenital absence of the left arm. The head at first refused to take him stating that 'this would place great strain and responsibility on a young teacher who already has many turbulent youngsters. . . . He would be a risk in the school.' The other two were more severely handicapped, one by thalidomide deformities and the other by diastrophic dwarfism.

Of the others refused places, three were children with spina bifida and hydrocephalus. The reasons given were 'too many steps', 'too crowded' and 'enough problems without a wheelchair'. Only in one case was the child's incontinence given as the reason. Of the infant group, most of whom were severely handicapped, five had been refused places by one or more infant schools, one being a haemophiliac and the others spina bifida children. In three cases incontinence was the main problem.

What must also be considered is how handicapped children fare when pre-school or nursery school provision is in question. Younghusband et al. (1970) noted the 'urgent need for more pre-school facilities for handicapped children; in particular day nurseries and nursery schools or classes which are prepared to take a proportion of handicapped children are in extremely short supply . . . what is now known about the importance of early learning applies with even greater force to the young handicapped child'.

In the infant group thirteen of the twenty-five children had attended nursery schools, in eight cases local authority schools and in five cases private ones. In six cases this had been arranged by the parents, in three by the local health authority and in other cases by the local education authority, the Spastics Society or teachers who were family friends. In three cases the child's incontinence had meant that he was refused by the local nursery school.

Where such provision is not available it is important that a child be admitted as early as possible to an infant class. However, of the twenty-five children only ten had joined an infant class before their fifth birthday, eight between the ages of five and five and a half, four between the ages of five and a half and six, and one after his sixth birthday.

In the junior group a comparison was made between the amount of nursery or other pre-school experience the handicapped and non-handicapped children had enjoyed, and the results are shown in Table 3.5 below.

TABLE 3.5. *Nursery school or other pre-school experience: junior group*

Groups	Nursery school experience		Other pre-school experience (excluding day nursery)	
	No.	%	No.	%
Controls (No. = 142)	49	34·5	17	11·9
PH group (No. = 74)	29	39·1	9	12·1
PH group without neurological abnormalities (No. = 48)	14	29·1	3	6·2
PH children with neurological abnormalities (No. = 26)	15	57·6	6	23·0

Overall the proportions of handicapped and non-handicapped children receiving such experience do not differ, although the PH children with neurological abnormalities were more likely to have been to nursery schools or playgroups, which is encouraging. When it is remembered, however, that handicapped children have a greater need than their peers for early stimulation the figures confirm the inadequacy of present provision.

(iii) *Unsatisfactory treatment within the ordinary school*
A child's being accepted by an ordinary school does not mean that his problems are over. The attitude the staff take towards him is of enormous importance. The question of special arrangements in

ordinary schools is the subject of chapters 8 and 9, and will only be touched on at this point. Hewett (1970) has noted that

> the willingness of teachers . . . to be flexible and helpful is some-times more important than the degree of handicap and we were given instances both of schools which exercised their imagination to accommodate children with quite considerable physical disabilities, and others where lack of imagination had made life more difficult than it need have been for children with minimal disabilities.

One illustration is given here of what can happen to a child in a crowded city school where no special provision is made. The boy concerned suffered from a congenital deformity which meant that he was only continent if he made frequent visits to the toilet. The local head was sympathetic and admitted him; the class teacher however was 'too busy to help' and would not even remind him to go to the toilet. As a result he often came home 'saturated'. The mother reported that the infant helper was instructed not to change the child as it was 'not her job': when she offered to come and change the child (and any other children who needed this) herself her offer was refused, no reasons being given. Fortunately the class teacher left, and thanks to the new teacher's cooperation the child's control is greatly improved.

Such cases seemed rare and most schools who accepted a handi-capped child were at least aware of their responsibilities towards him even though their resources were sometimes inadequate.

(iv) *The need to 'put up a fight' to obtain ordinary school placement*
As mentioned in chapter 1 it is official policy that 'no handicapped pupil should be sent to a special school who can be satisfactorily educated in an ordinary school' (DES *Circular No. 276*, 1954). The phase 'satisfactorily educated', however, leaves a great deal of room for interpretation. Different professionals may offer parents con-tradictory advice and the views of the parents themselves may fre-quently conflict with those of the person assessing the child, especially when assessment is carried out on the basis of a single visit to the home by a local authority medical officer who may never have seen the child before. Sometimes every attempt is made to avoid putting pressure on the parents, to inform them of the alter-natives available and to involve them as fully as possible in the final

decision. In other instances a rather subtle pressure may be exerted, in the sense that parents who in their hearts may be convinced that their children would be best placed in an ordinary school feel obliged to agree to the recommendations of a persuasive 'expert' who patently wants to 'do what is best for the child'. Finally pressure may be more obviously imposed, the parents being informed that their child 'will of course require special school placement'. As much of the success of a child's placement, whether in an ordinary or a special school, will depend on how the parents feel about that placement, unnecessary stress could probably be avoided if they were consulted more fully about their wishes and if there were a genuine attempt made to meet these. In this study fifteen parents had had to show considerable persistence and initiative to ensure the final placement of their children in ordinary schools while a much larger number, although they did not have to 'put up a fight', had had to have the courage of their own convictions in opposing the initial recommendation of a doctor. It is also significant that the first reaction of many parents to my carefully worded letter introducing the study and its aims to them was a defensive one of the 'I won't let him be moved to a special school' variety. In one area the fact that a day PH school was being constructed was causing great anxiety among almost all the parents whose handicapped children had been placed in ordinary schools. In the last part of this chapter the parents' attitudes and the reasons they offered for these are discussed in detail: in the following paragraphs examples are given of what the parents actually did to make sure that their children were placed in ordinary schools.

In a few cases parents anticipated a placement decision by making known their own views. One very sensible and articulate mother with a spina bifida child approached the local head when her child was 2 years old: he thought he could accommodate her, and advised her to return shortly before the child was due to start. When the child was nearly five, the paediatrician told the mother she need not worry as he would ensure that her child got a place in a residential PH school. The mother went back to the head (who 'wholeheartedly' agrees with the trend to keep PH children in ordinary schools) and after consultation with the local authority and some modifications to the school the child was accepted on a trial basis.

One of the children in the infant group (who had hydrocephalus with secondary spastic paralysis) is registered as a 'gifted' child. In her case a special school was suggested and to avoid this the mother herself made arrangements for the child to attend an ordinary school. Another child in this group has athetosis and quadriplegia. She walks slowly and shakily, her speech is slurred (dysarthria), hand control is considerably impaired and she has a high frequency hearing loss. Despite this, persistence on the part of the parents has meant that she has successfully attended ordinary nursery and infant schools. When transfer to the junior school came up the paediatrician considered her as 'ideal' for the new special school; once again parental determination was necessary before a six-month trial period in an ordinary junior school was agreed to.

It was not only rather severely handicapped cerebral-palsied children who had problems of this kind. The mother of a child with mild right hemiparesis reported that the local authorities recommended special schooling. 'It was a great surprise: I had him down for an ordinary school. It was not as if he couldn't speak. I couldn't make it out.' After the consultant's support had been enlisted the child was placed in an ordinary school.

Of the other children in the study whose parents had had to oppose placement in a special school rather actively, all but two came from London. Presumably this was because of the existence of a large number of special schools in London. One case concerns a child with upper limb thalidomide deformities. His mother reported that 'a lady and gentleman from the authorities came when he was nearly five and insisted on his going to a special school'. After visiting the school the mother felt most reluctant to accept the decision and was advised by her consultant to 'fight' for what she wanted. She therefore placed the child in a private school and when the family moved to another part of London was lucky in finding that the local head made no difficulties about accepting the child.

In the case of a child with spina bifida who was actually placed in a day PH school, the mother reported that 'someone just arrived at the door and said he was to go there . . . and that a bus would pick him up'. She thought it was 'quite a cheek' that she was not consulted first. It was not until the family moved out of London that a transfer to an ordinary school could be made.

Nearly all the spina bifida children in the study were in schools outside London. One exception was a child whose mother had taken the precaution of 'putting her down' for the local infant school when she was only three. When the question of transfer to a junior school

PLACEMENT PROBLEMS · 69

arose the mother was told that the child would have to go to a special school, but after she had enlisted the support of the consultant the junior school accepted her for a trial period. Only when the child had been in the school for some time did the mother reveal that she was suffering not from 'kidney trouble' but from spina bifida.

Clearly there are borderline cases where the recommendation for special schooling is very reasonable, and where success in an ordinary school could hardly have been predicted. One child in the study has severe diastrophic dwarfism. While on the waiting list for a day PH school (which the parents were reluctant about) she was admitted to an ordinary nursery school for a trial period. The head reported, 'she is in a group of forty-two 4 year olds and copes well with every aspect of nursery school routine. She needs no special attention from the staff . . . and shows great persistence and concentration in the mastery of tools such as scissors, brushes and pencils.' Following this she was, only because of her parents' insistence, given a trial period in an ordinary infant school. Here she coped very well. 'She tries most things . . . keeps up with her work . . . and is very happy.' At the next stage the parents faced further difficulties. The junior school head 'didn't say she would or wouldn't accept her . . . she thought she would be better off at a PH school'. Fortunately a new head was appointed who was 'altogether different . . . very understanding', and the child was accepted, although a place is being kept open at a day PH school for her.

(v) FUTURE PLACEMENT

(a) Infants

This chapter has been mainly concerned with problems relating to the children's present placement. It is equally important to look ahead to see whether any future problems were envisaged. The question was looked at in most detail for the twenty-five infants. Class teachers were first asked: 'Do you think this is the best school for X at the present time?' All but three answered yes. The case of the haemophiliac has been discussed. In the two other cases it was felt that there were no social problems but that the children needed the extra attention which could only be given in a smaller class, preferably in an ordinary school.

Teachers were next asked whether they thought the child would cope satisfactorily in an ordinary junior class. Replies are summarized in Table 3.6.

TABLE 3.6. *Likelihood that PH children now in infant classes will cope in an ordinary junior school*

Class teachers' views	No. of children
Will definitely cope	12
Will probably cope	7
Will probably not cope	4
Don't know	2
TOTAL	25

Of the six children about whom doubts or 'don't knows' were expressed, arrangements are being made for five to be transferred to special schools while the other (along with two more in the group) is being kept for an extra year in the infant class.

What problems precipitated the proposed transfers to special school? In one case it was very serious haemophilia. In another (a child with spina bifida and hydrocephalus) ordinary school placement had been only temporary and the child's need for intensive physiotherapy (which the mother was unable to arrange for locally) was the main precipitating factor. The child had also become very withdrawn, this being one of the very few cases where special school placement might have benefited social adjustment. Two of the other children to be transferred also have spina bifida. One is not getting enough physiotherapy at present, although socially and educationally his present placement has been most satisfactory, while the other was not getting enough individual help in class. The fifth child to be transferred is cerebral-palsied and is going to a school for delicate children.

The infant group's class teachers were also asked 'What do you think X's greatest difficulties will be?' (when he moves into a junior class). Replies are set out in Table 3.7 below. In some cases more than one difficulty was mentioned.

Many of the infant group had neurological abnormalities in addition to their physical disabilities and it is interesting that educational difficulties are mentioned most often, although it was not usually possible to say whether general backwardness or specific learning difficulties were responsible for these. Of the children with educational difficulties, six had spina bifida and hydrocephalus (there

TABLE 3.7. *Difficulties at junior level anticipated by teachers of handicapped infants*

Difficulties			No. of children	
Educational	1	specific learning disabilities	2	⎫
	2	general backwardness	6	⎬ 9
	3	works slowly	1	⎭
Poor mobility			8	
Other physical problems (excluding incontinence)			5	
Emotional difficulties			3	
Poor concentration			3	
Frequent absences			2	
Toileting			2	

were twelve such children in the study), two cerebral palsy and only one was without a neurological handicap. This was a child who was absent a great deal (for 30 per cent of the previous autumn and 50 per cent of the winter term) and had not yet made a start with reading. In no case did the teachers think the educational difficulties were sufficient to exclude the children from ordinary schools, but there is no doubt that all could have benefited from being in smaller classes, or in a special class within an ordinary school.

The physical difficulties mentioned were, apart from poor mobility, very varied. Two teachers were worried that the child would soon be too heavy to lift from the wheelchair, in another case the child's hand control was very poor, one child was a haemophiliac and one very small and delicate.

Although several children had emotional or behavioural problems teachers only mentioned these as major difficulties in three cases. In one, the child lacked motivation to work and only wanted to practise physical skills; another child was very clever but also very quick-tempered and 'might have difficulty in finding an outlet for his aggression'; the third child 'still finds it difficult to stand on his own feet'.

An interesting final point is that although fifteen of this group were incontinent, the appointment of a welfare assistant had proved so successful as a means of coping that in only two cases did teachers see toileting as a problem. In one of these an assistant has since been appointed; the other child's disability is so severe that it will prove a problem even in a special school.

Lastly, the teachers were asked whether they felt that more children with handicaps of this kind and extent could be placed in ordinary schools under similar arrangements. All but one (the severe haemophiliac's teacher) answered yes. When asked if they thought the majority of their colleagues would agree, twenty said yes, one no and four were not sure. These findings are encouraging and suggest that if sufficient extra help is given (a most important proviso), ordinary teachers are likely to be sympathetic about accepting handicapped children in their classes.

(b) Juniors

The question of future placement was not looked at in such detail in the case of the juniors. Teachers were, however, asked whether they thought the present placement was the most suitable for the child. Sixty-four (84·5 per cent) answered in the affirmative, two (2·7 per cent) were not sure and eight (10·8 per cent) thought the child would be better placed elsewhere. Details about this last group are shown in Table 3.8 below.

TABLE 3.8. *Children whom teachers thought would be better placed elsewhere: junior group*

Handicap	Type of school preferred by class teacher
Minor thalidomide deformities	Smaller class in OS
Severe thalidomide	Smaller class in OS or 'thalidomide school'
Bilateral talipes	Smaller class or special class in OS
Minimal cerebral dysfunction	'Very small class'
Congenital absence left arm	Maladjusted school
Left hemiplegia	Day PH school
Spina bifida and hydrocephalus	Day PH school
Spina bifida and hydrocephalus	Delicate school

In two cases teachers said specifically that they thought that 'children like this' (left hemiplegia and severe thalidomide) should be in special schools. The hemiplegic was the youngest in a class to which his twin also belonged. The teacher thought him 'rather swamped and confused' and that he 'feels rather inferior and resents the fact that others can do more'. The two children about whom teachers were 'not sure' were a child with brain damage (resulting from a fall) whose very sympathetic teacher felt she could not give him enough individual attention, and a child with minor congenital deformities who was also partially hearing and rather withdrawn. As in the case of the infants, educational rather than physical difficulties were felt to be the real problem in all but one case. Teachers were also asked about future placement, in this case whether they thought the child would cope in an ordinary secondary school (although since none of the children were yet in their last year, this question had not yet been seriously considered) and their views are shown in Table 3·9 below.

TABLE 3.9. *Likelihood that PH children now in junior classes will cope in an ordinary secondary school*

Class teachers' view	No. of children = 74	% of group	
Will definitely cope	39	52·0	} 80·0
Will probably cope	21	28·0	
Will probably not cope	9	12·0	
Don't know	5	8·0	

Of the nine children who teachers thought would probably not cope, seven were children about whose present placement doubts had been expressed, while the others were a haemophiliac and a child who could not manage stairs. The 'don't know' group comprised another haemophiliac, the partially hearing child, a paraplegic in a wheelchair and two cerebral-palsied children. Certainly at the secondary level many new difficulties are likely to arise, and this is an area where research is lacking and needed.

Parental attitudes to special school placement

At the beginning of this chapter, the need to consult the parents fully regarding the child's placement was stressed. Later in the chapter examples were quoted to show that this may not always be done, and that several parents felt they had had to put up a fight to obtain the type of provision they wanted.

It is generally accepted that the parents' attitude to the handicap determines to a considerable extent the child's own attitude; it also seems very likely that the greater their anxieties about schooling, the less easily the parents will be able to accept the handicap. If the child's education can be discussed early on and if the parents feel that real efforts are being made to meet their wishes, a major source of stress in the home will be, if not removed, at least diminished and the effects on the child are likely to be beneficial.

It is therefore of great importance to find out what parents really feel about the different kinds of special provision available and to try to understand the factors underlying their attitudes, without writing them off as 'unrealistic', 'emotional', 'unreasonable' or 'obsessive'. If, as I suggest is the case, the aspirations of the majority *are* for ordinary school placement for their handicapped children, it is worth considering whether it would not be both more realistic and more in keeping with our professed ideals of educational democracy to try to modify the system to meet those wishes, rather than to try to change attitudes which are often very deeply rooted.

In this study, attitudes were explored during my interviews with the mothers. Since these were mothers with children in ordinary schools, it is hardly surprising that they should be strongly in favour of ordinary school placement, just as one would expect that in a sample comprising mothers with children in special schools, the advantages of special school placement would be stressed. People need to maintain a consistency between beliefs and facts; a mother whose child is placed in a special school may 'rationalize' the situation by maximizing in her mind the advantages that have been pointed out to her and minimizing her anxieties. This makes it very difficult to investigate what people 'really' feel. It should be remembered, though, that over half the children in this study had been potential (or in a few actual cases) special school candidates and mothers were asked not only how they had felt about this suggestion but also what action they had taken in a situation in which they had a very real choice to make.

In order to make the picture as objective as possible, I have, at the end of the chapter, given a summary of the views of parents whose children were in a day PH school, based on the findings presented by Dr Joan McMichael in her book *Handicap* (1971).

Research findings

My interview with the mother in which these questions were investigated was, in over 50 per cent of cases, my second meeting with her, following a short preliminary visit. In the other cases prior contact had been by letter, and sometimes by telephone. In the rural areas the interview usually followed a day spent at the school, in urban areas it took place within a fortnight of the school visit. Questions about education came about halfway through the interview after a series of factual questions about the handicap itself. By this stage a fairly relaxed atmosphere had generally been established. The first questions were about pre-school and nursery education and these often triggered off a spontaneous account of the placement history including the parents' feelings about suggestions made by doctors and others.

Before attitudes to special schools were explored, all parents, including those in the control group, were asked how they would have felt if their child had had to go to a boarding school instead of to his present school. (In some cases it had to be explained to parents of handicapped children that the question referred to an ordinary boarding school.) The findings are shown in Table 3.10.

TABLE 3.10. *Mothers' views on boarding school placement*

Views	Handicapped group No. = 74		Controls No. = 139	
	No.	%	No.	%
Agreeable	14	18·9	34	24·4
Neutral/don't know	6	8·1	20	14·3
Not very pleased	28	37·8	47	33·8
Strongly against	26	35·1	38	27·3

The pattern of responses of parents of the handicapped children and of the controls is very similar; a slightly higher proportion of parents of non-handicapped children are willing to send their children to boarding school, whereas 72·9 per cent of the handicapped childrens' parents as compared to 61·1 per cent of the control group are opposed to this. These differences are not significant and PH parents are probably often simply being realistic in stating that their children needed individual care which would not be available in a boarding school.

Following this, the mothers of the handicapped children were asked, 'What about special schools, in particular schools for physically handicapped children. There are several questions I'd like to ask you about these. First of all has it ever been suggested by anyone from the health or education services that X should go to a special school?'

After details had been obtained the mother was asked, 'How did you (and your husband) feel about this?'

If a special school had never been suggested, parents were asked instead, 'What would your feelings have been if someone had suggested that X should go to a special school?'

In both cases, where opposition to such placement was expressed, the question was asked, 'Why did you not (would you have not wanted) X to go to a special school?' Answers were recorded verbatim: where they were very vague (e.g. 'It wouldn't be good for her') further probes were used (e.g. 'In what way, not good?'). The findings for the junior school group are shown in Table 3.11.

TABLE 3.11. *Attitudes of mothers towards special school placement: junior group*

Response	If actually suggested No. = 44		If had been suggested No. = 30		Overall total No. = 74	
	No.	%	No.	%	No.	%
In favour	1	2·3	2	6·7	3	4·0
Uncommitted	6	13·6	4	13·3	10	13·5
Slightly against	9	20·5	8	26·7	17	23·0
Moderately against	7	15·9	4	13·3	11	14·9
Strongly against	21	47·7	12	40·0	33	44·6

Overall only 4 per cent of the parents were in favour of special schooling, 13·5 per cent uncommitted and 82·5 per cent opposed, more than half of these quite strongly. One of the interesting findings s that, irrespective of whether special school placement was actually suggested or not, the proportion of parents giving each category of response is remarkably similar.

The same questions were put to mothers of children in infant classes. All these children were moderately or severely handicapped and for nineteen of the twenty-five children special school placement had been a strong possibility. Once again, however, only 8 per cent of the mothers were in favour of special school placement and 24 per cent uncommitted, while 24 per cent were slightly against it, 8 per cent moderately so and 36 per cent strongly opposed.

The parents' voices

In this final section I have attempted to fill out the bare bones of the previous statistics by letting the parents speak for themselves.

(i) THOSE 'IN FAVOUR OF' OR 'UNCOMMITTED' AS REGARDS
       SPECIAL SCHOOL PLACEMENT

In the junior group, two of the three mothers in favour of special school placement felt their children would 'get a better chance' in a special school, but the most common attitude of those in favour or uncommitted can be summed up thus: 'We think it's best to take the specialist's advice' or 'I know very little about special schools – I'd rather leave it to people who know better – I just want to do what's best for her.'

The other parents in this group tended to be those who anticipated problems in the ordinary schools. The father of a child with rudimentary legs was afraid that at secondary level, as sports became more important, his son would feel increasingly 'different' and 'left out'. Another parent, whose son's mobility was severely restricted, would 'love him to go to B [the local modern school] . . . but though our doctor is against a handicapped school . . . we don't want him to go to B if he's going to be that much different from the others and if people are going to point this out. We try to think of it from his point of view.'

Four parents whose children were due to move from infant to junior classes had decided to ask for a transfer to a special school. The reasons for this have been discussed earlier in this chapter. One parent had initially been opposed to special school placement but had come to realize that her child 'has very poor attention and won't work unless he has constant encouragement'. Others had realized that their children's physical needs could not be met in an ordinary junior school. One mother also referred to 'how cruel children can be'; although her child had been very happy in an ordinary infant school she was afraid he might be teased later and added, 'We couldn't bear him to be miserable at school or left out of things.' Despite this, her feelings about the transfer were very ambivalent and she still felt worried lest she was 'letting John down by moving him to a special school'.

(ii) THOSE OPPOSED TO SPECIAL SCHOOL PLACEMENT

The reasons given by parents for their opposition to special school placement were varied. In the junior group thirty-seven parents put forward one reason, twenty two reasons, and five three or more reasons. The complexity of the thinking underlying a strongly held attitude is illustrated by the views of one exceedingly sensible mother whose 8-year-old son (who is of average intelligence) is severely handicapped by arthrogryposis. He has contractures of the knees and club feet, but can walk slowly in calipers. His arms are only rudimentary and his fingers virtually useless; he has learnt to type using one finger of the left hand but prefers to write holding a pencil in his mouth. Despite these severe handicaps, and his placement when I visited him in a class of forty-four children, he was with the help of a welfare assistant making excellent academic progress and was very happy and well adjusted socially.

His mother had put up a strong fight to have him placed in an ordinary school, and the reasons she gave were threefold. The first was educational: 'I was afraid he'd be held back [in a special school] by backward children such as some spastics.' The second was social: '[I was afraid that] he'd lose his friends . . . you see he has his own friends around here [a small council estate]. From when he was two and a half, I sat him outside the door in a push-chair. He wasn't treated by the others as a handicapped child – I felt he would have been if he'd gone to a special school.' Thirdly, this mother was quite frank about her own emotions: 'One reason is "personal" – I suppose at first I wouldn't admit I had a handicapped child. After the initial shock I wanted to take him home and bring him up as normally as possible . . . also, I did a lot for him and didn't feel they should take him away. If a family are capable of bringing up a handicapped child I think they should be allowed to do so.'

As I was leaving, she added a little about her feelings at the time when his placement was in doubt. She hadn't known 'what rights parents had' and until placement had been decided, 'I dreaded the postman coming every day in case there was a letter to say he had to go to a special school . . . [though] I tried to keep the worry to myself.' I have quoted this mother in detail to emphasize the complex blend of constructive reasoning and strong emotion which may underlie an attitude. In the rest of this section I have tried to organize the material by picking out the main elements in parental opposition to special school placement and discussing these in turn.

One of the fears of several parents was that their children might have to go to a residential school. Seven mothers said that they might have been willing to consider a day special school for their children but not a residential one. Often the child was too young or, as one mother put it, 'he'd been away in hospital so often and through so much that it would have been a shame to have sent him to boarding-school.'

Most parents, however, were opposed even to day special schooling. Naturally, in a sample which contained a large number of only mildly or moderately handicapped children, many parents gave as their reason that the child was 'not handicapped enough' to require special schooling. Remarks such as these were common: 'He's not disabled as really disabled people go. I think he'd have got depressed being with other children like that' or 'he might have felt he was more handicapped than he really was' or 'it would be demoralizing for him to be put in with a lot of terribly crippled children if he's not that bad.'

Several parents mentioned the physical stimulus of an ordinary school. One child with polio had spent a week in a special school until the family were rehoused outside London. Her mother felt that 'if she was kept there she would get more into their ways. She'd fall back physically and wouldn't bother to do anything.' Another, whose spina bifida child was in calipers, 'knew she wouldn't attempt anything in the way of walking if most of the others couldn't'.

A second very common reason for opposition to special school placement was the effect parents felt this might have on the child's emotional or social development. Many parents specifically mentioned possible effects on the child's self-image. Three thought their children would have got 'an inferiority complex' through attending special schools, others that the child would be 'more self-conscious' or that such placement would 'plant in his mind that he's different'. The mother of a haemophiliac thought that 'he wouldn't feel like a normal person – he'd lose his self-confidence'. A Brazilian veterinary surgeon thought that if his son 'lives with other children with the same kind of problem this will convey to him that he's a real problem to society'.

The parents of children with 'invisible' handicaps were specially concerned. One mother, whose son was incontinent due to congenital deformities, had 'never treated him as a handicapped child'. She thought that 'if it's stressed too much they feel it – at present he doesn't class himself as handicapped'. She had noticed that when he was hospitalized he much preferred to be in an 'ordinary' children's ward. When placed with severely handicapped children 'he's been most aggressive and tearful'. One mother of an incontinent child puts this point of view particularly vividly: 'I was distressed [when a special school was suggested]... you see the special transport coming, with mongols and all. He's forward in his mind. I could imagine him sitting there thinking, "there's something wrong with them... there must be something wrong with me. After all, they're kids with funny faces and irons".'

Several parents took the attitude of 'it's not that I don't want her to mix with handicapped children... but more that I do want her to be with normal children'.

They frequently mentioned the social benefits to be gained from ordinary school placement. This sort of remark was common: 'The younger they live with normal people, the quicker they'll adapt. They're always going to get comments, and the younger they accept it the better.' The mother of a child with severe upper limbs thalidomide deficiencies puts it in almost the same words: 'I'm thinking of what happens when he comes out into the world. It's better that he gets hurt now than later, so that when he grows up and goes out he won't feel it.'

Often parents described how their children had grown up with the local children. A parent whose child has severe thalidomide deficiencies 'wanted her to be with the children she knows. After all, she's been at Sunday school with them since she was three.' The mother of a spina bifida girl thought it 'terribly important' for her child to mix with ordinary children and to be at school where 'all the local people know her. They treat her just like anyone else.' Five parents expressed anxiety about the fact that children tend to imitate those they are with; in three cases children placed in units or schools where there were cerebral-palsied children had very quickly picked up abnormalities of speech, gesture and expression.

One mother took another view and stressed the socially educative value of placing handicapped children in ordinary schools. 'I think it is wrong from the general public's point of view [to place children in special schools]. If they're herded out of sight, we'll never get the public, especially the next generation, to accept them.'

Once a child has been placed in an ordinary school, parents naturally worry about the effects of a transfer to a special school: 'He's so happy where he is . . . he says he wants to stay here . . I can't bear the thought of taking him away and seeing him crying.' Another mother 'wouldn't have known what to tell him if he'd had to leave . . . he'd have cried every day'. An athetoid child was 'used to ordinary children: she'd be upset if she was moved'. A child confined to a wheelchair (brittle bones) 'definitely wants to stay in an ordinary school'. The comment of a 7-year-old girl (severely handicapped by diastrophic dwarfism) on visiting a special school is probably, when it is a question of transfer, fairly typical: 'Oh Mummy, I don't want to come here.'

The other major reason for opposition to special school placement concerns the educational side. Two strands can be disentangled here. One is the association in some parents' minds between 'special schools' and 'mental handicap'. The other is the related belief that special schools have lower educational standards.

Regarding the first, many parents mentioned the fact that they knew there were 'mentally handicapped' or 'retarded' or 'backward' children in the special schools. Here is an example of how one mother's attitude was shaped. She and her husband 'didn't know much about special schools', although she had visited a residential home for cerebral-palsied children where her sister was a housemother. She discussed the matter with her consultant who was 'strongly against special schooling' and with her friends. One advised her 'not to send him to a special school if I could help it', another told her that P H schools have 'a mixture of physically and mentally handicapped children' and that this would 'hold him back'. She had seen for herself the 'green buses [special school buses] go past' and to her, 'some of the children looked very crippled . . . others are mentally retarded. I was afraid he might become mentally retarded if he went to school with them.' Lacking other information, she had become strongly opposed to special school placement. The special buses were mentioned by another mother: 'You feel as if everyone would be looking at her and saying "she's a bit simple" when they saw the special buses.'

There is considerable anxiety among parents about the number of backward children in PH schools. Some mistakenly thought that all the children in such schools were backward, as did this father of a haemophiliac boy: 'I thought he'd be backward in his studies if he went. All the children there are backward . . . they pay too little attention to studies.' The London mother of a thalidomide child thought that 'a good education is important for her so that she can stand on her own feet . . . children who go to those schools are mentally backward . . . though they can't help it. I can't see how mixing with them would help her.' A farmworker and his wife from a country village expressed an almost identical viewpoint: 'We'd accept a special school if there wasn't mentally handicapped children there . . . I've got nothing against them – these things just happen . . . but we feel he needs a really good education as he can't do manual work. We feel he wouldn't get this if he was with many other children of poorer ability.' He went on to ask some very pertinent questions about the extent of backwardness in special schools.

There is in fact a real problem here. At a time when poliomyelitis, tuberculosis and heart disease accounted for a very sizeable proportion of the special school population, PH schools probably did cater by and large for children of 'normal intelligence'. This pattern has changed and a recent study carried out by the head of a typical day PH school (Segal, 1971) produced the finding that backwardness in the basic skills was pronounced and extensive, and about 66 per cent of the pupils were 'clearly ESN in addition to their physical handicaps'.

Kellmer Pringle and Fiddes (1970) also point out that

> once in a special school there are a number of factors which are likely to depress still further the child's level of educational attainment: a shorter school day; fatigue due to a lengthier journey to school; and probably most important of all there is also likely to be not only a lower standard of work (because there will be a high proportion of dull children) but probably also a lower level of expectation on the part of the teachers. For the majority of pupils this is entirely appropriate . . . but . . . the severely handi-

capped intelligent child may not always find himself sufficiently stimulated educationally.

Views of parents whose children had been transferred from special schools

Four of the children had actually attended special schools. One of the children was transferred when only 5·4 years old. Of the other three, two parents were very dissatisfied with the education their children had received. One child with a severe metabolic disorder had been placed in a special school because of her strict dietary requirements. Her mother felt that 'she was learning nothing there and getting very backward'. The class teacher in the ordinary school fully endorsed this view: 'I feel she didn't have the basic work in the special school, although she did a lot of music. Her reading age was under 5 years when she got here (at 8·0 years) . . . she was probably the brightest in the class there and may have been left too much to her own devices, as she could manage.' There are forty children in her ordinary school class, but she is taken out three times a week for twenty minutes of remedial reading in a small group with a trained teacher, and after six months (when she was eight and a half) was reading at a 7½-year-old level with a comprehension age of 8·5 years (and a non-verbal IQ of 89).

Another mother whose spina bifida child had been transferred to an ordinary school when the family moved out of London thought that one problem at the special school had been that

> by the time they got them ready [for lessons] they lose a lot of of time . . . I worked out that he had about an hour's proper learning time in the whole day. He learnt more [at his new school] in six months than in two and a half years [in the special school]. His teacher was amazed at the things he couldn't do when he came here . . . I like him to have to fight to keep up with the other kids.

She also described her son's feelings about the special school: 'He hated it . . . I'm not sure why – perhaps he could see the other children were worse and couldn't play.' When a suggestion had been made that the child might be transferred to a new special school which was being built in the area, 'he said he wouldn't go . . . he'd rather stay at home. He really done his nut.'

D

The other child who had been transferred had multiple congenital deformities of the genito-urinary system, and had had a colostomy and an ileostomy. She had been institutionalized (after being abandoned) until the age of eight and a half, spending her first five years in a hospital, followed by placement in a residential PH school. She was then fostered by exceedingly sensible parents and since then has been coping very well in an ordinary school in an educational priority area. Her foster mother stressed that at the special school 'she wasn't getting enough encouragement to do all she could. For instance, she couldn't run when she came here. She had never had to, as none of the others did, but there was no physical reason for this. We soon encouraged her to run down on the beach' (where this family go camping most weekends).

Views of parents with children in special schools

In the introduction to this section, the difficulty of obtaining an 'unbiased' picture of parental attitudes was discussed, and Joan McMichael's study (1971) of the fifty children in a day PH school was mentioned. Dr McMichael (the school medical officer) assessed the parents' attitudes to the school. Each mother was asked 'Are you satisfied that, considering his defect, your child was reasonably excluded from ordinary school?' and forty-nine out of fifty answered yes. Parents were then asked what they thought were the main disadvantages of a PH school. Thirty-four thought there were no disadvantages: of the sixteen who mentioned drawbacks thirteen (i.e. 26 per cent of the sample) were concerned about educational standards. Ten mentioned 'not such good education' and similar themes while three thought their children 'could be pushed a little more'.

They were also asked about the advantages of the special school, and the main ones mentioned (those referred to by more than four parents) are listed in Table 3.12 below.

There is one very interesting feature here, which McMichael does not mention. The main justification of special school placement is surely that it can offer children the 'special educational treatment' they need. Yet out of fifty parents, only five refer (and then rather indirectly, i.e. 'smaller classes') to the educational advantages of the special school. For most parents (and they were not restricted to one answer) it is the 'supervision and care' and the 'special transport' aspects which are important, two needs which can be met in an

TABLE 3.12. *Advantages of the special school (from McMichael [1971])*

Advantages referred to	No. of parents
Good care and supervision	19
School transport	12
'The children are the same and not made to feel out of it'	9
Smaller classes	5
Having a nursing sister on the premises	5

ordinary school if a local authority is prepared to appoint a welfare assistant and to provide taxi transport. This is not to say that because parents fail to mention educational advantages these do not exist, but the omission is striking. Together with the other evidence presented in this chapter, it suggests that the opposition of many parents to special school placement is a more reasoned and reasonable opposition than they are always given credit for.

This chapter has been particularly concerned with placement problems as they are experienced by parents. While only a minority of parents reported difficulties of the kinds described here, it was a substantial enough minority to be disturbing. At the same time it must also be recorded that in many cases, some of them involving severely handicapped children, there was ample evidence that the doctors, educationists, administrators and others involved in the placement process had gone to considerable trouble to consult parents and to try to meet their wishes. Parents can be unreasonable, especially when they are not aware of the very real difficulties which local authority officials may have in placing a particular child. They can find it very hard to accept advice which may imply the acceptance of certain limitations in their children and cases were found in this study where the ordinary school was not meeting the child's needs.

All this is true and important, but it is also true that the views of parents have not always been well represented, and that until their problems are known, services cannot be improved.

REFERENCES

HEWETT, S. (1970) *The Family and the Handicapped Child*, Allen and Unwin, London.

MCMICHAEL, J. (1971) *Handicap, A Study of Physically Handicapped Children and Their Families*, Staples Press, London.

Ministry of Education (1954) *Circular No. 276.*

MITTLER, P. (1970) 'The concept of multiple handicap', chapter 12 in Mittler, P. (ed.) *The Psychological Assessment of Mental and Physical Handicaps*, Methuen, London.

PLESS, I. B., RACKHAM, K. and KELLOCK, T. D. (1967) 'Patterns in the admission of handicapped pupils to residential establishments', *The Medical Officer*, 3086, 118 (iii), 135–9.

PRINGLE, M. L. KELLMER and FIDDES, D. O. (1970) *The Challenge of Thalidomide*, Longmans, London.

SEGAL, S. S. (1971) *From Care to Education*, Heinemann Medical Books, London.

SHERIDAN, M. (1965) *The Handicapped Child and His Home*, National Children's Home, London.

YOUNGHUSBAND, E., BIRCHALL, D., DAVIE, R. and PRINGLE, M. L. KELLMER (eds.) (1970) *Living with Handicap*, National Bureau for Co-operation in Child Care, London.

II The Children in School

Chapter 4 · Social Relationships in School

'We thought it would be good for him to mix with normal children.'
Again and again, as the interviews with parents reported in the
previous chapter show, this was the reason given for the parents'
eagerness to send their children to ordinary schools. In the main
part of this chapter research findings relating to specific aspects of
'mixing with normal children' are discussed. Firstly, through the use
of sociometric techniques and through interviews with the class
teacher and mother, friendship patterns between handicapped and
non-handicapped children are examined. The sorts of questions
which the findings throw light on include the following: do handicapped children in ordinary schools have as many friends as their
peers? Is there any relationship between type or severity of handicap
and a child's chances of making friends? Do handicapped children
tend to be rather isolated in school? Are they left out, and why,
when children choose their own groups? How much do they see of
their friends outside school hours? The other aspect of social relationships in school examined here is the question of the extent and
nature of teasing, and of how the children, teachers and parents
cope with this, and also of whether curiosity about the handicap on
the part of the children's classmates is a problem.

Before coming to these very specific questions, however, it is
important to look in a more general way at what is involved in social
encounters between handicapped and non-handicapped people, and
it is with this more theoretical approach that the introductory part of
this chapter is concerned.

Social attitudes to disability
One of the most thoughtprovoking discussions of the effect of a
handicap on social encounters is Erving Goffman's book, *Stigma*

(1963). Normally when we encounter a stranger we try (often unconsciously) to assign him to a certain category; we also have certain expectations about the sort of characteristics ('abilities') which a person in that category will possess, and these give him a 'social identity'. We are not really aware of these expectations until we meet someone who possesses an attribute which makes him different from others in the same category: such an attribute Goffman calls a 'stigma'; it could also be called a 'failing', a 'short-coming' or a 'handicap'. Goffman distinguishes three very different types of stigma: first physical deformities, secondly blemishes of character and thirdly what he calls the 'tribal' stigma of race, nation or religion. In general, he states (Goffman, 1968) that the behaviour of 'normals' towards a person with a stigma is 'to exercise varieties of discrimination through which we effectively, if often unthinkingly, reduce his chances of a happy and successful life'.

It is perhaps worth noting here that the position of a person with a disability is sometimes likened to that of a member of an under-privileged ethnic or religious group, in so far as people have certain expectations about him by virtue of his membership of that group while he may aspire towards a 'normal' pattern of behaviour. There is an important difference, however, in that people born into min-ority groups learn from the minority culture how to deal with the majority culture; they also spend a considerable portion of their time in social interaction with members of minority groups and have learned appropriate social skills for doing this. A handicapped person is not, however, a member of a subcultural group; his position is not likely to be shared by many others and, unless he restricts his social contacts very severely, most of his social interactions will be with the non-handicapped majority group. In this respect he is in a less strong position to cope with any discrimination he may encounter.

Little work has been done on analysing the ways in which such negative attitudes to disability come into being. In Israel, Chigier and Chigier (1970) have looked at the cultural factors which influence attitude formation. They suggest that the actual significance attached to the presence of a disability stems from a combination of three sources. The first they label 'conditioning', meaning what is learned about disability from parents (in particular), friends, newspapers, jokes and casual remarks. The second source is 'exposure' to the disability: what one sees and feels for oneself on coming into contact with the disabled. The feeling is still sometimes experienced in this country that overt disabilities are unaesthetic and disturbing and that 'normals', especially children, should be shielded from exposure to the handicapped. Chigier and Chigier mention research which suggests that the nature of the initial exposure to the physical handicap (that is, whether this is pleasant or otherwise) is more significant than the amount of exposure or than the provision of verbal information. If this is so, then the first encounter between a severely handicapped child in a school and his new classmates should be much more carefully planned than is generally the case.

In some cases it seems true that exposure can, of itself, lead to a marked increase in the acceptance of different handicaps by the public. Goffman (1963) for instance notes that 'the immediate neighbourhood of mental hospitals may become places with high tolerance for psychotic behaviour; the neighbourhoods around some medical hospitals may develop a capacity for calm treatment of the facially disfigured who are undergoing skin-grafting'. On the other hand, many instances could be cited to show that familiarity, of itself, may do nothing to decrease fears and prejudices. Richardson (1961) found for instance that children attending summer camps where there were handicapped children did not differ in their attitudes to handicap from children who had not been exposed to disabled children in this way.

Thirdly, the Chigiers note the contribution positive teaching about disability and the 'correct' attitude to adopt towards it can make. They point out that it is still too often the case that attempts to educate the public are either very emotive (being sentimental, conscience-arousing, shockprovoking or evangelistic) or 'dully informative' and that too seldom are the public offered constructive alternative ways of looking at the disability. A great deal more could be done in this country using television as an educational device for this purpose, and books written for children, such as Camilla Jessel's informative story about a boy with spina bifida (1975) may also be helpful.

While the non-handicapped thus regard the handicapped person as 'different' it is essential to recognize the handicapped or 'stigmatized' individual's point of view. In Goffman's words 'his deepest feelings about what he is may be his sense of being a "normal person", a human being like anyone else ... who deserves a fair chance ... So the central feature of his situation is what is often, if vaguely, called acceptance.'

Difficulties in social encounters

What are the specific difficulties or barriers which people with physical disabilities encounter in establishing social relationships with others? In social encounters we categorize others by using a large number of 'cues' both verbal and non-verbal. Of the latter, appearance is of particular importance: a handicap such as a facial disfigurement, absence or deformity of a limb, clumsy gait or unusual uncontrolled movements often obtrudes itself upon the stranger's attention at the expense of the person's other 'normal' attributes, since it disturbs our unconscious expectations. A handicap may also have a 'halo effect' in that a wide range of imperfections of character may mistakenly be associated with a single physical difference. Davis (1961) summarizes very well the way in which a handicap may dominate a social encounter:

> whether it is overtly responded to as such . . . or whether no explicit reference is made to it, the underlying condition of heightened, narrowed awareness causes the (social) interaction to be articulated too exclusively in terms of it. This is usually accompanied by one or more of the familiar signs of discomfort and uneasiness: the guarded references, the common everyday words suddenly made taboo, the fixed stare elsewhere, the artificial levity, the compulsive loquaciousness, the awkward solemnity.

An experimental study carried out with American teenagers (Kleck *et al.*, 1966) showed that for these reasons the handicapped person does not receive normal and accurate feedback about his behaviour from his peers. It is difficult for him to know what others really think about him and so to develop the normal range of social skills. The authors also found that their subjects showed more emotional arousal (measured by the psychogalvanic skin response) when interacting with a handicapped person, as well as behaving in a more formal and inhibited way. Barker (1948) has suggested that stigmatized persons live on a 'social-psychological frontier', constantly facing new social situations in which they are uncertain what their status will be: this is aggravated by the unnatural behaviour discussed above.

In another American study Shears and Jensema (1969) tried to pinpoint the main factors underlying the acceptability of disabled or 'anomalous' people by getting ninety-four adults to state which of ten people with different 'anomalies' they would have as friends. The order in which these people were ranked was as follows (with the percentage of those willing to have them as friends in brackets). First, an amputee (80 per cent), next a wheelchair case (79 per cent), a blind person (77 per cent), someone with a harelip (69 per cent), a stutterer (55 per cent), a deaf mute (53 per cent), a cerebral-palsied person (38 per cent), someone mentally ill (28 per cent), someone retarded (24 per cent) and a homosexual (17 per cent). The authors concluded that the following six dimensions probably combined and interacted in producing stereotypes of anomalous persons: visibility of the affliction; interference with the communication process; amount of social stigma associated with the disability; the extent to which the person could be 'cured'; the degree of incapacity; and the difficulty in daily living the anomaly imposed. The last three dimensions were found to be particularly important at closer levels of intimacy.

Studies of a rather similar kind have been carried out with children by Richardson and his colleagues (1961). The subject is shown six drawings of a child of the same sex as himself: the only difference between the drawings is the presence or absence of a visible physical disability and the type of disability. The pictures are all laid in random order in front of the child and he is told to look at each picture carefully. He is then asked 'Which boy (or girl) do you like best?' After making his choice, the chosen picture is removed and he is asked again 'Now which boy do you like best?', the procedure being repeated until only one picture remains. In this way a rank ordering of each child's preferences is obtained. 640 American children aged 9–11 years old took part in the first study; later studies have been carried out in the United Kingdom, Germany, Israel and Mexico.

Richardson's main finding was that the children showed a 'remarkable degree of agreement' in their preference order for the different handicaps, the order from most to least liked being (a) the child without a visible handicap; (b) the child with crutches and a caliper on his left leg; (c) the child in a wheelchair; (d) the child with a left forearm amputation; (e) the child with a slight facial disfigurement; (f) the obsese child. Also interesting was the fact that physically handicapped children themselves ranked the drawings in the same way, that is, they had assimilated the same normative values as the majority group. In a later study (1968) in which race was looked at in addition to physical handicap, Richardson's results suggested that for all subjects physical handicap was such a powerful factor in establishing preference that it largely masked preference based on skin colour.

Although the degree of agreement found in the ranking order is important, it was not total and differences were found which were related to the sex, age and cultural group membership of the subjects. The child with a slight facial disfigurement, for example, was the second choice of most of the 6 year olds: this preference position dropped steadily with increasing age, the drop being earlier for girls than boys and most rapid round the onset of adolescence. Since the disfigurement was slight the face must have been scrutinized with particular care. In the 1963 study, Richardson included children from low income Jewish families whose immediate social environment or subculture exposed them less to the dominant cultural values, and more to different and sometimes conflicting values. He found that obese children received a much higher ranking from this group, such a child often being viewed as healthy and loved: the same result was obtained by myself from African boys in Uganda. It is also interesting to notice that whereas in the more affluent countries it is not the disabilities which are functionally more impairing which are least liked but rather those affecting expectations about a desirable appearance (although this was truer of the girls than the boys), the opposite was the case in Uganda where those children who were least liked were usually those least able to earn a living.

The main conclusion which Richardson draws from these studies is that the values or attitudes children generally hold towards the disabled will make them less inclined to initiate social relations with a handicapped than a non-handicapped child. In a discussion with one group of children after the testing, Richardson (1961) found that the children's expressed views were not compatible with the rankings, that is they denied judging the drawings on the basis of physical appearance, saying that children with handicaps were 'just as nice' as those without them. One or two children, however, made revealing remarks such as 'I don't feel comfortable with a handicapped child' or 'I don't know what to say to a handicapped child' and clearly there is sometimes considerable conflict between what a child thinks he ought to feel and his actual choice. While a disability may influence a social relationship in a very direct way by placing limits on mobility and on the range of activities which may be important in sustaining the relationship, less obvious factors are often operating. Thus Goffman (1963) has suggested that one reason for the tendency of the non-handicapped to avoid social encounters with the handicapped is the anxiety about 'the tendency for a stigma to spread from the stigmatized individual to his close connections'. In rather a similar vein Richardson (1969) reports that in the friendships he investigated in the summer holiday camps 'the non-handicapped child who is likely to initiate contact with a handicapped child is more isolated, has less general social experience, and has learned the values of his peers less accurately'. A child who is threatened by competence in physical skills or who is not fully accepted by his peers may feel handicapped children to be less threatening and less competent and more likely to accept him. Findings in the present study (reported more fully later in this chapter) suggest that this is not necessarily the case with children who have grown up at school together. Of the twenty (27 per cent) physically handicapped children whose choice of best friend was fully reciprocated by a non-handicapped peer, eighteen had non-handicapped friends who were of average or above-average popularity.

So far, discussion has been of the problems in social relationships of a person with a visible disability. A different set of problems arises when a person has a handicap which is not known to those present and not immediately perceivable. Goffman (1963) uses the term 'discreditable' (as opposed to 'discredited') to distinguish such persons and suggests that 'here the issue is not that of managing tension generated during social contacts but rather that of managing information about his failing. To display or not to display; to tell or not to tell; to let on or not to let on; to lie or not to lie; in each case to whom, how, when and where.' In this study such problems arose for only about 14 per cent of the children: this includes those with haemophilia (for whom the decision to 'tell' is usually made by the teacher and causes few problems); those with minor deformities of the hands and feet which can be hidden and the incontinent.

Such children may often 'pass' as not handicapped, and may be extremely anxious in case their disability is revealed, either through their own actions or by someone who knows about it. Among adults a common strategy is for the 'discreditable' person to handle such a 'risk' by dividing the world, as Goffman puts it, 'into a large group to whom he tells nothing and a small group to whom he tells all and upon whose help he then relies'. The major alternative is to disclose the handicap voluntarily, thus 'transforming his situation from that of an individual with information to manage to that of an individual with uneasy social situations to manage'. It is exactly such a choice which faces the child with an 'invisible' handicap in an ordinary school and it may be useful for the parent to discuss with the teacher the approach which it is best to take.

Social experience and the development of social skills

Although psychologists, teachers, doctors and others have, during the last two decades, done considerable research into the effects of early experience on later development, not a great deal is known about the specific social experiences which are necessary for a person to develop an adequate range of social skills. It seems likely, however, that handicapped children miss or only partially share such experiences. In cases of severe handicap the demands, in terms of time and energy, made on the parents in coping with the physical impairment alone means that social development is necessarily somewhat neglected: physical care at home or long periods of treatment and hospitalization may mean that the child has few opportunities for playing with his sibs or other children. Even when the handicap is not severe, social experiences may be restricted. A study of twins, one of whom had cerebral palsy, carried out by Shere (1956) showed that the handicapped twin was often assigned the role of a 'sick' child. He was often given less responsibility and had fewer restrictions placed on his behaviour, with antisocial behaviour being condoned, and he was often spoiled.

Although this situation can be avoided it is still true, as Barker (1948), Wright (1960), Richardson (1969) and others have pointed out, that physically handicapped children are not exposed to nearly as wide a range of physical and social settings as are their peers. Richardson (1969) quotes studies suggesting that although the young cerebral-palsied adult may, through intensive rehabilitation services (including special school placement), have developed considerable social independence, he is often socially immature and isolated.

All these authors suggest that specific training in social skills is needed to enable handicapped people to 'break through' social barriers. The concept of 'social skill' has been developed in particular by Michael Argyle (1967). He tries to show that in some ways social skills are like motor skills, since both can be analysed in terms of aims, selective perception of cues, central translation processes, response feedback and corrective action. He also shows that social skills have certain special features including the need to establish rapport with the other person and the need to motivate him and to reduce his anxiety and defensiveness. From these analyses arises the concept of 'competence' in social relationships, characterized by such factors as perceptual sensitivity, warmth and rapport, a good repertoire of social techniques, flexibility, energy and initiative, and a smooth response pattern.

Little work has yet been done on how such skills can be trained. Lectures and discussion may help, but what is essential is for handicapped people to gain active experience of desired ways of behaving in a relaxed situation and under careful guidance. Role-playing is a widely accepted approach for effecting changes in both behaviour and attitudes, or, suggests Wright (1960), it may be useful for a disabled person to accompany someone already well adjusted to a similar disability on various social excursions.

While PH children in special schools will be in special need of such training, teachers in ordinary schools with handicapped pupils should be aware that this may be an area in which the child needs specific guidance. The non-handicapped children in the class often also need advice on how to handle the socially awkward question of giving help. They can be told, for instance, that the disabled child may wish to limit his use of help to instances of absolute necessity. One social skill which can be taught to the handicapped child is how to reduce the uncertainty of the would-be helper by indicating clearly whether he wants the help and what form this can take. A research study carried out by Dembo et al. (1956) gives a useful summary of recommendations offered by the disabled to the non-disabled. These included the following 'dos' and 'don'ts': don't talk about the handicap unless the disabled person brings it up or unless he wants to; don't ask questions about it immediately; don't dwell on it; don't try to get him away from the subject if he raises it; do take into account his mood.

Although studies of the kind described here help us to understand some of the factors involved in the social relationships of disabled and non-disabled people, our knowledge in this area is still, as Richardson (1969) points out, partial and fragmentary. Does impoverishment of social relationships have greater consequences at one age level then another? Can such effects be reversed? Do we really know much about how the attitudes of 'normal' children towards disabled children are formed, how they differ at various age levels, especially at puberty, and how they can be modified? Even if our knowledge about such processes is still very fragmentary, what is important is that teachers and others should at least be aware of these problems and willing to explore ways of breaking down the social barriers which may be created both by the handicap itself and, to a much greater extent, by the reaction of others to it.

Social relationships: major findings

(i) THE SOCIOMETRIC TEST

One of the ways in which the social relationships of the handicapped group were explored was through the use of a sociometric test. Basically, a sociometric measure is designed to give an objective picture of the relationships between members of a given group by assessing the attractions (or attractions and repulsions) within it. It usually involves getting each member of the group to indicate privately which other members of the group he would like to have as a companion for a particular activity or occasion (and sometimes those with whom he would not like to participate). The limits of the group are specific and choices (the number allowed is usually restricted) are made in terms of specific criteria. A variety of ways in which the data can be analysed and represented are available. In a sense a sociometric test can be thought of as a variety of rating scale in which the group members are asked to rate their fellows in terms of their attractiveness as companions in certain activities.

Some controversy exists about the reliability, particularly in terms of consistency over time, of the results. Lindzey and Byrne (1968) suggest that such tests have a relatively high degree of temporal consistency particularly as the age of the participants increases or if the group has been in existence for a long time. In addition, the greater the strength or saliency of the choice, the greater the reliability: thus first choices are more stable than second, and second choices than third. Evans (1963) suggests that although changes in particular friendships occur, the general level of acceptability of the children relative to one another remains much the same. It may therefore be difficult to change the initial impression which a child makes on his group, acceptability at one age indicating that a child will be acceptable later in life. A follow-up study of 130 nursery schoolchildren carried out by Westman et al. (1967) suggests that early adjustment problems tend to persist in later life, one of the three main indices of later adjustment which they used being the nursery school child's relationship with his peers, including the extent to which he was accepted by them.

Before going further, the question of the research utility of socio-metric testing must be considered. Another way of putting this would be to ask, 'What does a child's sociometric status (that is whether he receives many or few choices) imply about that child?' Implicit in the work of T. L. Moreno, the pioneer in the use of this technique, is the idea that it is one way of measuring the social and personal adjustment of the subject. In a large number of studies positive correlations have been found between sociometric status and personal adjustment (Lindzey and Byrne, 1968) and this suggests that sociometric data might also be used as an index of changes in adjustment. It is not necessarily the case that the higher the socio-metric status, the better adjusted the child will be; however, a low choice status does usually correlate with poor social adjustment and the measure is particularly useful in drawing the teacher's attention to which children are 'isolates', that is, receive zero friendship choices from the others.

As Bonney (1943) points out, isolates are generally not discrimin-ated against in any overt manner, and this may cause the teacher to assume that they are better accepted than is really the case. A classic early sociometric study is Northway's 'Outsiders' (1942) in which characteristics of the children who fell into the lowest quartile (generally the ten 'least acceptable' children in the class) were looked at. Northway suggests that outsiders can be of three kinds: firstly they may be 'recessives', children who tend to be listless, lacking in vitality, of low intelligence and poor appearance; secondly they may be 'socially uninterested', that is, children who deliberately with-draw and neither wish for nor seek attention; thirdly outsiders may be 'socially ineffective', wishing to join in but not having the social skills to do so, and often being noisy, rebellious and delinquent. In a sociometric study carried out by E. A. Lunzer (1960) three specially selected groups were compared: these comprised children rated by teachers as 'aggressive' or 'withdrawn' or 'exceptionally well-adjusted'. As expected, very significant differences were found in the mean sociometric percentile rankings for the three groups. Of more interest was the fact that the aggressive and withdrawn children were rejected to an equal extent, even though when the same children were rated on the trait of sociability, the aggressive children were found to be far more dependent on company than even the well-adjusted group.

(ii) SELECTED STUDIES

Sociometric studies form a huge literature, and many examine the factors which affect social acceptability. They include studies concerned with environmental and social factors; those which relate sociometric status to intelligence and/or academic success; those concerned with personality characteristics; and those which study the status of individuals who are 'deviant' in some way, such as the physically handicapped. A few of the most interesting and relevant findings will be considered below.

Lindzey and Byrne (1968) suggest that there is much evidence showing that sociometric status is positively related to socio-economic status; however it is probably only very low socio-economic status which is a real disadvantage. Most studies relating sociometric status to intelligence have found a positive association. Heber (1956) found that a group of high IQ children was significantly higher in social status than an average IQ group, with low IQ children significantly lower. However, deviation from the average group was much greater in the case of the low IQ group and he concluded that 'the decremental effect on social status of a low IQ . . . [is] greater than the incremental effect of a high IQ'. In general it is probably true to say that provided a child's intelligence is not markedly below normal it has little effect on his popularity, while the influence of academic attainment on popularity seems similar. Grossman and Wrighter (1948) found that while children with low reading ability had low social acceptability scores, once a child was within the normal range additional ability did not add to his popularity. It should be noted that while correlations such as these are fairly well established they do not really explain why such associations should exist.

Unfortunately, little work has been done on the personality characteristics of socially successful and unsuccessful children, partly because of the inadequacy of our measures of personality. Bonney (1943), who studied 9 year olds, used trait ratings by teachers and pupils in conjunction with a sociometric test. She found that the traits most important in distinguishing between popular and unpopular children could be grouped into two clusters. The first included strong positive attributes such as leadership, enthusiasm and daring; the second, traits associated with friendliness. In an article called, 'Power in the classroom', Gold (1958) selected four groups of personality characteristics important to children in rating their peers. Firstly, and most important, were social-emotional characteristics centring around the concepts of 'friendliness' and 'fun to be with'. Next in importance was 'expertness', including 'being bright', 'having good ideas about how to do things', 'being good at making things' and so on. Thirdly, 'associational' characteristics were important, that is children were chosen who liked to do the same sort of things. Least important were 'coercive resources', of being strong and able to fight and of physical prowess. If these findings are accepted, they offer a useful analysis of why PH children might tend to have low sociometric status. They clearly have few 'coercive resources'; because of restricted experience, particularly where mobility or hand control is impaired, they may be lacking in 'expertness'; the handicap may restrict the amount and type of play possible with other children so that they may be low in 'associational characteristics'. This only leaves the child's social-emotional characteristics as potentially attractive to others and because such children often have a poor self-image there may be problems in this area too.

The number of sociometric studies which specifically examine relationships between handicapped children and their peers are very few. Bonney (1943) was one of the first to use this method to show that children who were 'different' were treated with great kindness and sympathy, but were not chosen as friends by their peers, while Soldwedel and Terrell (1957) looking at a small group of 12–14 year olds, including a group with mixed handicaps and a control group, found a tendency for the PH children to be chosen less often.

Centers and Centers (1963) used a social discrimination questionnaire (including such questions as 'who do you like most . . . least . . . etc.') with the classmates of children with amputations and the classmates of non-amputees, and found a significantly greater number of rejecting attitudes expressed towards the amputees. A near socio-metric measure was used by Dewey and Force (1956) to study the social acceptance and social relationships of a group of sixty-three orthopaedically handicapped children of normal intelligence placed in fourteen ordinary primary classes. The orthopaedically handi-capped children and those with visual defects received a signifi-cantly smaller number of choices on all criteria than the others, and particularly marked was the low number of choices received by cerebral-palsied children. Of the handicapped, those with heart defects or congenital abnormalities were most accepted as friends while those with hearing defects were chosen less often than any except the cerebral-palsied. The authors suggest the evidence indi-cates that the physical condition alone was sufficient to result in the child's being identified from as early an age as six (and continuously thereafter) as a member of a minority group based on the label 'handicapped'. Few PH children had enough assets to offset com-pletely the negative effects of this label. In this particular situation there were several PH children in each ordinary class and this, they suggest, may have hindered their social integration.

Research findings

(i) THE TEST ITSELF: PROCEDURE AND SCORING

In this study, the sociometric test was given to the class as a whole. All the classes visited were tested except for one very small class in a village school. The children were given standard forms and asked to write down the names of the three boys and girls they liked doing certain things with best. These included (a) who they would like to play with most during break; (b) who they would like best to sit next to; (c) who they would like to take with them if they were to be moved into another class. In each case the child was required to make a first, second and third choice. The same children could be chosen for each activity, allowing a minimum of three and a maxi-mum of nine choices. Class absentees were included, the names of all the children being written on the board. Full details of the procedure and wording are given in appendix F.

There are many ways of scoring sociometric tests, and the choices can be weighted or unweighted, Northway (1967) finding a high cor-relation between weighted and unweighted scores. Since first choices seem more significant and stable it was decided to give a score of three for a first choice, two for a second and one for a third. A simple quantitative method of scoring was then used. A matrix was drawn up for each class (with the names of the subjects along the left margin of the table, the order being reproduced along the top) and a score for each child obtained, made up of the total number of (weighted) choices he had received. In each class the children were then ranked on the basis of their raw score, these ranks being converted to percentile ranks (i.e. those with highest ranks would fall into the 91–100th percentile, those with the lowest into the 0–10th percentile and so on). In this way the status of children in classes of different sizes could be compared. Lindzcy and Byrne (1968) point out the need to be aware that different groups (here classes) do vary in the distribution and range of choices made. Despite this they conclude that 'the combination of data from different groups or the comparability of results from divergent samples probably does not involve any appreciable distortion of reality'.

Data such as these can be analysed in any number of ways. Three broad areas were of particular interest in this study. Firstly a comparison was made of sociometric status in different groups, for example between the control and PH groups, between children with and without neurological abnormalities, between children with different types of handicap, between children with different functional handicaps and between children with handicaps of different degrees of severity. Secondly, relationships between individuals within the groups were looked at, especially whether the choices made were reciprocated, partially reciprocated or unreciprocated (oneway choices), as well as the extent of what Moreno termed 'emotional expansiveness', that is, the amount of utilization of available choices. Thirdly, of particular concern in this study were the PH children who were either 'isolates' (receiving no choices) or of very low sociometric status, and comparisons were made on certain variables between these and the PH children who received high ranks.

(ii) GROUP COMPARISONS: FACTORS AFFECTING SOCIOMETRIC POSITION

It was felt that to compare mean sociometric ranks obtained by the different groups might reveal little of interest: instead it was the percentage of children in each group lying within each decile that was looked at, so that some idea of overall differences could be obtained. The results are shown in Table 4.1 below.

TABLE 4.1. *Sociometric rank in different groups (percentages)*

| Group | Percentile ranks | | | | |
	0–20	21–40	41–60	61–80	81–100
Controls (No. = 146)	13·6	13·0	20·5	23·2	29·4
All PH children (No. = 73)	26·0	28·7	21·9	15·0	8·2
PH without neurological abnormalities (No. = 47)	19·1	29·7	21·2	19·1	10·6
PH with neurological abnormalities (No. = 26)	38·4	26·9	23·0	7·6	3·8

When the control group and the PH group as a whole are compared, the main feature is that while 54·7 per cent of the PH group scored below the 41st percentile (and one quarter below the 21st percentile) only 26·6 per cent of the controls scored below this level; on the other hand 52·6 per cent of the controls scored above the 60th percentile but only 23·2 per cent of the PH group, differences which were significant at the 0·1 per cent level. However, it must also be pointed out that the control group was to some extent atypical: by chance 40 per cent of them (fifty-eight) might have been expected to score above the 60th percentile: the fact that over 50 per cent did so shows an upward bias which was significant at the 1 per cent level (x^2 with Yates correction = 7·40, df 1). Interestingly, there were three pairs of twins in these two groups. In one pair (where the handicap was mild) there was little difference in the sociometric status, but in the other pairs the differences were striking. A girl with a congenital amputation of the left arm scored between the 20th and 30th percentile, her twin between the 90th and 100th percentile. In the other pair, a mildly handicapped cerebral-palsied boy received zero choices whereas his twin was the second most popular child in the whole class. In both cases, intelligence level and attainments were similar.

When the PH group was divided into those with and without neurological abnormalities, clear differences were found. Although the children with purely physical disabilities still tended to receive lower rankings than the controls, the differences were not now so marked, whereas most of the children with neurological abnormalities had very low sociometric status. Only 11·4 per cent scored above the 60th percentile (but 52·6 per cent of the controls) with 38·4 per cent below the 21st percentile. Again these differences are significant at the 0·1 per cent level.

An interesting distinction was found between the PH and control groups when sex differences were looked at. For the control boys and girls, the mean percentile rank was the same (50th to 60th). In the PH group however, the girls (mean rank 30th to 40th percentile) were given a higher rank than the boys (20th to 30th percentile). As will be discussed later, of the seven PH children who received zero choices only one was a girl. Although one cannot generalize from such a small sample the results do suggest that handicapped girls may be accepted more readily by their peers than handicapped boys.

As it was possible that severity of handicap might be mediating some of the differences, this was also looked at in Table 4.2.

TABLE 4.2. *Severity of handicap and sociometric rank*

	Percentile ranks								
	0–20		21–40		41–60		61–80		81–100	
	No.	%	No.	%	No.	%	No.	%	No.	%
Mild handicap (No. = 13)	4	30·7	3	23·0	4	30·7	2	15·3	0	0·0
Moderate handicap (No. = 44)	12	27·2	14	31·8	8	18·1	6	13·6	4	9·0
Severe handicap (No. = 16)	3	18·7	4	25·0	4	25·0	3	18·7	2	12·5

The findings suggest that this is not an important factor and although the differences between the groups were not significant there was a very slight inverse relationship between social acceptability and severity of handicap. While the mean rank for the severely handicapped children was the 30th percentile, for the mildly handicapped group it was only the 26th percentile.

Although the number of children in each group was small, the relationship between type of handicap and sociometric status is of considerable interest (Table 4.3).

TABLE 4.3. *Sociometric rank and type of handicap (percentages)*

	Percentile rank					
Category of handicap	0–20	21–40	41–60	61–80	81–100	Total children
Controls	13·6	13·0	20·5	23·2	29·4	146
Cerebral-palsied	46·6	20·0	26·6	6·6	0·0	15
Spina bifida	25·0	50·0	8·3	8·3	8·3	12
Congenital abnormalities including thalidomide	17·3	21·7	30·4	17·3	13·0	23
Other, including haemophilia	21·7	30·4	17·3	21·7	8·6	23

The main finding here is not unexpected in the light of earlier studies: it is that the cerebral-palsied children are clearly the least well accepted of the PH group. Despite the small size of the groups, when the CP children are compared to those with congenital abnormalities, significantly more score below the 41st percentile (x^2 with Yates correction $= 3·46$, p $<$0·05). The children with spina bifida and hydrocephalus also have a comparatively low status, half being concentrated between the 21st and 40th percentile, and one-quarter below the 20th percentile. The children with congenital abnormalities on the other hand have a status which is not significantly different from that of the controls.

Another way of breaking down the figures is in terms of the main effect of the handicap on the child's functioning (children with several functional impairments being placed in the category in which they were most severely affected). The findings are shown in Table 4.4.

TABLE 4.4. *Relationship between major functional effect of handicap and sociometric status (percentages)*

Major effect	No. in group		Sociometric percentile rank				
			0–20	21–40	41–60	61–80	81–100
No handicap (controls)	146		13·6	13·0	20·5	23·2	29·4
Impaired mobility (including haemophiliacs)	33		28·1	28·1	21·8	12·5	9·3
Impaired hand control	27	72	28·0	20·0	32·0	12·0	8·0
Incontinence	12		7·6	46·1	7·6	30·7	7·6

These suggest that whether it was hand control or mobility which was primarily affected made little difference to the child's social acceptability. Very few incontinent children, however, fell below the 21st percentile and overall they were chosen more often as friends than were many other PH children. In several cases the fact that a child was incontinent and wore an appliance was not known to the majority of his peers. This finding should to some extent allay the fears of those who think that this group may be socially unacceptable.

(iii) INDIVIDUAL RELATIONSHIPS

Actual sociometric status may not, except in the case of those with very low ranks, be as important as the actual friendship patterns which exist between individual children, and a slightly different way of looking at the data is in terms of the total number of friends a child has, friends being defined here as those who choose him for specific activities. The findings are shown in Table 4.5.

As the results discussed already suggest, the PH children have, overall, a smaller number of friends than the controls. A greater proportion have no friends, or only one or two friends and a much smaller proportion have more than four friends. On the other hand, the positive aspect of these findings must not be ignored. Over half the handicapped group have three or more friends, and over a

TABLE 4.5. *Sociometric test: number of classmates choosing child as a friend (percentages)*

| Groups being chosen | Number of classmates naming child as a friend | | | |
	None	1–2	3–4	over 4
Controls (No. = 146)	3·4	17·8	24·6	54·1
Total PH (No. = 73)	9·5	35·6	28·7	24·6
PH children without neurological abnormalities (No. = 47)	6·3	31·9	31·9	29·7
PH children with neurological abnormalities (No. = 26)	15·3	42·3	26·9	15·3

quarter more than four friends and even in the case of children with neurological abnormalities nearly half the group have three or more friends.

A rather surprising result is obtained when what Moreno called 'emotional expansiveness' is looked at, that is the breadth of the children's choices (Table 4.6).

TABLE 4.6. *Sociometric test: number of classmates named as friends (percentages)*

| Groups choosing | Number named as friends | | |
	1–2	3–4	over 4
Controls (No. = 146)	1·3	48·9	49·6
Total PH group (No. = 73)	2·7	43·0	54·1
PH children without neurological abnormalities (No. = 47)	4·2	55·3	40·4
PH children with neurological abnormalities (No. = 26)	0·0	20·0	80·0

Here there is little difference between the controls and the PH children without neurological abnormalities, although the latter restrict the number of children they choose to a very slight extent. Quite the opposite happens in the case of those with neurological abnormalities, 80 per cent of whom name five or more different children as their friends, in many cases naming nine children, the maximum possible, rather than restricting their choice to three or four children as the others do. Interpretation of this result is difficult: discussion with the class teachers suggested that this group had fewer real close friends and tended to name children whom they would like to have as friends rather than those who actually were friends.

Evans (1963), discussing Bonney's work, has referred to the importance of helping a child to acquire at least one close personal friend who prefers his company to that of others, suggesting that unless a person is a preferred companion of at least a few other people he is likely to feel socially insecure all his life. It was therefore of interest to find out to what extent the handicapped group's choice of friends was reciprocated, and this is shown in Table 4.7 below. A reciprocated choice was one where a child's choice of 'greatest friend' (the friend to whom he awarded, as it were, the largest number of points) was mutual; a partially reciprocated choice one where the child was named as a friend at least once by the child he chose as 'greatest friend'; and a oneway choice speaks for itself (Table 4.7.)

TABLE 4.7. *Sociometric test: nature of choice (percentages)*

	Nature of choice			
Groups	Recipro-cated	Partially reciprocated	Not reci-procated	Not applicable
Controls (No. = 146)	36·9	33·5	21·2	8·2
PH group as a whole (No. = 73)	26·0	31·5	28·7	13·8
PH children without neurological abnor-malities (No. = 47)	29·7	34·0	27·6	8·5
PH children with neurological abnor-malities (No. = 26)	19·2	26·9	30·7	23·0

The results are quite encouraging. Statistically insignificant differences are found in the extent to which the friendship choices of the handicapped children and the controls are reciprocated, although the proportion of reciprocated choices falls in the case of the neurologically handicapped group.

This question was also investigated by asking the class teacher and the mother whether the child had a 'best friend' at school. There was quite good agreement in their answers and children were counted as having a close friend if either the mother or teacher reported this. The findings were in the expected direction: 73 per cent of the controls had a close friend, 60·4 per cent of the PH group without neurological abnormalities and 53·8 per cent of the children with such abnormalities.

(iv) ISOLATES

The sociometric test was also used so that the number and characteristics of the PH children who were 'isolates' (unchosen) could be examined. Of course, the description of an individual as an isolate refers to the choice behaviour of the group, and provides no evidence as to whether the child is isolated of his own accord or involuntarily. Also, as no negative choices were used (that is children were deliberately not asked who they liked least as is sometimes done) the sociometric test did not show whether the isolates were just ignored or actively disliked. Seven of the PH children (9·5 per cent) and five (3·4 per cent) of the controls were in fact isolates, a comparatively small proportion, and a difference which is statistically insignificant (x^2 with Yates correction = 2·47, df 1).

The features characterizing the isolated handicapped children were examined, and contrasted with those of the group of eight handicapped children who received the largest number of choices (above the 80th percentile). While all but one of the isolates were boys (the exception being a cerebral-palsied girl with marked involuntary movements described as a 'real tomboy') half the 'high status' group were boys and half girls. None of the isolates had a non-verbal IQ score of over 100, in three cases the score being below 80, whereas four of the 'popular' children had IQs of over 100, and the remainder IQs of over 85. As regards severity of handicap there was no difference in the distribution between the two groups and when type of handicap was looked at there was some overlap, each group containing a child with congenital abnormalities, a thalidomide child and a child with spina bifida and hydrocephalus. However, while there were three cerebral-palsied children in the isolates group, there were none in the high status group: instead there were three children with no visible handicap (one with rheumatoid arthritis and two who were incontinent). Two of the isolates came from very deprived homes, and in three cases the mothers were markedly overprotective and anxious, neither of these factors being true of any of the 'high status' group. Northway's study of 'Outsiders' (1944) has already been mentioned. If her classification is used, only two of the isolated handicapped children could be described as withdrawn; the others were anxious to join in but apparently lacked the social skills needed to make them attractive as friends. It is difficult to make generalizations from such a small group: all that can be said is that the P H children who appear to be most 'at risk' as regards social isolation are more likely to be boys, to be cerebral-palsied and to be of a low ability and attainment level. The five control group isolates also tended to be of below average ability and three came from very deprived homes. However, in their case all but one were girls.

(v) TEACHER RATINGS OF POPULARITY

In addition to the sociometric data, teacher ratings of popularity were also used, a rating of (1) being given to children of above average popularity (2) for average popularity (3) to 'not very popular' children and (4) to those the teacher considered 'isolates'. By combining (3) and (4) a simple three point rating was obtained for each child and this was compared with the sociometric ratings, children scoring below the 30th percentile being rated for this purpose as (3), between the 30th and 70th percentile as (2) and above this as (1). When the ratings were compared (using Spearman's rho), a correlation coefficient of 0·9994 was obtained. Where there were differences in ratings, teachers tended to rate the child a little higher than his classmates, but in general teachers had a good grasp of the social status of the handicapped children and also identified five out of the seven isolates as being children lacking in friends.

(vi) SOCIAL RELATIONSHIPS AND THE BEHAVIOURAL RATINGS

In the next chapter the behavioural scales given to parents and teachers to complete will be described. Two of the items on each scale refer specifically to social relationships. The rater is asked to say whether the statement 'not much liked by other children' applies (definitely/somewhat/ not at all) and also whether the child 'tends to do things on his own – rather solitary'. Not surprisingly, parents are unlikely to check the item 'not much liked by other children' and of the thirty-two children in the whole sample scoring below the 20th percentile, only three were picked out by parents on this item, whereas the same item on the teacher scale was a much better predictor of the children's sociometric status, half the children with low ratings being picked out.

Scores on the item 'tends to do things on his own' were also compared with the child's sociometric status. Here it is perfectly possible that a child who tends to play alone at home may have several friends at school and for the parent scale there was little correlation between this item and sociometric status. On the teacher scale, however, one-third of those scoring on this item had in fact a low sociometric status (below the 20th percentile).

(vii) OTHER ASPECTS OF SOCIAL PARTICIPATION

While the sociometric test was the main instrument used to investigate the children's social relationships, a number of items in the interviews with the class teacher and the mother, and a number of items from the Manchester scales of social adaptation (chapter 6), also throw light on this question.

Within the school setting teachers were asked about the extent to which the handicapped children were chosen in classroom group activities where the children were free to make up their own groups, for instance for projects, craftwork, drama, PE and games. Unfortunately it was not possible to break down this question into very specific activities as there was so much variety between schools. Findings are summarized in Table 4.8 below.

TABLE 4.8. *Social participation: extent to which handicapped children were chosen in group activities* (No. = 58)

How often chosen in group activities	No. of children	%
More frequently than most	2	3·4
Average number of times	40	69·0
Less than most	10	17·2
Hardly ever	6	10·4

The teachers felt that there were few problems here, the non-handicapped children generally being 'very good' about including the PH children. As regards the small number of children 'hardly ever' chosen, in two cases the reason was that they were enuretic (the actual physical handicap was, in both cases, talipes); two others were often unchosen because of the physical limitations of their handicaps; one child with hemiparesis after a head injury was left out because the others 'feel he's rather different' and in only one case (a child with congenital abnormalities) was it reported that the children found the handicap itself repugnant. While teachers only mentioned a small number of cases where the physical limitation of the handicap hindered participation in group activities, and while few children were noted by teachers as generally being left to play alone at break, there are bound to be occasions when handicapped children do, in periods when activity is unorganized, feel left out. As one spina bifida 10-year-old boy who wore calipers confided to me, 'They often won't let me play football with them as I'm too slow . . . I just hang around at playtime . . . I don't play with no one . . . well, sometimes I do.'

Mothers were also asked a number of questions about their children's friends and about how much time they spent with them outside school hours, and the main findings are shown below (Table 4.9).

TABLE 4.9. *Mother's report on time spent with friends: comparison between control and handicapped groups*

	Groups		
Nature of interaction	% controls No. = 142	% PH without neurological abnormalities No. = 48	% PH with neurological abnormalities No. = 26
Has 'special friend' at school	73·0	60·4	53·0
Plays with school friends 'frequently' outside school hours	70·9	43·7*	73·0
Has friends who attend other schools	32·6	54·1	26·9
Visits friends' homes once or twice weekly	44·6	37·4	38·4
Visits friends' homes more than twice weekly	25·5	22·9	23·0
Brings friends home to visit	81·4	75·0	88·5

* Difference from controls significant at the 0·1 per cent level

Most of the findings here are both encouraging and not unexpected. They suggest that while the control group tend to see more of their friends than do the PH children, the difference is not a very marked one. Two things are a little surprising. One is the high proportion of children with neurological abnormalities (73·0 per cent) whom mothers report as seeing their school friends 'frequently' outside school hours. The other is the rather high proportion of PH children without neurological abnormalities with friends attending other schools. The explanation for this seems to be that because of restricted mobility these children often play with the child next door who may be older or younger and so at a different school.

(viii) THE PROBLEM OF TEASING

The likelihood of a handicapped child being teased if he is placed in an ordinary school is a matter of considerable anxiety to parents and others. Since little information exists in the literature about the nature and extent of such teasing, in this study both parents and class teachers were asked a series of questions designed to give a clearer picture of what is happening and the major findings are summarized in Tables 4.10 and 4.11 below. The teachers were of course only able to describe the situation as it exists at present.

TABLE 4.10. *Extent of teasing of handicapped juniors: parent's report*

Present extent of teasing	Boys No. = 42		Girls No. = 32		Total No. = 74	
	No.	%	No.	%	No.	%
Not at all	22	52	15	47	37	50
Occasionally	20	48	16	50	36	49
Fairly frequently	0	0	1	3	1	1

TABLE 4.11. *Extent of teasing of handicapped juniors: teachers' report*

Present extent of teasing	Boys No. = 42		Girls No. = 32		Total No. = 74	
	No.	%	No.	%	No.	%
Not at all	37	88	25	78	62	84
Occasionally	5	12	7	22	12	16
Fairly frequently	0	0	0	0	0	0

The first thing to notice is that more teasing is going on than teachers are aware of: their reports indicate that only 16 per cent of the group are being teased whereas parents report this for half the group. With the exception of one girl, however, both parents and teachers agree that the children are only teased occasionally. Boys and girls seem equally likely to be teased, although the teachers are more aware that this is going on in the case of the girls.

Figures such as these are not, on their own, very informative and an attempt was made to discover whether the amount of teasing was correlated with factors such as type or severity of handicap. This was not the case, nor did size of class or of school have any effect. What was important, however, was the location of the school. Almost all the teasing reported was confined to London schools and schools in a nearby heavily industrialized area: in four out of the five LEA areas visited outside London parents and teachers reported no teasing whatsoever. These four areas included two where most of the schools were in new towns and two where the majority were in small towns or villages. This finding underlines the need to beware of such generalizations as 'all children are cruel . . .' (made in fact, by two parents in London). It also raises the question of whether, in urban areas well served by special schools, the fact that non-handicapped children are much less likely to meet severely handicapped children in school makes them less tolerant of physical deviance.

(a) The nature of teasing

In the following paragraphs, a number of very specific examples of the kind of teasing which does go on are given, as knowledge about what are likely to be problems may help teachers to anticipate them. The most common form of teasing was namecalling. The terms 'spastic' and 'mongol' are quite frequently used; amputees may be called 'one-armed bandits'; a thalidomide child with battery-powered prostheses was called 'the robot'; a child with rheumatoid arthritis who could only move slowly was made miserable by being known (at cubs, not in school) as 'grandad'. Namecalling was not always unprovoked and mothers would admit that their handicapped children were at times 'aggressive' or 'domineering'. Often children would be teased by newcomers to the school, or by older children (especially older boys) or by children in the street rather than by their classmates. Problems like these tend to die down quickly and, as one teacher put it, a handicapped child is usually 'only a nine days wonder'. Hurtful personal remarks about a child's appearance may also be made, such as 'what tiny hands you have' or 'why haven't you any neck?' but any initial repulsion children felt, for instance towards thalidomide deformities, in all cases but one disappeared very quickly. Spiteful remarks may of course be made: a child who is thwarted by losing a game, or has his toy taken away or is bossed by the PH child may retaliate with remarks like 'you can't do it . . . you're a cripple' or 'you won't be able to have babies as you won't be able to hold them' (of a child with rudimentary arms), but parents reported that retaliation of this kind was quite infrequent.

Parents of incontinent children (however this is controlled), especially those with spina bifida, often worry a great deal about the social problems and teasing which may ensue. In fact only three children in the study were teased because they were 'smelly', and two were not spina bifida children, but children who suffered from enuresis and were sent to school in unwashed clothes. Only one spina bifida child was teased and this ended after the ileal loop operation had been carried out. There is, however, often a great deal of anxiety (unrecognized by teachers) among spina bifida children lest the fact that they wear special appliances is discovered (three children with bags, for instance, had been followed by classmates into the toilet) and this problem is discussed more fully later.

Mimicking of handicapped children, for example of abnormal gait, occurred in the case of four children, two being hemiplegic. In a school where 'no teasing' was reported one child confided, 'they imitate the way my knees bend; they think it's like what I do but it isn't really.' More serious are cases of bullying. In the seventy-four schools visited, eight cases were reported. In almost all these the culprit was another child in the class who was disturbed or known to be a bully and who found the handicapped child an easy target. Placement in a small 'remedial' class may mean a handicapped child is thrown into contact with several disturbed children. One child came home 'covered in pinch marks', another with scratches on his arms, another constantly had his sticks knocked from under him. The only other incidents reported were those of a haemophiliac who was hit and kicked by the class bully who taunted him with not having 'enough stamina to fix me' – he retaliated by enlisting the protection of a strong friend. Most unpleasant perhaps was the case of the girl with minor hand deformities who was pulled to one side in the playground and held down while the others examined her hand.

These cases have been reported fully as they may alert teachers to possible problems. In case they make dispiriting reading, it should be noted that they were the only incidents reported by parents and teachers in visits to seventy-four schools, many of them in very deprived areas. It has also to be remembered that any child, whether handicapped or not, is likely to be teased at some stage, although parents usually felt the handicapped child was more vulnerable than their other children. In five other cases children had been exceedingly unwilling or refused to return to school until the parent had been to see the head or class teacher.

The examples above all come from junior schools: in the infant schools the problem of teasing rarely occurs. Infant school teachers reported none whatsoever, and only five mothers mentioned minor difficulties. Remarks such as 'you're a cripple' or 'you've got shoogly legs' may be made, and occasionally play may border on teasing. A spina bifida child in a low trolley was encouraged by the other children to chase them around the classroom and his mother felt this could easily develop into cruelty on their part and a frustrating situation for him. At this age incontinence raises fewer problems, although one spina bifida child whose bladder was manually expressed had been upset by remarks such as 'Her mummy comes and pushes her tummy' a situation which could have been prevented had toileting privacy been available.

(b) Coping with teasing

How is teasing generally coped with? In fourteen cases parents had felt it necessary to go to the school in person to report the matter to the class teacher or head, and in almost every case this had been very effective in halting the teasing. Others take direct action '[When they called him names] . . . I went over and cleaned them up' or used threats: 'his father will come and talk to you if there's any more trouble.' (There wasn't.) Sometimes the parents report being more disturbed than the child: 'I was so upset I was contemplating not sending her to school at all. I was thinking "to hell with the school and all of them".' Unfortunately a small number of parents feel unable to draw attention to the problems their children were having in case 'causing trouble' in this way might result in the child's being transferred to a special school.

(c) How do the children cope with teasing?

A common parental attitude is put succinctly by one mother: 'I feel he's got to fight his own battles, but if I feel it's unjust, I put my spoke in it.' While it is necessary for personality development that children learn to assert themselves, encouraging a child to stand up for himself may lead to problems. An infant who 'hits back' with an artificial arm or a 9 year old who resorts to kicking with heavy surgical boots may become very unpopular both with children and with other parents. Methods of active retaliation are only effective when PH children are stronger, which is rarely the case. As an 8-year-old girl with diastrophic dwarfism told me, 'I don't stand up for myself very much . . . only if they really hurt me . . . if I hurt them back they'll probably start arguing and hitting me and I don't like that.' Many handicapped children submit to or ignore the mild forms of teasing which occur, or resort to sarcastic retorts.

As far as teachers are concerned, three main methods of dealing with teasing are used. Several heads or class teachers anticipated the problem by speaking to the children in assembly or in the classroom beforehand. One village teacher of the old school 'took a tough line'. She first visited the home (the child was cerebral-palsied) to get an idea of his disabilities, then assembled the school and told them a little about him; that he was not to be called 'spastic' or 'cripple' and not to be pushed as he easily fell. Constructive suggestions from the teacher as to how the children should behave are often very effective with this age group and most parents thought some 'preparation' of this kind helpful although if the child has no overt handicap it may not be appropriate. The mother of an incontinent child who wore an appliance was strongly opposed to the teacher's suggestion that she should ask the class not to be rough with her: 'If they're told they mustn't hit her, they'll just go for her . . . the children around here are rough and cruel.' In this case, nothing was said and the child coped very successfully with the situation on her own.

A second method used by teachers is to talk to the class as a group after teasing has arisen, when the child is not present. This may be necessary when a teacher does not have any information beforehand about a child (as in the case of a non-English-speaking moderately handicapped hemiplegic who arrived without warning in a class of 8 year olds and who was ridiculed because he fell so easily, could not do what the others could and just appeared to be 'funny'). This could have been prevented had the teacher met the child in advance: as Wright 1960) points out, 'extraordinary care should be taken to cut down as far as possible exposure to ridicule, otherwise all too often the child will "learn" that he ought to be scorned.' Only in one case did a class teacher look aghast when it was suggested he should speak openly to the class about the thalidomide child with artificial legs in his class. He said that he 'wouldn't dare' to do this and instead tried to 'draw attention away from the handicap' when the others asked what was wrong with her.

Often there is no need for a teacher to speak to the whole class, and occasional teasing can be ended by a talk with the child involved. This teacher's comment was typical: 'I always talk to the culprit privately and try to help him to think how he would feel if he'd been born with her handicap.'

(ix) CURIOSITY ABOUT THE HANDICAP

While teasing as such may not be a problem, parents sometimes worry about their children being exposed to the curiosity of others. This question was difficult to investigate, since most of the children in the study had grown up with their classmates and in roughly 75 per cent of cases curiosity was now no problem at all (see Table 4.12 below).

TABLE 4.12. *Amount of curiosity shown by pupils about handicapped children*

Amount of curiosity	Reported by parent No. = 74		Reported by teacher No. = 74	
	No.	%	No.	%
None	52	70	58	78
A little in the past but no longer	11	15	10	14
Children still curious	11	15	6	8

When a child first arrives in school this may be a problem. One amputee's mother reported, 'The children used to crowd around him in the playground to look at his arm. Some of them kept on at him and asked him questions all the time, and he got a bit annoyed.' Another child who was pushed home daily in a wheelchair by his mother was preceded by several classmates who walked backwards in front of the chair staring, which both child and mother found more unnerving than actual teasing.

Normally, curiosity is of a reasonable kind. At the infant level children want to know why a child can't walk, what it feels like to use sticks, why one child is allowed to go to the toilet at any time, why another brings extra nappies to school, what was in the duffle bag (a change of clothes) one child always carried. After a PH child has been operated on, or fitted with a new pair of artificial legs, his classmates may take an interest in the sorts of things he can now do. Only occasionally does the sight of deformities lead to actual repulsion ('what horrible-looking hands'), although in the case of severe deformities children may be 'rather shattered' by the appearance of a newcomer if not previously told a little about him. Mealtimes may cause difficulties and a child may have to be placed in a particularly sympathetic group. Until this was done, for example, children seated at mealtimes beside a child with deformities of the upper limbs used to shudder, while in another school the messy eating habits of a cerebral-palsied child disturbed his neighbours. Fortunately such reactions were only very rarely reported.

The problem of incontinence has already been touched on. Children who wear urinary appliances may experience considerable anxiety about the potential reactions of their classmates: three methods of coping were used by the children in this study. One was to keep the matter strictly secret. One child insisted on keeping her foot against the door of the room in which she was being changed, while another experienced great anxiety when his sister's friends visited the home lest they see his nappies hanging out to dry. Some children cope by letting into the secret a few friends who will help them to ensure toileting privacy. A third method is to be entirely open. One child in the study would tell his classmates, 'I've got to go and empty my bag now'; another told her friends 'straight out' when they asked, and the latter 'accepted it quite naturally'.

The method of coping used depends very much upon the individual child, but the following comments will perhaps be helpful. Firstly, at least one adult in the school other than the head should have discussed the matter with the parent and should know how to attach and change the child's appliance and what to do in case of an accident, so that the child knows who he can go to. When he moves to a different class it may be necessary to make a different person responsible. Secondly, some arrangement must be made to ensure that the child can toilet himself or be changed in complete privacy. School toilets often do not lock, so some special modification or arrangement must be made. Lack of privacy was a very common problem in the schools visited and one generally reported by parents, teachers being unaware of the anxiety caused to the child. Finally the member of staff responsible should be aware that teasing may occur and should have discussed with the mother how to tackle this problem if it arises.

Conclusions: encouraging social integration in school

In this chapter difficulties of various kinds which handicapped children may and do experience in their social relationships in school have been discussed. It was necessary to focus on these in order to pinpoint areas where improvements can be made, but it would be quite wrong to ignore the fact that again and again teachers and parents were at pains to stress how considerate, helpful and kind a handicapped child's classmates were, how 'absolutely marvellous' they were to the children who had to be hospitalized and how 'cheerfully tolerant' they could be of apparently odd behaviour. In general there was also a very realistic awareness on the part of teachers of the dangers of overprotection which clearly can be a problem. If parental reports of their children's happiness at school can be relied on, there is little to choose between the handicapped and control groups (Table 4.13).

TABLE 4.13. *Happiness at school: junior group*

| | Handicapped group | | Controls | |
	No.	%	No.	%
Unhappy	1	1·3	3	2·0
Not altogether happy	8	10·8	19	12·8
Happy or very happy	65	87·8	116	78·3
Don't know	0	0·0	10	6·7

In the case of the infants, all twenty-five children were reported as being happy (ten) or very happy (fifteen) at school and handicapped children were, more often than controls, reported as being unhappy when for any reason they could *not* go to school.

It is nevertheless true that while few PH children are entirely isolated in school, being physically handicapped does in a great many cases make it more difficult for a child to establish satisfactory social relationships. The question inevitably follows of what teachers can do to help in this situation. An article which is useful in this context is the discussion by Lippitt and Gold (1959) of how children's perceptions of each other develop. In attempting to analyse what it is which maintains and aggravates the undesirable social situation of certain children in the (normal) classroom group, they found that difficulties appeared to be 'created and maintained' by a circular social process, contributed to by the individual, his classmates and his teachers. If the individual child is focused on, he is seen to contribute to the unhealthy situation by his negative self-evaluation and his response to this, by his hostility towards others, by his unskilled and unrealistic behaviour which may include either assertive aggressiveness or withdrawing non-contribution and by his insensitive and defensive reception of feedback from others which might potentially give him more guidance for his own behaviour. If his classmates are considered, the source of difficulty for the individual child is seen to be firstly, a very rapid evaluative labelling of the child, and a strong tendency to maintain this evaluative consensus despite further information; secondly, very inadequate skills of the group in providing the member with feedback which communicates sympathetic guidance rather than rejection or ignoring; thirdly, a lack of group standards concerning the acceptance and support of deviancy. Finally when the teacher's contribution was considered, Lippitt and Gold found a lack of teaching effort that focused on developing personal attitudes and group standards about good human relationships, a lack of any attempt to group the children in such a way as to help the unaccepted children and a lack of any clear presentation of constructive behaviour patterns towards low status children which could be imitated by the other pupils.

This clear analysis suggests a number of different points at which the problem could be attacked and gives some idea of its complexity. Simple solutions are unlikely to be effective. As Northway (1967) points out, simply 'placing isolated children in existing groups is not always the best way to help them. It is not likely to result in the child's being accepted unless he has a definite contribution to make to the activities of the group.' What is important is that the teacher approaches the question with a clear and constructive policy right from the start. Each teacher will have a somewhat different approach, but four points are worth considering. One concerns giving the class sufficient and appropriate information (in terms of the children's ages) about the handicapped child before he enters the class. Practice in Scandinavia is discussed in chapter 9 and some examples are given, and in this study a number of cases were found where this had been done to good effect. In the infant study, for example, the head or class teacher had spoken to the other children in advance in 28 per cent of the cases, and in the junior study in 13 per cent. In all cases where there were special 'units' for PH children, heads had discussed with the other pupils and sometimes with the parents the new class. In one school the head first talked to all the children, then took sixty of them on a visit to a local Cheshire home and finally invited handicapped adults in wheelchairs to visit the school and talk to the children.

Webb (1967) points out that it is unrealistic to expect very young children to show compassion, and better expectations are for courtesy, ordinary kindness and tolerance. Long talks about the handicapped child are dangerous as the children may repeat the patter without understanding it, and may dislike the child who gets so much of an adult's attention. Usually it is sufficient to explain quite simply that a child cannot balance or walk or talk very well or needs to go to the toilet rather frequently and to give the children a positive lead about how to behave. While there is an obvious need to prepare children for the arrival of a haemophiliac in the school, it is equally important that there should be very careful preparation when cerebral-palsied children are to join a class since their behaviour may seem 'odd' to the others. It is also important to ensure that children with very obvious handicaps, especially those in wheelchairs, are not overprotected and this can be explained to even quite young children. To be able to prepare the children adequately the head and the class teacher must themselves have sufficient information and have met the child and his mother beforehand at the school or at his home (preferably both).

Further information can be provided at a later date. With young children, this will usually mean simply answering their questions, for instance, about the special aids and how they work. With older children the staff may want to go further than this. In one school where there was a young spina bifida pupil, older children who wished to saw a film of the local 'opportunity class' for handicapped pre-school children which had a follow-up section on integration in ordinary schools.

A second useful approach, which is suggested by Lippitt and Gold (1959), is for the teacher to work in conjunction with the 'high-power' children who have the most influence on the social-emotional structure of the class. This is in fact quite often done and a carefully planned example is given in chapter 9. It is easier to do this with older children and an obvious problem is that, faced by a new class, a teacher may not know which children to select. Since much of the teasing of handicapped children comes from older children in senior classes it is probably worth considering how to enlist their co-operation, although the obvious danger is that of drawing undesirable attention to a handicapped child and in this way actually creating a 'difference'.

The third point may appear to be a minor one: it relates to the choice of seating position for the handicapped child and it may be controlled by physical factors (if the child is in a wheelchair) or by the child's attainment level. What Lindzey and Byrne (1968) in their discussion of the antecedents of interpersonal attractiveness have to say is relevant here: 'There is evidence that individuals who are physically near to one another in terms of classroom seats, dormitory rooms, suburban houses (etc.) are more likely to choose one another as friends than persons who are more remote.' Too often PH children are seated next to other children who are 'deviant' in some way through, for instance, being low in reading ability or lacking in social skills. Careful selection of seating partners can do much to help newly arrived handicapped children to make real friendships.

A final point which Lippitt and Gold (1959) among others have suggested is that teachers should try to work directly outside the classroom with children in need of help, to assist them to initiate changes in an unsatisfactory social situation. Clearly teachers with large classes have limited time available to do this, although in this study many teachers were going out of their way to help both withdrawn and aggressive children who lacked social skills. The contribution which non-teaching staff, such as the school meals staff and the welfare assistants, can make is considerable, particularly since they are often in a better position to observe what goes on outside the organized classroom situation than are the teachers themselves.

REFERENCES

ARGYLE, M. (1967) *The Psychology of Interpersonal Behaviour*, Penguin Books, Harmondsworth, Middlesex.

BARKER, R. G. (1948) 'The social psychology of physical disability', *Journal of Social Issues*, 4, pp. 28–38.

BONNEY, M. E. (1943) 'Personality traits of socially successful and socially unsuccessful children', *Journal of Educational Psychology*, 34 (7), pp. 449–72.

CENTERS, L. and CENTERS, R. (1963) 'Peer group attitudes towards the amputee child', *Journal of Social Psychology*, 61, pp. 127–32.

CHIGIER, E. and CHIGIER, M. (1970) 'Cultural factors in early education of the handicapped in Israel', in *Proceedings of the 4th International Seminar in Special Education*, Cork, Ireland, International Society for the Rehabilitation of the Disabled, New York.

DAVIE, R., BUTLER, N. and GOLDSTEIN, H. (1972) *From Birth to Seven: The Second Report of the National Child Development Study (1958 Cohort)*, Longmans, London.

DAVIS, F. (1961) 'Deviance disavowal: the management of strained interaction by the visibly handicapped', *Social Problems*, 9, p. 123.

DEMBO, T., LEVITON, G. L. and WRIGHT, B. A. (1956) 'Adjustment to misfortune: a problem of social psychological rehabilitation', *Artificial Limbs*, 3, pp. 4–62.

DEWEY, G. and FORCE, D. (1956) 'Social status of the physically handicapped child' *Exceptional Children*, 23 (3), pp. 104–7 and 132.

EVANS, K. M. (1963) 'Sociometry in schools – I sociometric techniques: II applications', *Educational Research*, 6, pp. 50–8 and 121–8.

GOFFMAN, E. (1968) 'Marked for life', *New Society*, 28 November 1968, pp. 795–7.

GOFFMAN, E. (1963) *Stigma: Notes on the Management of Spoiled Identity*, Prentice-Hall, New Jersey.

GOLD, M. (1958) 'Power in the classroom', *Sociometry*, 2, pp. 50–60.

GROSSMAN, B. and WRIGHTER, J. (1948) 'The relationship between selection-rejection and intelligence, social status and personality amongst sixth grade children', *Sociometry*, 11, pp. 346–55.

HEBER, R. F. (1956) 'The relationship of intelligence and physical maturity to the social status of children', *Journal of Educational Psychology*, 47, pp. 158–62.

JESSEL, C. (1975) *Mark's Wheelchair Adventure*, Methuen, London.

KLECK, R., ONO, H. and HASTORF, A. H. (1966) 'The effect of physical deviance upon face to face interaction', *Human Relations*, 19, pp. 425–36.

LINDZEY, G. and BYRNE, D. (1968) 'Measurement of social choice and interpersonal attractiveness', chapter 14 in Lindzey, G. and Aronson, E. (eds.) *The Handbook of Social Psychology*, II, Addison Wesley, Reading, Mass.

126 · THE DISABLED SCHOOLCHILD

LIPPITT, R. and GOLD, M. (1959) 'Classroom social structure as a mental health problem', *Journal of Social Issues*, 15 (1), pp. 40–9.

LUNZER, E. A. (1960) 'Aggressive and withdrawing children in the normal school', *British Journal of Educational Psychology*, pp. 1–10 and 119–23.

NORTHWAY, M. L. (1944) 'Outsiders: a study of the personality problems of children least acceptable to their age-group', *Sociometry*, 7, pp. 10–25.

NORTHWAY, M. L. (1967) *A Primer of Sociometry* (2nd edition), University of Toronto Press.

RICHARDSON, S. A. *et al.* (1961) 'Cultural uniformity in reaction to physical disabilities', *American Sociology Review*, 26 (2), pp. 241–7.

RICHARDSON, S. A. (1968) 'The effect of physical disability on the socialization of a child', in Goslin, D. A. and Glass, D. C. (eds.), *The Handbook of Socialization Theory and Research*, Rand McNally, New York.

RICHARDSON, S. A. (1969) 'Contributions of social science to paediatrics', prepared for the XII International Congress of Paediatrics, Mexico, December 1968.

SHEARS, L. M. and JENSEMA, C. J. (1969) 'Social acceptability of anomalous persons', *Exceptional Children*, 36 (2), pp. 91–6.

SHERE, M. O. (1957) 'The socio-emotional development of the twin who has cerebral palsy', *Cerebral Palsy Review*, 17, pp. 16–18.

SOLDWEDEL, B. and TERRELL, I. (1957) 'Sociometric aspects of physically handicapped and non-handicapped children in the same elementary school', *Exceptional Children*, 23, pp. 371–2 and 381–2

WEBB, L. (1967) *Children with Special Needs in the Infants' School*, Colin Smythe, London.

WESTMAN, J. C., RICE, D. L. and BERMANN, E. (1967) 'Nursery school behaviour and later school adjustment', *American Journal of Orthopsychiatry*, 37, pp. 725–31.

WRIGHT, B. (1960) *Physical Disability – A Psychological Approach*, Harper, New York.

Chapter 5 · Emotional and Behavioural Difficulties

In the previous chapter the children's social relationships were considered in detail but little was said about their emotional or behavioural problems, although these clearly influence personal relationships. It was pointed out that social acceptability was not closely related to the severity or functional effect of the handicap, one implication being that it must be related to aspects of the personality other than physique.

It would be both interesting and useful to be able to 'measure' in some way the personality of a physically handicapped child and to relate this to his social success in an ordinary school. Unfortunately, personality tests are probably less well developed than any other type of psychological test, especially for young children. It is also true and understandable that much greater emphasis has been laid by psychologists on measuring abnormal rather than normal behaviour. This chapter is therefore concerned more with the emotional and behavioural problems of the children rather than with the positive personality traits associated with social acceptability.

In the first part of the chapter there is a short discussion of some of the ways in which a physical handicap may affect emotional development. Following this the question of the child's attitude to his handicap is looked at in more detail; material collected during interviews with teachers and parents is presented to illustrate in a specific way some of the problems facing a handicapped child in an ordinary school. In the final and longest section of the chapter, the extent and nature of behavioural disorders in physically handicapped children, particularly in those with neurological abnormalities, is examined more systematically and the findings of this and of earlier studies are discussed.

The effect of a physical handicap on emotional development

Although a good deal has been written about the effect of a physical handicap on emotional and social adjustment, the amount of systematic research has been limited. It has been difficult to select representative subjects and to secure adequate controls, and appropriate tests for assessing behaviour and personality problems have been lacking. Kellmer Pringle (1964) has carried out a comprehensive review of studies prior to 1962 and this has recently been updated (by Pilling, 1972, 1973a, b, 1974).

In summing up the findings of the early studies, Kellmer Pringle (1964) concluded that

> while most comparative studies show handicapped children to be less mature and more disturbed than those without any disabilities, the consensus of opinion and weight of evidence seem fairly clearly balanced against the view that the handicapped are inevitably maladjusted. Most would agree that physique is only one factor in an extensive context of environmental and personal conditions working together. Available data have failed to show any evidence of a definite association between a particular disability and a particular behaviour characteristic.

One reason for the expectation still held by many people that physically handicapped children will show more emotional disturbance than their peers is the feeling that they are very likely to be frequently frustrated (a frustrating situation being defined as one in which some obstacle prevents the satisfaction of a desire). If frustration is present it may be expressed in a variety of ways. Aggressive behaviour or blaming others is common, repressing one's desires or withdrawing into fantasy another possibility.

But are physically handicapped children necessarily frustrated? Wright (1960), in her very comprehensive account of the emotional problems of the disabled, thinks not. She argues that 'some governing apparatus is functioning to prevent the weak and disabled from too great negative psychological consequences of their limitations'. Two aspects of the situation, she suggests, tend to decrease the amount of frustration a child feels. Firstly there are changes in the environment (for instance allowances made by a teacher for slow handwriting) and secondly changes in the handicapped person who may, for example, either lower his goals or substitute new attainable ones or find ingenious ways of circumventing the difficulties. She also thinks that it may be possible to foster a child's tolerance of frustration by exposing him to only small amounts which he can cope with.

It might be useful for a teacher in an ordinary class to list the frustrations which the handicapped child is likely to experience and to observe in what way and how successfully he is coping, or how he could be helped to do so. A great deal of sensitivity may be needed, as children often hide their frustrations. One child in the study, who was severely handicapped by spina bifida, had recently had his feet amputated and was still unable to manipulate his prostheses. His teacher reported that he was 'quite content to watch PE lessons from his wheelchair'. His mother's story was different. He was 'inwardly seething with rage' at not being allowed to participate as he knew that within his limits there were things that he could do. Here the frustration had been imposed by the environment rather than by the handicap itself.

Another common but quite different emotional problem which being handicapped can give rise to is a feeling of uncertainty. Parents and teachers frequently reported, for instance, that physically handicapped children were reluctant to participate in new situations, for example to go on a school expedition. Meyerson (1956) accounts for such uncertainty in terms of the handicapped child's having to face many more 'new psychological situations' than his peers, a new psychological situation being, for example, what every child experiences when he goes to school for the first time.

Three kinds of new psychological situation may face the PH child. First, the situation may be new in that (if his environment has been more restricted than a non-handicapped child's) he has never experienced it before. Secondly, it may be new or may cause uncertainty if he lacks the required physical tool. He may refuse to go on a school expedition in case he encounters steps or cannot keep up. Thirdly, he may be unsure of his reception by others. In a PE lesson, for instance, the child with deformed feet may wonder how others will react when he takes his socks off. Often physical and emotional uncertainty will occur together, as in the case of the armless thalidomide girl faced with eating in the school dining-room for the first time.

Avoiding the situation may seem, for some children, the easiest way out. One incontinent child in the study was so afraid of being laughed at when he emptied his appliance in the school toilets that he never did empty it: as a result the teacher complained that he was 'smelly'. A much better way of coping is for the child to be taught the specific skills, whether physical or social, needed to cope, and for minor environmental changes to be made where possible (in this instance a lock put on the toilet door). If they are well informed about the child's problems, teachers are often able to anticipate the situations in which a child is likely to feel uncertain and to decide in advance how he can be helped to cope.

The child's attitude to the handicap

Although the presence of a handicap may give rise to frustration and uncertainty, why is it that different handicapped children react in entirely different ways to potentially frustrating or anxiety-causing situations? There is a great deal of agreement that the key factor determining the child's attitude to the handicap and the likelihood that he will develop related emotional disorders is the parental attitude to the handicap. A very clear statement of this comes from Allen and Pearson (1928): 'The child seems to adopt the same attitude to the disability as his parents do. If they worry about it, so does he. If they are ashamed, he will be sensitive too. If they regard it in an objective manner, he will accept it as a fact, and will not allow it to interfere with his adjustment.' A corollary of this is that it is as essential to treat the relationship between the child and his parents, and the attitude of the latter towards the disability at the time of its occurrence, as it is to treat the disease itself.

Parental attitudes were explored in a Canadian study carried out by Gingras and his colleagues (1964) in which the psychological development of forty-one children with congenital limb abnormalities was investigated. The authors found that the child's success or failure in understanding the world and in mastering motor activities was determined not so much by physical limitations as by the more or less anxious attitudes of the mothers. The children tended to perceive their disabilities through the parental attitudes of acceptance or rejection. For example, those whose parents were least affected by the presence of a congenital limb defect adjusted with much less resistance to the use of a prosthesis.

In the previous chapter the importance of society's reactions to a handicapped person was pointed out; this must be reiterated in relation to emotional handicaps. These, at least in the case of children without brain damage, do not spring directly from the physical handicap but are mediated by social values. The process is probably as follows. A child lacks a required tool for behaviour, such as an arm. Others notice this, and devalue him. The child accepts the norms of society, and devalues himself. In some handicaps such as facial disfigurement the handicapping factors are at most entirely social rather than physical.

The effect of such a devaluation can be minimized if the negative aspects of the handicap along with the coping aspects are brought to the notice of the child in the accepting atmosphere of his own home. This is quite crucial, for as long as a physical disability is linked with shame and inferiority a child cannot realistically accept his own self. At the same time, as Wright (1960) points out, parents must not enter into too great a 'conspiracy of cheerfulness', otherwise the child may have the devastating experience of being brought face to face with his shortcomings in a hostile rejecting environment. Generally the first time that a child is brought face to face with this environment is when he first goes to school, or at least when he enters junior school at 7 years old. As Gingras et al. (1964) point out, it is then that the child has to face the responsibility for his own adjustment to the new school world: he has to establish a new type of relationship with adults, he has to ward off possible attacks (verbal or otherwise) of classmates, and to make himself acceptable to them. The school environment is a complex one, and especially if the handicap is not well accepted by the parents it is at this point (and even more so at adolescence) that an increase in emotional problems can be expected.

At this stage the child's image of himself (his self-concept), particularly those aspects of the self-concept relating to attitudes and experiences involving the body (the body image), is likely to be intensified as he makes comparisons between himself and his non-handicapped peers. A handicapped child will share the peer values, particularly as regards physical activity; that is, he will hold up to himself 'normal' performance as the model of behaviour to aspire to and the handicap will, at least to some extent, be a more or less latent source of self-devaluation. At the same time, even quite young children may have a quite realistic acceptance of their handicaps. Gingras et al. (1964) studied the self-portraits of amputee children aged six to thirteen interpreting their inclusion of the limb-deficiency

or prosthesis in the drawing as indicating acceptance of the handicap. They found that an artificial leg or foot was accepted much
earlier on than an artificial upper limb. Richardson (1964) in a
study of handicapped and non-handicapped 9–11 year olds at a
summer camp for underprivileged children in the USA explored
self-concepts by asking the children to 'tell me about yourself'.
He found they were very realistic in their self-descriptions and that
they shared the aspirations of their age-mates but knew they could
not live up to them.

Aspiring to the normal has obvious disadvantages since, by holding up 'normal' performance as a model, a person exposes himself to
repeated feelings of inferiority and failure, and this argument is
sometimes put forward by those who feel uneasy about placing PH
children in ordinary schools. On the other hand, the advantages in
striving towards the normal should not be forgotten. Social relationships will be smoother if a handicapped person knows, through daily
contact with his peers, what normative behaviour is. It may also be
necessary for a person to cling to the normal before he can give it up
through a realistic knowledge of what is involved, and it is likely
that children in ordinary schools have fewer unrealistic job aspirations than do those in special schools. Holding up 'normal' performance as a model may also lead to a change in attitude where a person
can see that the effects of his disability are restricted, not pervasive,
and that in certain aspects of life, normal performance can be
achieved. It may be easier for girls than boys to find other goals than
those related to physique. One of the findings of the study was in
fact that a higher proportion of PH girls than boys made a satisfactory social adjustment in the ordinary school.

Research findings

In the study an attempt was made to assess the children's attitudes to
their handicaps. The mother was asked how the child felt about his
handicap, and how much he appeared to worry about it and talk
about it. Replies were recorded verbatim and on this basis (combined
with my own observations during the individual testing sessions) the
children were rated on a four-point scale ranging from very well
adjusted to poorly adjusted. In the infant group all the children but
five (i.e. 80 per cent) appeared to be well adjusted to their handicaps,
while in the case of the juniors 73 per cent were well or very well

adjusted, 19 per cent (fourteen children) were moderately well adjusted but had some difficulties in accepting the handicap and 8 per cent (six children) were poorly adjusted.

Teachers who felt they knew the mothers well enough were asked to rate the mother's attitude to the handicap. In 53 per cent of the fifty-eight cases which were rated the mother's attitude was 'very sensible', in 24 per cent 'fairly sensible', in 14 per cent 'overprotective', in 5 per cent 'overdemanding' while 4 per cent were rated as rather ambivalent. Because the rating was a very subjective one, and did not include all the mothers, no attempt was made to correlate the child's adjustment to his handicap with his mother's attitude to it: however it was noticed that few of the 'very sensible' mothers had poorly adjusted children.

The main finding was thus that for almost three-quarters of the juniors, and an even higher proportion of the infants, the handicap appeared to be well accepted. Here is one typical response: 'she hardly talks about it at all – of course, you never know what goes on in their minds, but outwardly she's a very happy person.' Most parents found that the handicap was usually taken for granted or not noticed. The severity of handicap did not seem important. The mother of a 9 year old child with only vestigial arms reported, 'she doesn't seem to worry . . . certainly she never lets me know if anything's upset her. She's very friendly . . . in a group she'll push herself forward rather than back.' A boy of the same age with a similar handicap, who used powered prostheses, was described as cheerful, outgoing and very persistent in overcoming his difficulties, 'altogether a very normal boy'.

Even when the handicap is well accepted, children will occasionally ask such questions as 'why can't I walk?' (when the new baby starts walking) and the handicap may be commented on at an early age. A 5 year old achondroplasic child (a form of dwarfism) asked why she was smaller than her friends. On being told by her mother 'God made you like that' her response was, 'Well, it was jolly unfair of him.' However, the same child was quick to notice the things she could do that others couldn't, such as being chosen for the coveted role of the cat in the pantomime. One particularly well-adjusted child was a boy with severe arthrogryposis (see appendix N). Walking was very difficult for him and hand control severely impaired. At 4 years old he asked his mother 'Why are my arms like this?' In her words, 'I explained as near to nature as I could how a baby grew and how some grew a bit different, and he accepted that. Once or twice he has said, "I wish I had a proper arm so that I could do such and such" but I said, "well you haven't but make the most of what you have".'

Even well-adjusted children may suffer from temporary depression. A 10 year old with rheumatoid arthritis was reported by his teacher to be 'cheerful, uncomplaining and very well-adjusted' and his mother confirmed that he had 'a real gift' for putting up with pain and hospitalization. At times, however, he had 'terrible fits of depression' and was very sensitive to the fact that his mother had to be with him more than was normal for a boy of his age.

About a quarter of the juniors had difficulties of some kind in coming to terms with their handicaps, and most of these appeared to be related to one of four things; appearance, anxieties about incontinence (an 'invisible' handicap), frustration at not being able to join in and worries about the future.

It is not surprising that handicapped children may be sensitive about their appearance but what is interesting is that it is often not the child with severe handicaps who is most sensitive but rather the child who can almost pass as 'normal'. A child with peripheral neuritis, for example, accepted cheerfully the loss of strength which attacks of the disease caused, but was very worried because the steroid treatment made him fat in the face. One of the least handicapped children in the study, a girl with minor congenital abnormalities of the hands, became very worried if anyone looked at these. While most of the amputees accepted their handicaps well, two boys, both in their first year of junior school and both with forearm amputations, showed a similar pattern of markedly aggressive behaviour. In both cases the parents clearly had great difficulty in accepting the handicap. In one case the child wore a glove over his artificial hand and became extremely disturbed on the occasions when the glove slipped off. The other child had entirely rejected his prosthesis (as his mother also appeared to have done) and his behaviour problems had become so severe that he was being considered for admission to a school for maladjusted children.

A different situation exists in the case of the hidden handicap of incontinence. While not all incontinent children worried about this handicap, discussions with parents revealed a great deal of hidden anxiety, even in children who were well-adjusted. An awareness of the potential social shame which incontinence may give rise to appeared in children of all ages. A bright 5 year old with severe bowel incontinence 'nearly had a blue fit' according to his mother when he was told in front of the class to go and fetch his welfare assistant (whose job it was to change him). The mother of a 7 year old who had to be changed at school said that he refused to carry a parcel with spare pants and trousers, as 'the other children will know what they are'. An 8 year old girl always insisted on keeping her foot firmly against the door of the room in which she is changed until a key was provided; a 10 year old is terrified that children visiting his home will find out that he wears an appliance and gets very upset when his mother hangs up nappies outside.

With the exception of the 5 year old these children were all happy at school, they had friends, they were outwardly well-adjusted socially and their teachers did not realize these strong hidden anxieties existed. Two things seem essential, first that the head or class teacher ensures that the child has toilet privacy, and secondly that the teacher regularly has a word with the mother about whether any problems exist. It is also often helpful if a child knows that he can turn to the teacher if an accident occurs.

An abnormal appearance or the existence of a hidden handicap like incontinence cause anxiety because they are socially stigmatizing. Of a different kind are the problems caused when a handicap prevents a child from joining in with his peers. The only child with polio in the study became very upset at one stage when the other children were 'rushing around the school and playing games' and she would come home crying every day. For boys, the problem can be even more acute, although often non-handicapped children are thoughtful about including the child whose mobility is poor. A rather timid boy, paralysed on one side, plucked up courage to join his classmates for football in the park, but soon gave up as he hardly ever got the ball; a child with artificial legs often finds at playtime that the other children forget about him, and 'he's left hanging around outside the classroom on his own'.

As children approach puberty, this kind of problem is likely to worsen. The oldest children in the study were 10 year olds, and several parents reported that they were 'beginning to feel different' and to be more aware of things they could not do. With girls, appearance matters more. One 10 year old with a very minor hand deformity has suddenly started 'finding fault with her hand all the time'. Another, with an artificial arm, until recently very well adjusted, has become self-conscious, refusing to go swimming or to go out without a cardigan. Questions begin to be asked, too, about jobs or marriage.

With boys there is more anxiety about what physical activities they will and won't be able to participate in at school. Two of the 10 year old boys in the study had recently developed school phobias. The mother of one, a haemophiliac, reported that 'up to six months ago he took it in his stride. Recently he seems more thoughtful about it and has been rather moody, not wanting to go to school and not as happy as before.' She wondered if he had 'started thinking about the future'. The other boy, who is paralysed on one side, appears to have 'got over' his sudden recent fear of school, but his parents are for the first time seriously considering the possibility of a special school at secondary level.

Extent and nature of emotional and behavioural disorders

Material of the kind presented in the last section is useful in illustrating some of the practical problems faced by physically handicapped children at school. It is also important, however, to look much more systematically at the incidence of behavioural problems in different groups of children: the remainder of this chapter is concerned with the question of the extent and nature of the disorders found in handicapped and non-handicapped children of primary school age. There is also the question of the effect of neurological abnormality to be considered. While the absence of a definite association between a particular disability and particular behavioural characteristics was noted earlier in the chapter, evidence is accumulating to show that behaviour disorders are much more frequent in the neurologically abnormal group.

One of the problems in the early studies was that this distinction was rarely made, physically handicapped children often being considered as a unitary group. A few studies exist, however, where the nature of the handicap was specified. The Gingras (1964) study of forty-one children with congenital limb deformities has already been mentioned: here no major emotional disorders were found. In a more recent study, Kellmer Pringle and Fiddes (1970) used the well-known Bristol social adjustment guide to investigate emotional problems in eighty thalidomide children aged from $4\frac{1}{2}$–$8\frac{1}{2}$ years old. A comparison was made with the non-handicapped 7 year olds in the National Child Development study (1958 Cohort) and it was found that the incidence of problem behaviour was very similar and that emotional maladjustment 'was no more prevalent among the thalidomide group (despite many severe physical and sensory handicaps) than among the non-handicapped'.

Although these studies suggest that for children without neurological abnormalities the rate of disorder does not tend to be much higher than in non-handicapped children, a largescale study carried out in the Isle of Wight (Rutter, Tizard and Whitmore 1970b) showed that the incidence of psychiatric disorder in children with physical handicaps resulting from damage below the brainstem (i.e. without neurological abnormalities as defined in chapter 2) was twice that of non-handicapped children. The handicapped group was a very diverse one, however, and included a large proportion of children with heart conditions and with asthma and other respiratory disorders who could be thought of as falling into the category 'delicate' rather than 'physically handicapped' and so were rather different from the sample in this study.

(i) BEHAVIOUR DISORDERS IN NEUROLOGICALLY ABNORMAL CHILDREN

While the results of studies comparing children with purely physical disorders and non-handicapped children are somewhat inconclusive, there can be much less doubt about the higher rate of disorder which is found in neurologically abnormal children. In the ordinary schools most of these children tend to be either cerebral-palsied or children with spina bifida and hydrocephalus. Early studies on cerebral-palsied children have been well reviewed by Nielsen (1966). Her 'tentative' conclusion was that 'emotional disturbances are more common among cerebral-palsied than among "physically healthy" children, but the actual disturbances found are not specific for cerebral palsy'.

Less is known about the emotional problems of children with spina bifida and hydrocephalus, although information is being systematically collected in a current study in south Wales where Laurence and Tew (1967) have been reviewing these children. Earlier studies do suggest quite a high rate of disturbance in children with infantile hydrocephalus (generally not, in these studies, associated with spina bifida). Laurence and Coates (1962) found that about a third of those they were able to rate were emotionally unstable, 'the principal deviation from normality being excessive shyness, anxiety or nervousness which led to withdrawal, inaction and difficulty in tackling problems'. In a Swedish study Hadenius and his colleagues (1962) also found that behaviour disorders were common in this group, only about half of the children they tested being 'well-adjusted in school and society'. However, such comments must be taken with caution since they are not based on clearly defined criteria as to what constitutes emotional stability. Also they refer to children with spontaneously arrested hydrocephalus whose problems may differ from those of spina bifida children whose hydrocephalus generally has a different causation and has usually been controlled very early on by the insertion of a valve.

Probably the most systematic and detailed recent study in which behaviour problems in children with brain disorders were examined was the Isle of Wight study, where this group showed a rate of psychiatric disorder (34·3 per cent) five times as high as the non-handicapped group (6·6 per cent) and more than twice as high as handicapped children with no brain dysfunction (11·6 per cent) (Rutter, Graham and Yule 1970a). Such a relationship was not explained by severity of handicap since, 'although there was a slight tendency for the most handicapped children to show psychiatric disorder more often, the association fell well short of statistical significance', nor by intelligence, as the relationship was found when only children with IQs over 86 were included, nor by age or sex. The authors were led to conclude that 'the most important feature in relation to the much higher rate of disorder [in this group] . . . was dysfunction specifically of the brain'.

This is not to say that the neurological abnormality is a direct cause of the behaviour disorder, and there is a great deal of disagreement between people who view the brain-damaged child's psychiatric problems as arising largely from environmental circumstances and those who lay much greater stress on factors within the child associated with the actual brain dysfunction. Birch (1964), for example, emphasizes that

the disturbed behaviour said to be characteristic of such children is [often] not a direct consequence of the brain damage. It is rather the fact that the primary disorganization, for example in perception, and also the frequently accompanying motor deficits, mean that the child develops untypical relationships with the environment in which he is developing.

Rutter, Graham and Yule (1970a) list the factors which may lead to the development of psychiatric disorders in cerebral-palsied children as including the presence of a visible disability, frustrations inherent in the physical restrictions, adverse parental reactions to the child's handicap, perceptual abnormalities, poor speech and language, visual defects, low intelligence, common prejudices, the child's and his peers' reaction to the disability, impaired emotional control and so on. Many of these are factors which have been discussed in the earlier part of this chapter and many are factors whose damaging effects can, since they are environmental, be diminished by understanding and well-informed parents and teachers.

Just as there is probably a multiplicity of factors which may account for the comparatively high rate of disturbed behaviour in this group, so too is the nature of the disorders very varied. One way of looking at the behavioural effects associated with neurological abnormality is to group them in three categories. First are the symptoms which are also shown by 'normal' children who are emotionally disturbed. Second are those which appear to be rather more common in children with neurological impairments, including lability of mood (for instance outbursts of aggression or a tendency to tearfulness), periods of 'regression' of behaviour during which the child falls back into old safe habits, perseveration (the persistent repetition and continuance of an activity once begun) and impairments in the self-image, particularly the body image.

Third are the behavioural syndromes most commonly associated with neurological damage – hyperactivity and distractability. The first of these, hyperactivity, is extremely striking, but fortunately occurs only in a minority of neurologically impaired children and, in its most extreme form, is very rarely seen in the ordinary classroom. Also known as the hyperkinetic syndrome, it is characterized by severe and disorganized overactivity. These children tend to be impulsive and meddlesome and their lack of inhibition may extend to all aspects of social functioning so that they are often aggressive and generally unpopular. The syndrome is well described by Stewart (1970) who notes that it tends to diminish in later childhood and to disappear in adolescence.

Much more commonly seen, even in children with minor neurological abnormalities, is distractability or poor concentration, a problem which is also very commonly found in non-handicapped children with behaviour disorders, as well as having a high rate of occurrence in the general (non-psychiatric) child population. Parents, teachers, clinicians and others frequently comment on the association between neurological damage and distractability, although whether the causal link is direct or indirect is not known. Schulman and his colleagues (1965) report a study in which they set out to discover significant patterns of behaviour in children with neurological abnormalities. They only found one symptom which significantly characterized this group, distractability. In its most extreme form, the child seems unable to attend to a given stimulus for a sufficient period to make an appropriate intellectual response. Instead he appears to be reacting continuously to inessential stimuli which may be visual, auditory or tactile. Overall he seems to have difficulty in focusing his attention selectively, in inhibiting responses to competing stimuli and in maintaining his attention on a particular item. His behaviour is, in one sense, rather like that of a normal infant.

(ii) RESEARCH FINDINGS

What sort of findings did the present study throw up? The main questions under investigation were firstly whether there were differences in the extent and nature of emotional and behavioural disorders between the PH and control groups, and secondly whether there were differences between the children with and without neurological abnormalities. It was also decided that an analysis of the individual items of deviant behaviour should be made to discover whether any particular items tended to characterize the behaviour of any particular group.

(a) Terminology, measures and methods

A few words are needed about the terminology. The term 'maladjustment' has been avoided because of its association with the need for treatment and with a particular type of school placement, and the term 'psychiatric disorder' has also not been used since the findings were based only on questionnaires and not on supporting clinical evidence. Instead, as in the Isle of Wight study, the terms 'behaviour disorder' or 'deviant behaviour' were used. 'Deviant' simply has a statistical connotation; a child is considered 'deviant' if he shows behaviour known to be unusual in children of his age. The term 'behaviour disorder' was used of a child with a score above the critical cut-off point on either of the behavioural scales described below.

Two measures were used to assess emotional and behavioural disturbances in the junior group, a thirty-one item questionnaire completed by the child's parents and a twenty-six item questionnaire completed by his class teacher. The questionnaires were devised by Rutter (1967) for 7–13 year olds and were used in the Isle of Wight study. They will be referred to as the IOW A (parental) and IOW B (teacher) questionnaires. They consist of a series of behavioural descriptions and the person completing the scale has to note whether the description 'certainly applies', 'applies somewhat' or 'does not apply' to the child. For the parental scale only, there are also a few items in which the frequency of the behaviour has to be noted. A score of one is given for each statement marked 'applies somewhat' and of two for 'certainly applies'. Children scoring above the cut-off points of thirteen on the parental scale and nine on the teacher scale are said to show a 'behaviour disorder'. In a few cases what could be termed 'deviant behaviour' in a non-handicapped child (for example a tic, speech disorder or bedwetting) resulted directly from a handicap, and the item was not included in the child's overall score.

The questionnaires may of course produce 'false negatives' (children who don't score above the cut-off point but really have a behaviour disorder) or 'false positives' (children whose scores suggest a disorder, but who are in fact well adjusted) but taken together (the overlap between deviant children selected on the scales is quite small) they pick out about four-fifths of the 'true positives'.

The scores on particular items are grouped together to obtain a neurotic subscore (items such as 'often worried', 'unhappy', etc.) and an antisocial subscore (items such as 'tells lies', 'is often disobedient', etc.), the classification used being one developed by Rutter which divides childhood psychiatric disorders into the predominantly antisocial, the neurotic and the mixed antisocial/neurotic. The term antisocial (or conduct) disorder refers to abnormal behaviour which gives rise to social disapproval; neurotic disorder to an abnormality of the emotions (such as disproportionate anxiety). When the total score indicates some disorder, scores on the neurotic and antisocial items can be compared.

The *A* scales were left with the mother at the end of the interview, with a request that they should be returned as soon as possible. This gave both parents the opportunity to discuss the item at leisure. The interview itself took place after the visit to the school either later the same day or within the next week. The *B* scales were handed to the teachers during the school visit and again it was requested that they be returned as soon as possible.

(b) Extent of behaviour disorders in the 7–10 year olds

One of the ways in which the handicapped and non-handicapped children were compared was by looking at the average deviance scores made by the different groups, a *t* test being used to test the significance of the differences. On the parental scale the main feature was the lack of significant differences between the different groups. The highest mean deviance score (6·75) was obtained by the neurologically abnormal group, followed by the controls (6·49) and then by the PH children without neurological abnormalities (5·69). A similar pattern of results was found on the teachers' scale, the mean deviance scores being 6·70, 4·52 and 4·17 respectively. None of these differences between the groups were statistically significant.

Of greater importance than the mean deviance scores was the extent of behaviour disorders in the different groups. In Table 5.1 below the groups are compared on both scales, and the control group scores are also compared with the 'general' (non-handicapped) Isle of Wight population, a slightly older group (10–11 year olds).

On the parental scale the findings for the handicapped and control group are almost identical, as regards both the extent and type of disorders. Although the proportion of controls showing such disorders (11·5 per cent) is higher than in the Isle of Wight study (6·8 per cent) this difference just falls short of statistical significance. The findings on the teacher scale show a higher rate of disorder in both groups. This is particularly marked for the controls, nearly one in five of whom show a behaviour disorder. The rate for the handicapped group is slightly lower (but not significantly different) and as in the case of the controls antisocial disorders are much more common than neurotic disorders. The difference between the rate of disorder in the control group (19·6 per cent) and in the Isle of Wight general population (7·1 per cent) is very striking (and significant at the 0·1 per cent level), the main difference lying in the much higher rate of antisocial disorders. Rutter *et al.* (1970b) did

TABLE 5.1. *Extent of behaviour disorders in the control and handicapped groups and in the Isle of Wight 'general' population*

Parental questionnaire	Physically handicapped group		Controls		IOW general population
	No.	%	No.	%	%
Total with a score of 13* or more	8	11·9	15	11·5	6·8
Neurotic	3	4 5	6	4·6	3·0
Antisocial	5	7·5	9	6·9	2·7
Undesignated	0	0·0	0	0·0	1·1
TOTAL CHILDREN FOR WHOM QUESTIONNAIRE OBTAINED	67		130		1940
Teachers' questionnaire Total with a score of 9* or more	10	14·5	27	19·6	7·1
Neurotic	3	4·3	9	6·5	2·5
Antisocial	7	10·1	18	13·0	3·9
Undesignated	0	0·0	0	0·0	0·7
TOTAL CHILDREN FOR WHOM QUESTIONNAIRE OBTAINED	69		138		2186
OVERLAP: CHILDREN DISTURBED ON BOTH QUESTIONNAIRES	2		5		not available

* Cut-off points for deviant children

predict that the figures they obtained for the Isle of Wight were likely to be an underestimation of the extent of such disorders, since on the island the major social problems of England's large cities do not appear.

In the Isle of Wight and other studies behaviour disorders have been found to be more common in boys than in girls, although Rutter *et al.* (1970b) point out that 'sex ratio means little unless diagnosis is taken into account', antisocial disorders being much more common in boys and neurotic disorders slightly more common in girls. In the present study a similar trend was found on the parent scale, both control and handicapped boys showing a higher rate of disorder than the girls, but on the teacher scale this was only true of the handicapped group, both the boys and the girls in the control group showing a high rate of disorder (appendix G.1).

What about differences between children with and without neurological abnormalities? These are shown in Table 5.2, and are compared with the findings for the two roughly similar groups on the Isle of Wight, the 'physical disorder group' (which included children with heart and chest disorders as well as the motor-handi-

TABLE 5.2. *Extent of behaviour disorders in children with and without neurological abnormalities*

Parental questionnaire	Physically handicapped without neurological abnormalities		Physically handicapped with neurological abnormalities		IOW 'physical disorder group'	IOW 'brain dysfunction group'
	No.	%	No.	%	%	%
Total with a score of 13 or more	4	9·3	4	16·7	13·3	23·5
Neurotic	1	2·3	2	8·3	5·7	11·8
Antisocial	3	7·0	2	8·3	5·1	8·8
Undesignated	0	0·0	0	0·0	2·5	2·9
TOTAL CHILDREN FOR WHOM QUESTIONNAIRE OBTAINED	43		23		158	34
Teachers' questionnaire						
Total with a score of 9 or more	4	8·9	6	25·0	15·5	30·6
Neurotic	0	0·0	3	12·5	7·5	16·7
Antisocial	4	8·9	3	12·5	5·2	5·6
Undesignated	0	0·0	0	0·0	2·9	8·3
TOTAL CHILDREN FOR WHOM QUESTIONNAIRE OBTAINED	45		24		174	36

capped) and the 'brain dysfunction' group which largely comprised cerebral-palsied, spina bifida and epileptic children. In the Isle of Wight study both ordinary and special schoolchildren were included, so that they tended to be more heavily handicapped and to be of a much wider range of intelligence. Deviance, and frank psychiatric disorder, were notably more frequent in the subnormal children included in the Isle of Wight sample: subnormal children were, however, excluded from the present one.

The most striking finding here is that on both scales the neurologically abnormal group show a consistently higher rate of disorder than the other PH children, although the actual numbers involved are very small and on neither scale was the difference statistically significant. Nevertheless, on the teacher scale one in four of the neurologically abnormal children showed a behaviour disorder compared to only one in eleven of the other PH children.

As was expected in view of the different composition of the groups, the children in both the Isle of Wight groups showed higher rates of disorder, but the extent and direction of the differences between the brain dysfunction and physical disorder groups followed a similar pattern in both studies and on both scales.

When the type of disorder shown is considered, it is very striking that in this study only one child in the group without neurological abnormalities showed a neurotic disorder, whereas in the neurologically abnormal group, antisocial and neurotic disorders appear equally frequently on both scales. Once again the numbers involved are too small for these differences to be of statistical significance but they do suggest that most PH children without brain damage in ordinary primary schools are unlikely to develop neurotic disorders and that any emotional disturbance related to the handicap is more likely, at least at this age, to take the form of aggression than of withdrawal.

(c) Individual items of deviant behaviour in 7–10 year olds

In addition to looking rather globally at overall rates of disorder, a more detailed analysis of individual items of deviant behaviour was made. The main aim was to calculate the percentage of children who showed deviant behaviour on any particular item, and to compare the results for the different groups. A child was counted as showing deviant behaviour if either the 'applies somewhat' or 'certainly applies' column was scored. The detailed results, along with an account of their exact statistical significance and of how this was tested, are shown in appendices G.2–G.4. Boys' and girls' scores were considered separately since there were likely to be considerable sex differences on certain items. The proportion of the Isle of Wight 'normal' children scoring on any particular item was also included in these tables as this helps to give some idea of the representativeness of the control group. It has already been noted that the overall rate of disorder was higher in the control group than among the Isle of Wight children. Where individual items of behaviour were concerned, the control boys were on the parental scale significantly more destructive, fought more and told more lies, and on the teacher scale showed up as more restless, fought more, were more disobedient and bullied others more. A significantly greater proportion of the control girls fought, lied and were fussy (parent scale) and on the teacher scale fought, were disobedient, lied, bullied, were restless, were solitary and were fearful. There were also a few differences in health problems, but it was mainly on antisocial items of the type listed above that both control boys and girls showed a higher rate of disturbance than in the Isle of Wight 'general' population.

What of the differences between the handicapped and control groups? Of particular interest in the context of placing handicapped children in ordinary schools were the items relating to peer relationships (i.e. 'not much liked by other children' and 'tends to do things on his own – rather solitary'). On the parental scale there were no differences between the control and handicapped groups on these items; it is, anyway, probably very difficult for parents to be objective about this. On the teacher scale there were few differences between the PH and control girls. Although 30·0 per cent of the PH boys were 'not much liked' compared to 17·8 per cent of the controls and 35 per cent were 'rather solitary' compared to 23·0 per cent of the controls, these differences are not statistically significant.

The only important significant differences between the handicapped and control groups were as follows. On the parent scale the handicapped girls showed a lower rate of lying and stealing, while on the teacher scale they showed up as less miserable and less fussy than the controls. Most significant of all, both the handicapped boys and the girls showed significantly poorer concentration than the controls on the teacher scale.

These findings confirm what was suggested earlier, that apart from poor concentration there is no particular syndrome of deviant behaviour which characterizes PH children. Instead, the disorders they show are very similar to those of their classmates. Once again, however, it was felt necessary to look separately at the children with and without neurological abnormalities. Since the numbers were so small the only items selected for analysis were those on which at least one-quarter of the children with neurological abnormalities made a score. On the parent scale (appendix G.5), although the neurologically abnormal children tended to have more temper tantrums, to be more solitary, more disobedient and more fearful, the only statistically significant difference was that they worried more (54 per cent) than did the other PH children (30·9 per cent).

On the teacher scale more differences were found and these are shown in Table 5.3 below.

TABLE 5.3. *Comparison of children with and without neurological abormalities on selected items of deviant behaviour: teachers' scale*

Behaviour	Children with neurological abnormalities No. = 24		Children without neurological abnormalities No. = 46		Controls No. = 140	
	No.	%	No.	%	No.	%
Fidgety	9	37·5	10	21·7	36	25·7
Worries	9	37·5	15	32·6	35	25·0
Not liked	7	29·1	9	19·5	25	17·8
Solitary	13	54·1*	12	26·0	25	17·8 ‖
Poor concentration	21	87·5‡	20	43·4	50	35·7 ‖
Fearful	12	50·0*	10	21·7	34	24·2 §
Complains of aches or pains	6	25·0†	1	2·1	14	10·0

* Difference from children without neurological abnormalities significant at 5 per cent level
† Difference from children without neurological abnormalities significant at 1 per cent level
‡ Difference from children without neurological abnormalities significant at 0·1 per cent level
§ Difference from children with neurological abnormalities significant at 1 per cent level
‖ Difference from children with neurological abnormalities significant at 0·1 per cent level

Here the main items which characterize the children with neurological abnormalities are that they are more solitary, more fearful and, most marked of all, that 87·5 per cent showed poor concentration compared to 43·3 per cent of the other PH children and 35·7 per cent of the controls, a finding which fully confirms those of other studies discussed earlier in this chapter.

(d) Behavioural and emotional difficulties: the infant group

Very little work appears to have been carried out on the behavioural and emotional difficulties of physically handicapped infants. The Kellmer Pringle and Fiddes study (1970) of 4½–8½ year old thalidomide children, using the Bristol social adjustment guide, has already been mentioned. The proportion of 'maladjusted' children found in this study was 13 per cent while approximately a further 25 per cent were 'unsettled', these rates being identical to those for children in the National Child Development study (1958 Cohort). The symptoms most frequently reported were 'anxiety or uncertainty about adult interest and affection' followed closely by restlessness and unforthcomingness (defined as a lack of confidence before any new or difficult situation) together with a lack of assertiveness and curiosity. Overall the authors found that at this age the most common emotional reaction to a handicap was 'a deep concern and fear about adult love and acceptance. In about one quarter of the whole group this was a marked feature, but this same anxiety was also felt to a lesser extent by one in every two children.'

In the present study the infant version of the Isle of Wight *A* and *B* scales was used with the infant group. The infant scales are very similar to the scales used with the juniors and only a small number of items differ. At the time of writing, no validity data allowing the construction of either a cut-off point or diagnostic subscales existed, but raw frequency distributions for 440 5 year old school entrants on the Isle of Wight were made available (Yule, personal communication, 1972) and were used for comparison purposes.

As the group was so small, only items on which five or more children made a score are considered, details being given in appendix G.6. On the parent scale, the only significant differences found between the PH infants (mean age 6 years 8 months) and the Isle of Wight 5 year olds was that the latter were more disobedient at home. The other major difference, which just fell short of statistical significance, was that the PH children tended to be more solitary.

On the teacher scale there were two highly significant differences (p. < 0·001) between the PH and Isle of Wight children. One, which is hardly surprising, is that the former complained more of aches and pains. The other was that 76·0 per cent of the handicapped children showed poor concentration compared to only 23·4 per cent of the Isle of Wight group. As two in three of the PH infants had neurological abnormalities, this finding offers further evidence that attentional difficulties are closely associated with neurological abnormality.

No attempt was made to assess the overall incidence of disturbed behaviour in such a small group. There were, however, two boys who appeared on the basis of these scales and of information provided in the parent and teacher interviews to have serious behavioural and emotional problems, and three others (one girl and two boys) who also showed difficulties. To end this chapter a little will be said about each of them.

Most disturbed was Richard, a 6½ year old of above average intelligence with multiple congenital internal defects which had resulted in very poor bowel control. In appearance he was a completely 'normal' child. Provision of a full-time welfare assistant meant that Richard could remain in an ordinary school, but even before he started school he had shown signs of disturbance and had been receiving psychiatric help from the age of four and a half. His security had been undermined by constant surgical manipulations and he had become a very tense child who reacted to difficulties by frequent temper tantrums at home and by aggressive uncooperative behaviour at school. He was also very restless and distractable.

Roger, who was nearly 7 years old and of average intelligence, was also clearly disturbed but in most ways provides a complete contrast to Richard. Severely handicapped by spina bifida and hydrocephalus, his handicap is very apparent since he is confined to a wheelchair for most of the time. He is doubly incontinent and needs complete toilet assistance, and he has a slight stutter. His mother reports that at home he becomes frustrated very easily and has frequent screaming fits when he does not get his own way. At school he has become very withdrawn and moody over the past year. He makes few attempts to help himself physically, spends much time staring listlessly into space and does no work unless someone stands over him. The school staff feel that his disturbed behaviour results from an inability to accept his handicap. This was one of the few cases where it was felt by the staff and the mother that the child would be better placed in a special school and Roger is to be transferred at the end of the school year when he moves into the juniors.

Of the other infants in the study who showed some behavioural disturbance, one was a girl with a moderate degree of spastic diplegia and athetosis and a slight speech difficulty. She was an only child whose mother tended to overprotect her and her main problems were those already noted as characteristic of cerebral-palsied children, including a marked degree of restlessness, poor concentration and lack of persistence in her work, and a tendency to play on her own. Another child with rather similar symptoms was a 6 year old boy with spina bifida and hydrocephalus. One of the least handicapped infants, his main physical difficulties were poor hand control and occasional incontinence. He clearly found it difficult to mix with the other children and tended to be afraid of new people and situations, although he could also be quite aggressive. He too showed extreme restlessness and poor concentration.

The other somewhat disturbed infant was a 7 year old boy with severe defects of the urinary system (hydronephrosis and hydroureters), another 'invisible' handicap, which resulted in his case in occasional bladder incontinence. When first placed in an ordinary school he had received unsympathetic handling from his teacher and his new teacher found him 'very anxious and oversensitive about his handicap'. He tended to be a worrier, to be afraid of new situations, to be rather solitary and occasionally would refuse to go back to school after an accident. His difficulties seem to be decreasing, however, and there is little doubt about his being able to cope at junior level.

These cases show that apart from restlessness and poor concentration the type of disturbed behaviour shown by PH infants varies widely from marked aggression to almost total withdrawal. They also show an absence of any clear association between on the one hand the severity of handicap, its visibility or invisibility and the actual functions impaired, and on the other hand the presence or absence of a behaviour disorder.

REFERENCES

ALLEN, F. H. and PEARSON, G. H. J. (1928) 'The emotional problem of P.H. children', *British Journal of Medical Psychology*, 8, pp. 212–35.

BIRCH, H. G. (1964) *Brain Damage in Children*, Williams and Wilkins, New York.

DAVIE, R., BUTLER, N. and GOLDSTEIN, H. (1972) *From Birth to Seven: The Second Report of the National Child Development Study (1958 Cohort)*, Longmans, London.

GINGRAS, G., MONGEAU, M., MOREAULT, P., DUPOIS, M., HERBERT, B. and CORRIVEAU, C. (1964) 'Congenital abnormalities of the limbs: II, psychological and educational aspects', *Canadian Medical Association Journal*, 91, pp. 115–19.

HADENIUS, A., HAGBERG, B., HYTTNAS-BENSCH, K. and SJOGREN, I. (1962) 'The natural prognosis of infantile hydrocephalus', *Acta Pediatrica*, 51, pp. 117–18.

LAURENCE, K. M. and COATES, S. (1962) 'The natural history of hydrocephalus', *Archives of Disease, in Childhood*, 37, pp. 345–62.

LAURENCE, K. M. and TEW, B. J. (1967) 'Follow-up of 65 survivors from the 425 cases of spina bifida born in South Wales between 1956 and 1962', *Developmental Medicine and Child Neurology*, Supplement 13, pp. 1–3.

MEYERSON, L. (1956) 'Somatopsychology of physical disability', in Cruickshank, W. M. (ed.) *Psychology of Exceptional Children and Youth*, Staples Press, London.

NIELSEN, H. H. (1966) *A Psychological Study of Cerebral-Palsied Children*, Munksgaard, Copenhagen.

PILLING, D. (1972) *The Orthopaediacally Handicapped Child. Social, Emotional and Educational Adjustment: An Annotated Bibliography*, NFER, Windsor, Berks.

PILLING, D. (1973a) *The Child With Cerebral Palsy, Social, Emotional and Educational Adjustment: An Annotated Bibliography*, NFER, Windsor, Berks.

PILLING, D. (1973b) *The Child With Spina Bifida, Social, Emotional and Educational Adjustment: An Annotated Bibliography*, NFER, Windsor, Berks.

PILLING, D. (1974) *The Child With Chronic Medical Problems: An Annotated Bibliography*, NFER, Windsor, Berks.

PRINGLE, M. L. KELLMER (1964) *The Emotional and Social Adjustment of P.H. Children*, Occasional Publications No. 10, NFER, Slough, Bucks.

PRINGLE, M. L. KELLMER and FIDDES, D. O. (1970) *The Challenge of Thalidomide*, Longmans, London.

RICHARDSON, S. A. (1964) 'The effect of physical disability on a child's description of himself', *Child Development*, 35 (3), pp. 893–907.

RUTTER, M. (1967) 'A children's behaviour questionnaire for completion by teachers: preliminary findings', *Journal of Child Psychology and Psychiatry*, 8, pp. 1–11.

RUTTER, M., GRAHAM, P. and YULE, W. (1970a) *A Neuropsychiatric Study in Childhood*, Clinics in Development Medicine, 35/6, Spastics Society/Heinemann.

RUTTER, M., TIZARD, J. and WHITMORE, K. (ed.) (1970b) *Education, Health and Behaviour*, Longmans, London.

SCHULMAN, J. L., KASPAR, J. C. and THORNE, F. M. (1965) *Brain Damage and Behaviour : a clinical-experimental study*, C. C. Thomas, Springfield, Illinois.

STEWART, M. A. (1970) 'Hyperactive children', *Scientific American*, 222, pp. 94–9.

WRIGHT, B. (1960) *Physical Disability – A Psychological Approach*, Harper and Row, New York.

YULE, W. (1972) Personal communication.

Chapter 6 · Social Competence and Overall Social Adjustment

This chapter falls into two quite separate sections. In the first, one last aspect of social adjustment is considered, the social competence of the children. In the second section an attempt is made to assess the overall social/emotional adjustment of the children, taking into account all the different aspects of social adjustment (such as relationships with other children, emotional and behavioural difficulties and social competence) which have been considered in this and the preceding chapters.

1 Social competence

(i) MEASURING SOCIAL COMPETENCE: JUNIORS

The material presented in this section is based on the results of the Manchester scales of social adaptation (Lunzer, 1966) on which all the juniors were tested individually, and of the Vineland scale of social maturity (Doll, 1947) which was used with the infants.

The Manchester scales of social adaptation aim at a direct assessment of social competence. This has been defined by Doll (1953) as 'the functional ability of the human organism for exercising personal independence and social responsibility'. Lunzer (1966) points out that he has used the term scales of adaptation rather than of social maturity to emphasize the fact that underlying a child's social competence level are not only innate cognitive and personality factors but also the effects on him of different environmental experiences. The term 'adaptation' is thus used in a Piagetian sense to describe the ways in which organisms modify their mode of response to the environment according to experience, and Lunzer regards his scales as 'useful measures of the comparative adaptation of individuals to the social requirements of their own societies' (Lunzer,

1966). He points out that scores will reflect the effects of a stimulating or impoverished environment; for physically handicapped children, the extent to which the social environment is impoverished is likely to be related to a considerable extent to the severity of the physical handicap and to the resulting restrictions on activities of different kinds.

Lunzer's main intention in producing these scales was 'to provide an instrument for measuring subnormal degrees of social adaptation', and they offered a useful tool for comparing the level of social competence of PH children and their non-handicapped classmates. They are basically adapted from the Vineland scale of social maturity (Doll, 1947) which is better known and widely used in this country as well as in the USA where it was developed and standardized. Lunzer's scales cover a smaller age range (six to fifteen) than do the Vineland scales (which tend to concentrate on children at the lower end of the scale) and include more items for this age range. Lunzer also points out that the kinds of social opportunities experienced by children in Britain above the age of about six are sufficiently different from their American counterparts to justify the construction of new scales. The Manchester scales are not yet fully standardized but since they were to be used for an 'internal' comparison of the control and handicapped groups this was not a serious defect and for this age group they are the best scales available.

The Manchester scales have two separate parts, a scale of 'social perspective' and one of 'self-direction'. The first bears more on cognitive aspects of social competence, that is on social 'know-that'. It has five subscales: general social perspective (A), knowledge of sport (B), knowledge of current affairs (C), cultural and aesthetic knowledge (D) and scientific knowledge (E). In this study only scale A was used. There were two reasons for this. One was that, as Lunzer points out, scale A discriminates most satisfactorily in the earlier range, while scales B to E are more suited to adolescence. The other reason was that while the social perspective scale as a whole closely reflects intellectual differences, the correlation between scale A and measured intelligence is lower than are the correlations between intelligence and scales $B-E$ (Akhurst, 1970). Scale A itself contains thirteen items which test, for example, the child's ability to give his name and address, birthday and year of birth, to tell the time, draw a simple map of the area he lives in, write letters and show a simple knowledge of the news.

The other main scale, the self-direction scale, is concerned with the more practical aspects of social competence, that is, social 'know-how'. It has five subscales all of which were used. Scale *F* investigates socialization of play and leisure, scale *G* freedom of movement (for instance, going to a park alone, or on a bus), scale *H* different aspects of self-help (mainly related to dressing, washing and eating), scale *I* handling of money, including shopping, and scale *J* responsibility in the home. Finally an overall self-direction score can be calculated.

(ii) FINDINGS ON SOCIAL COMPETENCE: JUNIORS

In this study comparisons were made below between the handicapped children and the controls, and also within the handicapped group. The children's mean scores on each of the subscales were compared and an analysis of performance on a number of specific items was also made. In Table 6.1 the mean scores of the PH group as a whole and the controls are compared. Details are shown in appendix H.1.

TABLE 6.1. *Comparison of mean scores of controls and PH children on Manchester scales* A *and* F–J

		Scales					
	A	F	G	H	I	*J*	
Groups	Social perspective	Sociali- zation of play	Freedom of move- ment	Self- help	Hand- ling of money	Respon- sibility in home	Total self- direc- tion
Controls (No. =148)	8·96	11·87	3·57	15·95	5·06	2·54	38·85
PH group (No. =74)	7·71	9·51	1·98	11·69	3·81	1·75	28·0

In all cases the controls were superior and the differences between the groups were statistically significant (for scale *A* at the 1 per cent level, for *F–J* at the 0·1 per cent level). The differences were least for *A*, which depends more on intellectual than on physical ability, and greatest on the self-help scale.

Next comparisons were within the handicapped group. Severity

of handicap is likely to be an important factor in social competence
and so the mildly, moderately and severely handicapped groups
(whose mean ages of 8·6, 8·9 and 8·11 years did not differ significantly) were compared. The mean scores for these groups are given
in appendix H.3 and the results are presented in the form of a graph
below (Figure 6.1).

FIGURE 6.1. *Social competence and severity of handicap*

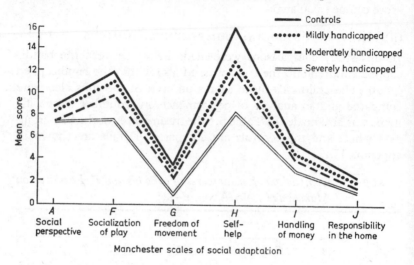

This clearly shows that with the exception of the general social
perspective scale where the mean scores of the three groups did not
differ much the mildly handicapped children do best on all the scales
and the severely handicapped least well. In fact, the differences
between the mildly and moderately handicapped children were not
statistically significant (see appendix H.3), the significant differences
lying between the severely handicapped children and the other two
groups. The former had significantly lower scores on all the self-
direction subscales except for J (responsibility in the home). Since
the children in these three groups did not differ significantly in age or
intelligence, severity of handicap does seem to be, as was expected,
a major factor affecting most aspects of social competence.

In other areas of social adjustment the presence of a neurological
abnormality has been shown to be important and a comparison
between children with and without such abnormalities was again

made. The children in the neurologically abnormal group did not differ significantly from the others either in age or in severity of handicap, though they were of lower intelligence. Details are given in appendix H.2 and the main differences are shown in the graph below (Figure 6.2).

FIGURE 6.2. *Social competence and neurological abnormality*

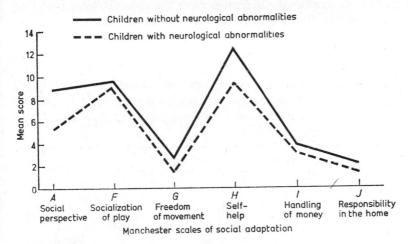

While the mean scores of the neurologically abnormal group were lower on all the scales, the only differences of statistical significance were on scale *A* (an expected difference since this scale is related to intellectual ability) and on scales *H* (self-help) and *J* (responsibility in the home). It is rather interesting that these children show a lower level of social competence on activities carried out inside the home (eating, washing, dressing, helping generally) than on those done outside (measured by scales *F* and *G*) and a possible reason is that this group, in particular the cerebral-palsied children, tend to be protected at home. Their lower scores cannot be explained by differences in intelligence since most had scores between 80 and 89, a level more than adequate for looking after themselves and helping in small daily routines.

Not only were the mean scores made by the groups on each scale compared but an item analysis was also carried out. Altogether there are forty-eight items on scales *A* and *F–J* and half of these (those considered most important for this age group) were selected for individual analysis. The percentage of each group 'passing' a particular item was calculated and comparisons then made between the groups. Since age differences are important, the children without neurological abnormalities were compared with their particular controls (rather than with the control group as a whole) and a similar procedure was followed for those with such abnormalities.

When the scores of children with purely physical handicaps were looked at, significant differences from the controls were found on eleven of the twenty-four selected items. In one case the PH children were superior and in ten cases the controls. Details are shown in Table 6.2.

TABLE 6.2. *Analysis of selected items on Manchester scales: significant differences between proportion of PH children without neurological abnormalities and their controls who made a full score*

| | Groups | | |
| | Controls No. = 96 % | Children without neurological abnormalities No. = 48 % | Significance level |
Scale and item			
Scale A			
Telling the time	56·3	81·3	1%
Scale F			
Ball games	96·9	75·0	0·1%
Club membership	38·5	16·7	1%
Expedition I (park)	68·8	45·9	1%
Expedition II (walk, cinema, etc.)	30·2	14·6	5%
Scale G			
School unaccompanied (score 1 or 2)	93·8	75·0	1%
Bus alone (score 2 or 3)	34·3	16·7	5%
Scale H			
Cutting with knife	49·0	27·0	1%
Tying laces or bow	83·3	70·8	5%
Pouring tea	80·2	62·5	5%
Washing	95·8	75·0	1%

On the following items however, no significant differences were found: scale *A*, giving address, spatial orientation, knowing birthday, addressing an envelope, writing letters, relating news seen on TV or heard on the radio; scale *F*, participation in 'adolescent' games (football, table tennis, etc.); scale *H*, having a bath, dressing; scale *I*, shopping (involving both one and several shops) and saving; scale *J*, responsibility in the home (minor routines such as washing up). The general impression given by the results was that there were no real differences in social perspective (social knowledge) and that where self-direction was concerned the children were as independent as their handicap allowed, particularly within the home.

The same type of comparison was made between the children with neurological abnormalities and their controls. In this case the controls were significantly better (often at the 0·1 per cent level) on eighteen of the twenty-four items as shown in Table 6.3 below.

The only items on which there were no significant differences were scale *A*, addressing an envelope, writing letters, relating the news; scale *F*, club membership; scale *G*, taking a bus; and scale *H*, saving pocket money.

Not only were the children in the group with neurological abnormalities poorer than the controls on many individual items; they were also poorer than the children without neurological abnormalities, as can be seen if the proportions of children 'passing' each item on Tables 6.2 and 6.3 are compared. Some of the differences were very striking and again suggest the neurologically abnormal children may be overprotected. For example, only 3·9 per cent went to school unaccompanied compared to 75 per cent of the other handicapped children and 90 per cent of the controls. Only 69 per cent had been into a shop alone (compared with 91·7 per cent and over 96 per cent respectively of the other groups) and only 15 per cent helped in simple household chores (compared to 56 per cent and over 63 per cent of the others).

(iii) SOCIAL MATURITY IN THE INFANT GROUP

To end this section, the infant group will be considered very briefly. In their case social maturity was assessed by the well-known Vineland social maturity scale (Doll, 1947). The aspects of social development which are covered on this scale include self-help

TABLE 6.3. *Analysis of selected items on Manchester scales: significant differences between the proportion of neurologically abnormal and control group children who made a full score*

Scale and item	Groups		
	Controls No. = 52 %	PH with neurological abnormalities No. = 26 %	Significance level
Scale A			
Address	88·5	69·2	5%
Telling the time	46·2	11·5	0·1%
Spatial orientation (score of 2)	30·8	3·9	0·1%
Birthday	77·0	57·7	5%
Scale F			
Ball games	94·2	61·5	0·1%
Adolescent games	13·5	0·0	5%
Expedition I (park)	73·0	42·3	1%
Expedition II (walk, cinema etc.)	40·4	3·9	0·1%
Scale G			
School unaccompanied (score 1 or 2)	96·0	3·9	0·1%
Scale H			
Cutting with knife	46·1	11·5	1%
Tying laces or bow	90·4	34·6	0·1%
Pouring tea	86·5	38·4	0·1%
Washing	96·1	65·4	0·1%
Bathing (score 3 or 4)	38·0	0·0	0·1%
Dressing	19·2	3·9	5%
Scale I			
Shopping – simple	96·1	69·2	1%
Shopping – complex	30·8	3·4	1%
Helping at home (minor routines)	63·5	15·4	0·1%

generally, eating, dressing, self-direction, occupation (mainly play activities at this age), communication, locomotion and socialization. The individual child can be assessed on this scale in relation to other children in terms of a social maturity quotient (comparable to an intelligence quotient). This not only provides practical knowledge about the child's level of social competence but can also be compared with the intelligence quotient. In cases of intellectual subnormality the social quotient (SQ) is likely to be considerably higher than the IQ; in cases of physical handicap the disparity is likely to be in the opposite direction, the extent of the disparity reflecting the severity of the handicap.

This was in fact found. The distribution of SQs is shown below in Table 6.4 and is compared to the distribution of IQ scores.

TABLE 6.4. *Comparison of distribution of Vineland social maturity quotients with intelligence quotients: infant group*

Measure	Standardized scores				
	100+	90–9	80–9	70–9	below 70
Vineland social maturity quotient	6	5	6	7	1
Ravens coloured matrices standardized scores	16	4	4	1	0
English picture vocabulary test standardized scores	19	3	2	1	0

The differences between the level of intellectual ability and level of 'social maturity' are very striking. In the cases of all the children but one the social quotient was lower than the child's standardized score on both the matrices and the EPVT. At this age the majority of the items on the Vineland scales are closely tied to normal physical development. For example, many children failed on such items as cuts with scissors, walks downstairs, cares for self at toilet, goes about neighbourhood unattended and plays competitive exercise games, items which are normally passed by younger children. The results confirm the fact that the majority of the children in the group were severely physically handicapped and emphasize once more the close interdependence of social and physical development.

2 Overall social adjustment

(i) CALCULATING THE OVERALL SOCIAL ADJUSTMENT SCORE

In this and the two preceding chapters different aspects of the child's social and emotional adjustment were discussed as shown by tests, questionnaires and interviews. Such measures indicated that a particular child was, for instance, exceedingly popular, or that he showed an antisocial type of behaviour disorder, or that he made a rather low score on the self-direction scale. Measures such as these provide important information about certain rather specific aspects of social functioning. It would be useful if they could also in some way be combined to produce an overall picture of the child's social adjustment. This might be more satisfactory than simply to equate social adjustment with emotional stability or sociometric status or some other single measure.

An attempt was therefore made to combine the children's scores on a number of these measures in such a way as to produce an overall social adjustment score. After such a score had been calculated each child could then be placed in a 'well-adjusted' or 'less well-adjusted' group, and a study made of the factors which appeared to be correlated with good or less good adjustment and of their relative importance. This investigation was confined to the junior group.

The way in which the overall social adjustment score was calculated is described in some detail below, since it was devised solely for the purposes of this study. To those who are suspicious of 'overall' measures the following justification is offered for this procedure. Clearly it is important to discover how PH children are adjusting socially to ordinary school life. How are we to measure this? The sorts of measures available have already been described, but is any one of them adequate to measure social adjustment? Some might make this claim for the sociometric test, but does a low popularity ranking necessarily mean that a child is poorly adjusted? Social adjustment is surely related to social competence, but does a social competence score such as that obtained from the Manchester scales accurately reflect a severely handicapped child's overall social adjustment? Clearly this is not the case, although such a score should be taken into account. For some people scores on behavioural scales such as the Isle of Wight A and B scales offer the closest approximation to social adjustment scores. However, a child may score above the cut-off point and yet be making a satisfactory social adjustment, especially in schools where antisocial behaviour is to some extent the norm. There is, then, quite a strong case for combining the results of several measures of adjustment, so tapping a number of different aspects of social functioning. Combining several measures also has the advantage that several sources of information about the child (his peers' judgements, his class • teacher, his parents, the tester and the child himself) are all utilized.

A combination of ten measures was therefore used to give the overall social adjustment score. On each measure a child was given a score of 1 (superior), 2 (average) or 3 (low). The scores were allocated in such a way that only children doing exceptionally well or exceptionally badly would score a 1 or 3, a score of 2 reflecting a position in a broad middle range. The scores on each measure were added and a simple average computed to give the overall social adjustment score, which could range from 1·0 (high) to 3·0 (low). If data were missing, an average score was computed on the items available.

Of the ten measures, two were based on the sociometric test results, three on the Isle of Wight behaviour scales, three on the Manchester scales and two on information from the parental interviews. In this way all these measures contributed a roughly comparable proportion to the child's final score. This also meant that several sources of information about the child were used. Another advantage of using several measures was that the extent to which the child's score was directly affected by the physical handicap varied from one measure to another, considerably on the Manchester scales, for example, and very little in the case of the behavioural scales.

The ten measures used, and the way in which they were scored were as follows:

1 *Sociometric status* – the child's percentile rank on the sociometric test was noted and a score of 1 given for rank 91–100, 2 for 11–90, and 3 for 0–10.

2 *Sociometric test* – nature of choice. A child scored 1 if his choice of best friend was reciprocated, provided that he was also chosen by five or more different children, 3 if he was an isolate and 2 in all other cases.

3 *IOW scale A* (parental) – a child scored 1 for a total deviance score of 0–4, 2 if it was 5–12 and 3 if it was 13 or more.

4   *IOW scale B* (teachers) – a child scored 1 where the total deviance score was 0–3, 2 where it was 4–8 and 3 if it was 9 or more.

5   *IOW scale A, items 5 and 7* and *IOW scale B, items 6 and 8* – these items, 'not much liked by other children' and 'tends to do things alone, rather solitary' were selected as being particularly important measures of social adjustment. The suggestion of Rutter *et al.* (1970a) that difficulty in getting along with other children is the symptom most commonly associated with general maladjustment has already been noted. A child scored 1 if his total score on these four items was 0, 2 if it was 1–2, and 3 if it was 3 or more.

6   *Manchester scales: scale A* – general social perspective. Lunzer (1966) has provided standardization tables for converting the raw scores to percentiles, depending on the child's age. A child scored 1 if he scored in the 90–100 percentile, 2 for the 10–90 percentile and 3 if the score lay in the 0–10th percentile.

7   *Manchester scales: scale F* – socialization of play. This was included separately as it was considered an important practical measure of social adjustment. Scoring was as for item 6.

8   *Manchester scales – total self-direction.* This was scored as for items 6 and 7 above.

9   *Parental interview* – items relating to the child's friendships. During this interview a number of questions were asked about the child's friendships. Nine of these questions were selected and points awarded on the basis of the answers, the maximum score possible being 15. A child who scored 13–15 points was given a score of 1, 4–12 points meant a score of 2 and 0–3 points of 3.

Details of the questions and the points awarded are shown in appendix I·1.

10 *Parental interview* – behaviour difficulties. During the interview with the mother (usually from one to one and a half hours) a number of questions were asked about nervous troubles and behavioural problems. The design of this section of the questionnaire was closely based on that used in the Isle of Wight study where the authors (Rutter *et al.*, 1970) mention finding the interview the most useful and reliable tool in the assessment of

psychiatric disorder. Mothers were first asked if their children had any emotional or behavioural difficulties and later were asked a number of specific questions. The total number of difficulties mentioned (either spontaneously or after a specific probe) was recorded. (In fact, few differences were found between the PH and control groups: 42 per cent and 49 per cent respectively mentioned 0–1 difficulties, 46 per cent and 42 per cent 2–4 difficulties and 12 per cent and 9 per cent 5 or more.) For the overall social adjustment assessment, a score of 1 was given if 0–1 difficulties were mentioned, 2 for 2–4 and 3 for 5 or more.

(ii) OVERALL SOCIAL ADJUSTMENT: MAIN FINDINGS AND RELATED FACTORS

The mean overall social adjustment scores for the different groups are shown in Table 6.5 below.

TABLE 6.5. *Mean overall social adjustment scores (low score = good adjustment)*

Group	No.	Mean overall social adjust- ment score	SD
Controls	148	1·86	0·30
All handicapped	74	2·04	0·24
Handicapped without neurological abnormalities	48	1·97	0·24
Handicapped with neurological abnormalities	26	2·18	0·20

As expected, the controls did best and the children with neurological abnormalities least well. The significance of the differences between the groups were tested by t tests and differences which were significant at the 0·1 per cent level were found between the controls and each of the other groups. The difference between the children with and without neurological abnormalities was also significant at the 0·1 per cent level.

Mean social adjustment scores, however, can be misleading and the next step was to rate each child as 'well adjusted' or as 'less well adjusted'. To obtain this dichotomy the mean overall social adjustment score of all the controls (i.e. 1·86) plus one standard deviation

(0·30) was taken as the cut-off point, that is children with scores of 2·1 or higher were regarded as 'less well adjusted' and those with scores of from 1·0 to 2·0 as 'well adjusted'. As there is nothing magical about a cut-off point the term 'less well adjusted' was used in preference to alternatives such as 'poorly adjusted'.

The next step was to compare the proportions of children in the different groups falling into these two categories, and this is done in Table 6.6 below.

TABLE 6.6. *Comparison of social adjustment in control and handicapped groups*

Groups	Well adjusted		Less well adjusted	
	No.	%	No.	%
Controls (No. = 148)	107	72·2	41	27·7
Handicapped without neurological abnormalities (No. = 48)	32	66·6	16	33·3
Handicapped with neurological abnormalities (No. = 26)	8	30·7	18	69·2

Just under three in four of the controls fell into the well-adjusted group, compared to two out of three children without neurological abnormalities, not a significant difference. The proportions are reversed for the neurologically abnormal children, only one in three of whom are 'well-adjusted', the difference between these and the other PH children being significant at the 0·1 per cent level ($x^2 = 7·36$, df 1).

One of the reasons for assigning children to these two categories was so that a study could be made of the main factors which appeared to be related to social adjustment. The presence of a neurological abnormality has already been considered. Other factors examined included intelligence, severity of handicap, type of handicap, age, sex, family factors (including social class, size of family and separation experiences) and factors related to the school (such as size of school, size of class and the location of the school). Each of these will be considered briefly.

A number of writers have suggested a correlation between intelligence and social adjustment, and this was examined although IQ scores were not available for all the children. The findings for the PH group as a whole are shown below in Table 6.7.

TABLE 6.7. *Overall social adjustment and intelligence, PH group*

Groups	IQ Level (NFER non-verbal test 5)	
	90+	below 90
Well adjusted	30	8
Less well adjusted	8	21
TOTAL CHILDREN	38	29

The significance of the association was tested by an x^2 test, and a value of x^2 (with Yates correction) = 15·64 was obtained, which was significant at the 0·1 per cent level. Since in the PH group intelligence and neurological abnormality were correlated, the same analysis was carried out for the control group. A highly similar pattern of results was obtained (x^2 with Yates correction = 17·14, df 1, p < 0·001) and an equally significant association between overall social adjustment and intelligence found. These results confirm what other writers have suggested, that children of lower intelligence (here below 90 on a non-verbal group test) tend to be less well adjusted socially.

The next factors examined were those related to the handicap. First, severity of handicap was looked at. Its effects have been examined in a number of studies. Wright (1960), for example, discusses the problem in some detail and points out that the findings have been rather inconclusive. Some studies show a relationship between degree of disability and poor adjustment, others no relationship, and in yet others it is reversed. Such differences may depend partly on the criterion of good adjustment used. The relationship is anyway probably not a simple one. A mild handicap may, suggests Wright, make adjustment easier by imposing fewer restrictions on a child, but on the other hand a person with a minor disability may be more anxious to hide it, thereby thwarting his own adjustment. The results in this study are shown in Table 6.8 below.

TABLE 6.8. *Overall social adjustment and severity of handicap*

	Mildly handicapped (No. = 13)	Moderately handicapped (No. = 45)	Severely handicapped (No. =16)
Well adjusted	7	24	9
Less well adjusted	6	21	7

The results in this table suggest that severity of handicap has little effect on overall social adjustment, the children in the different groups being very evenly divided between the well-adjusted and the less well-adjusted categories.

What about the actual type of handicap? It was felt that this was worth looking at, even though the number of children in each group would be very small. The results are shown in Table 6.9 below.

TABLE 6.9. *Type of handicap and overall social adjustment*

Type of handicap	Well-adjusted No.	%	Less well-adjusted No.	%
No handicap	107	72·7	41	27·7
Congenital abnormalities including thalidomide	15	68·2	7	31·8
Haemophiliacs and 'miscellaneous'	15	62·5	9	37·5
Spina bifida (with or without hydrocephalus)	6	50·0	6	50·0
Cerebral palsy*	4	25·0	12	75·0

* Cerebral palsy vs congenital abnormalities, $x^2 = 5·28$ df 1, p $< 0·02$

This table is arranged so that the best-adjusted groups come first. Children with congenital abnormalities are shown to be most like the control group and children with cerebral palsy least like them, four out of five being less well adjusted, even though fourteen of the fifteen cerebral-palsied children were only mildly or moderately handicapped.

Age was considered next. It is sometimes suggested that PH

children may at first make a good social adjustment to ordinary school placement but that as they become older the strain on them increases and social adjustment suffers. This was not the case. There was, on the contrary, a slightly (although not significantly) higher proportion of well-adjusted children in year 3 than in years 1 or 2 of the junior school. A very similar pattern of results was obtained for the control group.

Differences in social adjustment related to sex have been touched on at various points in this book and it was the next factor considered (Table 6.10).

TABLE 6.10. *Social adjustment and sex: controls*

| | Well adjusted | | Less well adjusted | |
	No.	%	No.	%
Boys (No. = 84)	63	75·0	21	25·0
Girls (No. = 64)	44	68·7	20	31·3

As Table 6.10 shows there were no marked sex differences as far as the control group was concerned. A slightly, but not significantly higher proportion of boys were well adjusted, but this may reflect the fact that an unusually high proportion of control girls had behaviour difficulties. When the PH group is considered (Table 6.11) a different picture is obtained.

TABLE 6.11. *Social adjustment and sex: PH group*

| | Well adjusted | | Less well adjusted | |
	No.	%	No.	%
Boys (No. = 42)	20	47·6	22	52·3
Girls (No. = 32)	20	62·5	12	37·5

These results indicate that nearly two in three of the PH girls are well adjusted compared to fewer than one in two of the PH boys. The numbers are small and the difference not statistically significant (x^2 with Yates correction = 1·075), but it is still an interesting one. It ties up with what Richardson (1964) found in a study of 9–11 year olds in an American summer camp for the 'underprivileged' attended by handicapped and non-handicapped children of both sexes. A handicap did not have the same consequences for boys and girls. The boys in the camp experienced more difficulties in interpersonal relationships and expressed more concern about the aggression of others than did the girls. Richardson thought that this might have been because girls could turn more easily to non-physical recreations where they were less disadvantaged, whereas for the boys physical activity was highly valued.

Next the relationship of a number of family factors to social adjustment were looked at briefly. First was social class. In the group as a whole, a correlation of 0·2 was found between social class and good adjustment (appendix I.2), few differences in this pattern being found between the handicapped and control groups. As expected there was a tendency for a greater proportion of less well-adjusted children to come from social class V. Unexpectedly, however, they also tended to come from social class III (non-manual), a finding which could not be explained. The number of children in these two classes was, however, very small. The relationship between social adjustment and size of family was also examined and a slight but statistically insignificant tendency was found for less well-adjusted children to come from larger families. The child's position in the family (oldest, youngest and so on) and whether the mother went out to work or not were factors which appeared to be quite unrelated to social adjustment.

Quite a different family factor which was examined for the handicapped children only was the separation experiences of the child, information about this being collected in the interview with the mother. A great deal has been written on this subject, particularly since Bowlby's 1953 monograph on the effects of maternal deprivation was published. It is now generally accepted that the infant of 7–11 months old is particularly vulnerable to the disruption of newly formed ties (both as regards a later capacity for personal attachments and in vocalization and language development) but that normally recovery from a single comparatively short period of separation is fairly prompt and complete.

For the purposes of this study, two kinds of separation experiences were recorded (a) separation through hospitalization at the ages of 0–3, 3–5 and 5 years old and (b) separation from the mother for reasons other than hospitalization. Since very few cases of the latter were found, only separation through hospitalization was considered in the analysis. For the majority of the children the longest periods spent in hospital had been between the ages of 0–3 ,this span including what appears to be the most 'critical' period of from about 7–11 months. Details of time spent in hospital and its relationship to overall adjustment are shown in appendix I.3. The main finding was that there was no relationship between overall social adjustment and early hospitalization: if anything, there was a slight tendency for the better-adjusted children to have spent slightly longer in hospital. This may have been partly because the cerebral-palsied children as a group had spent very little time in hospital and they tended to be less well adjusted. This lack of measurable ill-effects of early hospitalization should be encouraging to those whose children have to spend either long or frequent periods in hospital at an early age.

Finally a number of factors related to the schools themselves were considered. Size of school and size of class appeared to be of little importance for overall social adjustment and a more interesting factor was the location of the school. It has quite often been suggested (for example, Barker, 1948) that children living in towns are more likely to have problems in social adjustment than are those in rural communities since the latter are fairly well known whereas the former come into contact with more strangers and have to cope with more stereotyped attitudes to the handicap. The fact that more teasing went on in London schools than elsewhere has already been commented on.

To explore this question, schools were placed in three categories – London schools, village schools and town schools – and the proportions of well-adjusted children in each were compared. The results are shown in Table 6.12 below.

TABLE 6.12. *Overall social adjustment and location of school*

| | | % of well-adjusted children | |
| | No. of | Controls | PH |
Location of school	schools	(No. = 107)	(No. = 40)
London schools	41	72·0	46·3
Urban schools	19	71·4	68·4
Village schools	14	73·7	50·0

These are very interesting findings although the differences between the groups fail to reach statistical significance. For the control group, the location of the school is clearly unrelated to overall social adjustment; the proportions of well-adjusted children in each kind of school are almost identical. For the PH children, however, the picture is different. In both London schools and village schools about half the children fall into the well-adjusted and half into the less well-adjusted groups. In the urban schools, however, over two-thirds of the PH children are in the well-adjusted group. Moreover, the urban schools had a much higher proportion of neurologically abnormal children (56 per cent) than either the London (29 per cent) or the village (25 per cent) schools, yet despite this a higher proportion of children were well adjusted. How can this finding be explained? It may be relevant that several of the nineteen urban schools lay in areas where the local authority had a very positive approach to the integration of PH children and was prepared to spend time and money (for example, through the provision of a special welfare assistant) to achieve this. It is also the case that although the classes were not smaller the urban schools, many of which were in new towns, often had better amenities than did either the London or village schools, and provided more satisfactory conditions for teachers. This may have meant that they had more time and energy available to help the PH children to 'fit in' socially and to meet their parents. Whatever the reason for this finding, and although the numbers involved are admittedly small, one implication is that the situation in London (or in cities whose schools face similar problems) is not necessarily a good guide to what is happening elsewhere as regards social integration and should not form the sole basis for major policy decisions on this issue.

To sum up this whole section, the findings suggest that the two factors most closely related to overall social adjustment were firstly the presence or absence of a neurological abnormality, particularly when this is cerebral palsy, and secondly intelligence level. Social class, size of family and the location of the school were also of some importance and PH girls tended to be better adjusted than PH boys. Being physically handicapped *per se* was not, however, an important factor.

Finally, some case history material is presented which highlights the relative importance of the factors. A list was made of the PH children with the highest and lowest social adjustment scores, on which type and severity of handicap, intelligence level and social class were all included (see appendices I.4 and I.5). The fourteen children with the highest overall social adjustment scores had a great variety of handicaps ranging from mild to severe, but only one child had a neurological abnormality and all but three (of the thirteen tested) had IQs above 90. These children tended to be girls and to come from social classes I–III.

When the seventeen children with the lowest overall social adjustment scores were considered, one striking feature was that over half had neurological abnormalities and another was that only one had an IQ above 90. Nearly two out of three were boys and more came from social classes III (non-manual), IV and V than was true of the well-adjusted group.

Children most 'at risk' as far as social success in an ordinary school is concerned (although of course there will be exceptions) seem likely to be boys, to be neurologically abnormal and in particular cerebral-palsied and to have IQs below 90. Their chances of success will be greater if they come from social classes I or II and from small families, but these chances bear little relationship to the severity of handicap; teachers should be aware that a child with only a minor handicap may be as much at risk, socially and emotionally, as one whose handicap is much more apparent.

REFERENCES

AKHURST, B. A. (1970) 'The relationship between the social perspective scales of the Manchester scales of social adaptation and the Mill Hill vocabulary scale', unpublished study.

BARKER, R. G. (1948) 'The social psychology of physical disability', *Journal of Social Issues*, 4, pp. 28–38.

BOWLBY, J. (1953) *Maternal Care and Mental Health*, World Health Organization Monograph, Geneva.

DOLL, E. A. (1947) *The Vineland Social Maturity Scale*, Educational Test Bureau, Minneapolis, Minn.

DOLL, E. A. (1953) *The Measurement of Social Competence*, Educational Test Bureau, Minneapolis, Minn.

LUNZER, E. A. (1966) *The Manchester Scales of Social Adaptation*, NFER, Slough, Bucks.

RICHARDSON, S. A. (1964) 'The effect of physical disability on a child's description of himself', *Child Development*, 35 (3), pp. 893–907.

RUTTER, M., TIZARD, J. and WHITMORE, K. (eds.) (1970) *Education, Health and Behaviour*, Longmans, London.
WRIGHT, B. (1960) *Physical Disability – A Psychological Approach*, Harper and Row, New York.

Chapter 7 · School Attainment

Very few systematic studies have been carried out of the educational consequences of chronic physical disorders in children. One recent exception was the study of thalidomide children in Scotland carried out by Kellmer Pringle and Fiddes (1970). In investigating the children's educational needs and progress they found that although the majority were severely handicapped 'more than half could well hold their own in ordinary day primary schools', and only about a third needed special schooling. The recent Isle of Wight study (Rutter, Tizard and Whitmore, 1970) has already been referred to. Here the physically handicapped children were placed in two subgroups, one being a 'physical disorders group' containing 114 9–11 year olds with a variety of disorders (almost half were asthmatics) not involving any brain abnormality and the other being a group of 48 children with 'brain disorders'. These groups and the controls were compared on a number of educational measures.

Studies such as these include children attending both ordinary and special schools, and there do not appear to be any major studies which have looked specifically at physically handicapped children in ordinary schools, as for instance Johnson (1962) did with the hearing-impaired.

A major aim of the present study was therefore to investigate the educational progress of PH pupils attending ordinary schools, in particular in relation to the progress of their non-handicapped peers. Interviews with the mothers of the PH juniors elicited the fact that 91·8 per cent were 'satisfied' with their child's progress, 1·3 per cent 'fairly satisfied' and only 6·7 per cent 'dissatisfied'. If these feelings reflect the true state of affairs the situation would be very satisfactory.

A second important function of this part of the study was to investigate differences within the PH group between children with and without neurological abnormalities. In the case of disorders which do not involve the brain, any intellectual or educational difficulties experienced by the children could result indirectly from the physical disorder or be quite independent of it, whereas if neurological abnormalities exist they are more likely to produce direct intellectual and educational consequences. Phillips and White (1964), for example, compared twenty-three cerebral-palsied children with motor handicaps appearing early in life with thirty-two physically handicapped children without congenital brain injury, the children being selected from the same school and matched as accurately as possible for age and physical handicap. Allowing for age and IQ differences, the differences in attainment in reading and arithmetic (especially the latter) between the two groups remained significant. In the Isle of Wight study the rate of specific reading retardation was nearly twice as great in the brain disorder group as in the group of children with physical disorders which did not involve the brain (Rutter *et al.*, 1970).

In this chapter it has been necessary to discuss findings for the children in junior schools and those in infant schools in two quite separate sections, as different intellectual and educational measures were used for the two groups, and since it was only with the juniors that a control group was used. In the case of the juniors the first section is concerned with intelligence and this is followed by sections on arithmetical ability, reading accuracy and comprehension, and reading backwardness. In the last section the children's overall academic attainment and progress is assessed and some of the main factors contributing to this are examined. Findings for the small group of twenty-five rather severely handicapped infants are discussed in the last part of the chapter.

The junior group

(i) INTELLIGENCE

(a) *Choice of test*

A number of factors suggested that the most appropriate test would be a group test of non-verbal ability, the one eventually selected being the National Foundation for Educational Research non-verbal test 5 (Pidgeon, 1968). This test (also known as non-verbal test BD) consists of 100 items aiming to provide a measure of children's ability to reason with diagrammatic material. It includes four timed sub-tests (cypher, similarities, analogies, series) each preceded by a practice test. While not dependent on the medium of words or language, it is nevertheless dependent on children's perceptual awareness of detail and their knowledge of simple spatial relationships. The test's reliability (K-R formula 20) is quoted in the manual as 0·966.

The test has been standardized for children aged 8·0 to 11·0. It was therefore suitable for all those participating in this study except for a number of children in junior 1 classes. It was decided that for such children the giving of this test should be postponed until they had moved into junior 2 classes. This meant in fact a return visit to the school either one or two terms later in the case of 69 of the 188 children tested.

A group test was chosen for several reasons:

1 The limited time available in the schools made it necessary for the control children and the PH child to be tested simultaneously.

2 The study was partly concerned with how the PH children were functioning within group situations, i.e. within normal-sized classes of non-handicapped children where comparatively little individual attention was available. Despite possible attentional difficulties, especially in the children with neurological abnormalities, it was necessary for them to be able to follow instructions as members of a group and it was felt appropriate to use a test which included this requirement.

3 A third reason for choosing a group test concerns the procedure used in this study. Parents and teachers were most anxious that the PH children should not be 'singled out' for attention. The usual procedure was to tell the class the study was concerned with 'the sorts of things which children can do at different ages'. The group test thus served the incidental purpose of helping the PH child to become used to my presence in the class in the company of the other children before he was tested individually.

A non-verbal test was selected partly because many of the schools in the study were in areas of London with large numbers of immigrant children (many being comparative newcomers to the country) and it was felt that such a test would cause fewer problems than a test of verbal ability. A second reason was that reading skills even in 8 and 9 year olds may still be poorly developed. It was felt that a substantial number of the PH children might have such difficulties and that a test of non-verbal ability would be more suitable.

A test of this kind does, of course, depend on perceptual skills and on the analysis of spatial relationships, and it is such skills rather than verbal abilities which are likely to be impaired in children with neurological abnormalities. Such a child's score on a non-verbal test is therefore likely to give a lower estimate of overall intelligence than a verbal test would do. It was felt, however, that provided it was borne in mind that the possible attentional, perceptual and spatial difficulties of the neurologically abnormal children might result in a non-verbal test giving an under- rather than an over-estimate of their overall ability, such a test would nevertheless provide a useful measure of their actual level of functioning in relation to their peers.

The only motor component in the test is the underlining of selected digits or figures. Two of the PH group normally used electric typewriters for some of their work but all were able to underline by hand or, as in one case, holding a pencil in the mouth, and also to turn over the pages independently. The test is timed but the act of underlining occupies such a small fraction of the total time that it could only have made a very minor difference to the scores of a handful of PH children.

(b) Findings

Table 7.1 below shows the distribution of non-verbal intelligence scores among the different groups for the 188 children who were tested. Scores were not available for 7 of the PH group and 27 controls. These were children who were not present when a later visit to the school was made. The reasons for this were varied, and included cases where the child had been moved to another school, changed classes, left the county, was in hospital or was simply absent.

The distribution of scores does not differ markedly between the control group and the PH group without neurological abnormalities. 66 per cent of the former are concentrated in the range of 85–114 and 61·2 per cent of the latter. This is in line with the Isle of Wight study findings that 'the intelligence of the total group of children with physical disorders not involving the brain was closely

TABLE 7.1. *Distribution of NFER non-verbal test 5 scores for the different groups*

Standardized score	Controls (No. = 121)		PH group without neurological abnormalities (No. = 44)		PH group with neurological abnormalities (No. = 23)	
	No.	%	No.	%	No.	%
Below 75	5	4·1	2	4·5	5	21·7
75–84	8	6·6	3	6·8	6	26·0
85–94	19	15·7	12	27·2	10	43·4
95–104	22	18·1	9	20·4	1	4·3
105–14	39	32·2	6	13·6	1	4·3
115–24	18	14·8	10	22·7	0	0·0
125+	10	8·2	2	4·5	0	0·0

similar to that of the control group'. The group with neurological abnormalities is strikingly different, with 48 per cent below 85 and only 52 per cent above, and only two children having scores over 95.

In Table 7.2 the mean scores for the three groups are shown with the significance of the differences between them, while the mean scores for the PH children in the mildly, moderately and severely handicapped groups are also compared.

TABLE 7.2. *Mean NFER non-verbal test 5 standardized scores for the different groups*

Group	Size of group	Mean standardized score	SD
Controls	121	104·7	15·5
Total PH group	67	95·9*	16·2
PH without neurological abnormalities	44	102·2†	15·3
PH with neurological abnormalities	23	83·3*	9·3
Mildly handicapped group	13	91·0	15·8
Moderately handicapped group	40	97·6	15·4
Severely handicapped group	14	95·1	19·1

* Differences from controls significant at the 0·1 per cent level
† Differences from the neurologically abnormal group significant at the 0·1 per cent level

G

The main feature of the results is that there are no significant differences between the controls and the PH group without neurological abnormalities. The mean figure for the controls is a little higher than that obtained on the same test in the Isle of Wight study (Rutter *et al.*, 1970b) for 9 year olds (103·4) and 10 year olds (102·0). The slightly lower mean score of the group without neurological abnormalities may reflect slight motor difficulties in carrying out the tests, the social class differences already noticed or early deprivation of experience. When the mildly, moderately and severely handicapped groups were compared, no significant differences were found although there was a wider range of ability among the severely handicapped children.

The difference between the neurologically handicapped children and the controls, and between this group and the other PH children is highly significant and the narrower range of ability within the neurological group is also interesting, the scores tending to cluster in the range 80–90. Most of the neurologically abnormal group were either hemiplegics or children with spina bifida and hydrocephalus and the low mean score was entirely in accordance with the findings of many largescale surveys of such children. Ascher and Schonel (1950), for example, found a mean of 77 for the IQ of hemiplegics in their study, this figure being somewhat higher for those who were mildly handicapped, while Floyer (1955) gives a mean of 80·0 for hemiplegics and Perlstein and Hood (1956) of 82·5 for hemiplegics without epilepsy.

A recent review (Anderson, 1973) of surveys of children with spina bifida and hydrocephalus suggests that the majority in this group fall into the IQ range 70–90. Thus Badell-Ribera, Shulman and Paddock (1966) found a performance mean on the Wechsler intelligence scale for children of 79 for the more severely handicapped and 89 for the less handicapped children, Laurence and Tew (1967) a mean of 86 and Lorber (1971) a mean of 79 with 33 per cent of this group falling into the range 80–99 and only 19 per cent having scores above this. As already mentioned the perceptual and spatial components of the non-verbal test may also have proved difficult for some of the hydrocephalic and cerebral-palsied children.

The difference between the neurologically abnormal group and the other groups was large enough to make it necessary to partial out the effects of intelligence when differences in attainment were looked at. There is considerable disagreement about the means by which intelligence can be taken into account when deciding how well a child's performance reflects his potential ability. As the authors of the Isle of Wight surveys point out (Rutter *et al.*, 1970) there is not a one-to-one relationship between intellectual ability as assessed by conventional intelligence tests and reading attainment, and in many instances, particularly perhaps in the sheer mechanics of reading, children do achieve more than might have been expected of them in terms of measured intelligence. Clearly, however, a bright child is likely to do better academically than a dull one and it was therefore decided to take intelligence into account on all the measures of attainment used in this study by means of a simple analysis of co-variance with intelligence as the co-variate and the child's performance as the dependent variable.

(ii) ARITHMETICAL ABILITY

Since methods of teaching arithmetic now vary so widely, and since most of the tests available when this study was designed had recently become out of date with the introduction of decimalization, it was decided to ask teachers to rate children for arithmetical ability on the five-point scale used in the National Child Development study (Kellmer Pringle *et al.*, 1966, Davie *et al.*, 1972). The scale was as follows:

Rating	Description of rating
1	Extremely good facility with numbers and other mathematical concepts. Grasps new processes very quickly. Shows insight and understanding.
2	Understanding of number work well developed. Grasps new processes without difficulty.
3	Average ability in this sphere.
4	Rather slow to understand new processes. Rather poor ability with numbers, although able to do some things by rote.
5	Little, if any, ability in this sphere. Shows virtually no understanding at all.

Teachers were given these descriptions on a printed form and asked to rate the handicapped children and the controls accordingly. The findings for the different groups are shown in Table 7.3 and in addition findings for the 7 year olds in the National Child Development study (Davie *et al.*, 1972). Although the junior group children were older (mean age 8 years 9 months) the ratings are age-related and this comparison with a large national sample gives an idea of the representativeness of the control group.

TABLE 7.3. *Teachers' ratings of arithmetical ability in the different groups and in the National Child Development study (percentages)*

Rating	National Child Development study No. = 15 049	Control group No. = 136	Total PH group No. = 67	PH without neurological abnormalities No. = 44	PH with neurological abnormalities No. = 23
1	3·1	9·5	1·4	2·2	0·0
2	17·8	23·5	11·9	15·9	4·3
3	43·5	36·0	40·2	52·2	17·3
4	31·6	25·7	32·8	22·7	52·1
5	3·9	5·1	13·4	6·8	26·0

Clearly the PH group as a whole perform less well than the controls (although the comparison between the controls and the National Child Development study group suggests that the controls may as a group have been somewhat above average in attainment). When the PH group is split, however, the performance of the children without neurological abnormalities becomes more like that of the controls, and very similar indeed to the 'national' group while the poor arithmetical ability of the neurologically abnormal group becomes very evident.

Another way of looking at the differences is to compare the percentage of children of below average arithmetical ability (ratings 4 or 5) in the different groups. In the national study 35·5 per cent of the children were below average, in the control group 30·8 per cent, in the PH group without neurological abnormalities 29·8 per cent and in the neurologically abnormal group 78·1 per cent, that is, roughly four in every five children with a brain disorder were experiencing some difficulty in arithmetic, the difference from the other PH children being significant at the 0·1 per cent level.

How can the very poor arithmetical ability of this group be accounted for? A useful account of the arithmetic difficulties of 'normal', physically handicapped and cerebral-palsied children has been given by Haskell (1972). He points out that where attempts have been made to explore the relationship between neurological disorders and poor arithmetic attainment the findings are 'occasionally contradictory and generally inconclusive' and considers that the best strategy is to look first at the factors which are known to affect arithmetical ability in all children.

A major factor is of course intelligence and, as described earlier, its effects were partialled out by use of an analysis of co-variance. (It should be noted that only the scores of the children for whom IQ results were available are shown in this and other tables where the effect of IQ is partialled out.) Table 7.4 shows the mean arithmetic ratings for the children in the different groups before and after they have been adjusted according to intelligence.

TABLE 7.4. *Mean arithmetic ratings before and after adjustment of scores according to non-verbal IQ*

Group	No.	Mean non-verbal IQ	Mean arithmetic rating* before adjustment	Adjusted mean arithmetic rating
Controls	121	104·7	2·76	2·83
PH group without neurological ab-normalities	44	102·2	2·88	2·90
PH group with neuro-logical abnormalities	23	83·3	3·73	3·36

* The lower the rating the better the performance

Before the mean ratings were adjusted, the neurologically abnormal group had a rating (3·73) which was significantly poorer (at the 0·1 per cent level) than that of the other groups: when intelligence is taken into account this difference is reduced considerably and is in fact no longer statistically significant (F = 1·692 [df 2, 184] not significant at the 5 per cent level).

Apart from intelligence it is likely that other factors were operating to account for the difficulties of the neurologically abnormal children, particularly as their scores were poorer even when this was taken into account. Haskell (1972) in his review of the literature shows that emotional factors, especially anxiety, may contribute to poor performance in arithmetic and it has already been shown in the discussion of the behaviour disorders of the children in this study that one of the behavioural items which tended to characterize the neurologically abnormal group was 'worried more'.

Schonell and Schonell (1957) list school absence as one of the most important causes of lack of ability in arithmetic (a subject which is particularly susceptible to the influences of absence). The neurologically abnormal children were not only – as expected – absent more frequently than the controls, but also than the children with congenital abnormalities.

A number of other factors are listed by Haskell as applying specifically to the cerebral-palsied group (each of these factors being also applicable to children with hydrocephalus). These are:

1 Not only deprivation of sensory-motor experience (which will affect other PH children) but also abnormal feedback from disordered movements.

2 A higher incidence of ocular defects, especially squint, leading to less efficiency than normals in simple tasks (for example, computations) involving movement of the eyes (Abercrombie, 1960). In fact seven of the neurologically impaired group did have squints.

3 Disorders of perception leading to difficulties in recognizing shapes, in matching and discriminating forms, in distinguishing figure from ground and in integrating the constituent elements to form the whole (Abercrombie, 1964; Wedell, 1964; Miller and Sethi, 1971a, 1971b).

4 More frequent disturbances in visuo-motor skills leading to a generally poorer performance on visuo-motor tasks such as copying or constructing shapes than among non-brain-damaged children (Abercrombie, 1964; Wedell, 1964; Spain, 1970).

5 A greater distractability than in children without brain disorders which will particularly affect arithmetic attainment since 'one of the major determinants of success in working sums is the degree

to which the pupil can keep his mind persistently on the task in hand' (Schonell and Schonell, 1957).

In the analysis of behaviour disorders (chapter 5) 87·5 per cent of the neurologically impaired group were noted by their teachers as showing poor concentration compared with 43·4 per cent of the other PH children and 35·7 per cent of the controls, a highly significant difference.

There are then a number of reasons, the most important probably being the lower intelligence of the group, to explain the finding that half the neurologically abnormal group had 'rather poor ability with numbers'. What is more disturbing is that in addition nearly one-quarter (six children) showed 'little, if any ability' or 'virtually no understanding' in this sphere. Very little remedial help with arithmetic was available, a problem which is discussed in the next chapter.

(iii) READING ACCURACY AND COMPREHENSION:

Two main measures of the children's reading ability were used, one being the class teacher's ratings (of a similar kind to those used for arithmetic) and the other a well-known standardized reading test, the Neale analysis of reading ability.

The main pattern of findings is shown by the teacher's ratings (Table 7.5); once more the national sample of 7 year olds has been included for comparison purposes.

As was noted in the arithmetic ratings, the control group appears to contain a greater proportion of very able children than does the national sample. The main feature of these results however is that there are few differences between the controls and the PH children without neurological abnormalities, whereas over two-thirds of the neurologically abnormal group are reading at a below average level, and none are rated as above average.

The main measure of reading attainment was the Neale analysis of reading ability (Form A), this test being given to the handicapped child and the controls individually. Neale (1966) devised the test 'to meet a practical need for a diagnostic measure which, while yielding scores of a traditional nature concerning a child's progress in reading, would provide a sympathetic and stimulating situation in which his difficulties, weaknesses, types of error, persistence and attitudes could be assessed'. In this test the child is asked to read aloud a

TABLE 7.5. *Teachers' ratings of reading ability in the different groups and in the National Child Development study (percentages)*

Description of ratings	PH with neurological abnormalities No. = 23	PH without neurological abnormalities No. = 44	Control group No. = 136	National Child Development study No. = 15 029
1 Avid reader. Reads fluently and widely in relation to his age	0·0	9·0	14·7	6·6
2 Above average ability. Comprehends well what he reads	0·0	20·4	20·5	24·0
3 Average reader	30·4	43·1	37·5	43·1
4 Poor reader. Limited comprehension	52·1	22·7	19·1	23·2
5 Non-reader or recognizes very few words	17·3	4·5	8·0	3·2

series of passages graded in difficulty and after each passage is asked some questions to test his understanding of what he has read. On the basis of this, reading ages for accuracy and comprehension are calculated. A reading age of 7 years or less on the test means that the child still has difficulty in reading a very simple short passage with understanding, while making only minor errors, while with a reading age of 8 years he would manage to grasp the meaning and make few errors in a relatively easy reading task. The comprehension score is not independent of the accuracy score, since testing is stopped once the child reaches a certain error level.

In computing the mean reading scores, non-readers were treated as if they had scored at the floor level of the test, i.e. at 6·0 years. As all the children could read a few words and were making progress, this seemed more reasonable than omitting them from the analysis.

The results of the different groups for reading accuracy are summarized in Table 7.6.

TABLE 7.6. *Neale's analysis of reading ability: mean accuracy scores in the different groups*

Group	Size of group	Mean chronological age (months)	Mean accuracy score (months)	SD (months)
Controls	148	105·4	103·8	19·5
Total PH group	74	105·9	99·1*	19·9
PH without neurological abnormalities	48	106·4	104·5	21·0
PH with neurological abnormalities	26	105·0	89·2†	12·7

* Difference from controls significant at the 2 per cent level
† Differences from controls and group without neurological abnormalities significant at the 0·1 per cent level

The mean reading age of the controls and the PH group without neurological abnormalities was very similar (confirming the accuracy of the teacher ratings). In both cases it was approximately a month below their chronological age. The picture was not as satisfactory for

TABLE 7.7. *Mean reading accuracy, before and after adjustment of scores according to non-verbal IQ*

Group (mean CA months)	No.	Mean non-verbal IQ	Mean reading accuracy score (months)	Adjusted mean accuracy score (months)
Controls (107·16)	121	104·7	106·0	104·2
PH group without neurological abnormalities (106·7)	44	102·2	106·3	105·9
PH group with neurological abnormalities (106·08)	23	83·3	93·2	103·8

the neurologically abnormal group who were, on average, reading at a level nearly fifteen months below their chronological age, the difference between this and the other two groups being significant at the 0·1 per cent level. Once again, however, when the effect of intelligence was partialled out through an analysis of co-variance, these differences disappeared (F = 0·354 [df 2, 184] not significant).

Although these results suggest that the neurologically abnormal children were reading as well as might have been expected on the basis of their IQ level, the findings must be treated with some caution. The IQ scores only reflected non-verbal ability, and the children's verbal intelligence may have been higher. In the section on reading backwardness other factors which may have been affecting this group are discussed.

For reading comprehension, the results were very similar (Table 7.8).

TABLE 7.8. *Neale's analysis of reading ability: mean comprehension scores in the different groups*

Group	Size of group	Mean chrono- logical age (months)	Mean accuracy score (months)	SD (months)
Controls	148	105·4	103·5	20·2
Total PH group	74	105·9	97·7*	20·0
PH without neurological abnormalities	48	106·4	104·1	21·1
PH with neurological abnormalities	26	105·0	86·0†	10·2

* Difference from controls significant at the 1 per cent level
† Difference from controls and group without neurological abnormalities significant at the 0·1 per cent level

Once again there is no significant difference between the control group and the PH children without brain disorders. The mean comprehension age of both these groups is close to their chronological age whereas in the neurologically abnormal group it is nineteen months below. However the partialling out of the effects of IQ

(Table 7.9 below) again negates the difference between the groups (F = 0·239 [df 2, 184] not significant).

TABLE 7.9. *Mean reading comprehension, before and after adjustment of scores according to non-verbal I Q*

Group [mean CA months]	No.	Mean non-verbal IQ	Mean reading compre-hension score (months)	Adjusted mean compre-hension score (months)
Controls [107·16]	121	104·7	107·3	104·9
PH group without neurological abnormalities [106·7]	44	102·2	102·0	101·5
PH group with neurological abnormalities [106·08]	23	83·3	88·6	101·8

To sum up, when reading ability was investigated, no differences were found regarding either reading accuracy or reading comprehension between children with physical disorders but no neurological involvement and their non-handicapped peers. On average the children were reading at a level only a few weeks below their chronological ages. There was of course a wide distribution of reading ability but this was similar in both groups. The children with neurological abnormalities formed a more homogeneous group as far as both reading accuracy and comprehension were concerned and on average their level of reading accuracy was about fifteen months below their actual ages, retardation being even greater in the case of comprehension. The fact that most of these children had IQs in the range 80–90 has already been noted. It is also likely that several had specific learning disabilities which affected progress in reading and would have benefited from extra help, this question being discussed in the following chapter.

(iv) READING BACKWARDNESS

(a) Extent of backwardness

The extent of actual reading backwardness in the different groups is a question of major importance. The terms 'backward' and retarded are often used very loosely and mean different things in different studies of reading ability. Here the term 'backward reader' is used (as was done in the Isle of Wight study) to refer to a child whose reading accuracy age or whose reading comprehension age was at least twenty-eight months below his chronological age. I have also introduced the term 'borderline backwardness' to refer to those children with reading accuracy or comprehension ages which are from 19–27 months below their chronological age.

A large number of studies of reading now exist and only a few of the more important ones will be referred to here. In the Isle of Wight study the rate of reading backwardness was 6·64 per cent among 9 and 10 year olds. Morris (1966) found that, at 8 years old, 14 per cent of a sample of Kent schoolchildren were reading not at all or extremely poorly while Pringle et al. (1966) found that 10 per cent of children in their last term of infant school had hardly started to read. In Scotland, Clark (1970) carried out a major community study of reading difficulties in 1,544 Dunbartonshire primary schoolchildren. 15 per cent of the 7 year olds were 'without any independent reading skill', while at 8 years old 15·3 per cent of the sample had reading quotients of 85 or less on the Schonell graded word reading test. Most of these, however, 'were of lower than average intelligence and came from the lower end of the social class distribution'. When they were retested at 9 years old on the Neale reading analysis it was found that among those of average intelligence (defined as children who had at least one IQ on the WISC within the normal range, i.e. fullscale verbal or performance IQ of 90 or above), only 1 per cent of the population were found to be backward by two years or more.

In the present study when reading accuracy alone was considered, the extent of backwardness was 8·1 per cent in the control group, 13·6 per cent in the PH group without neurological abnormalities and 22·9 per cent in the group with such abnormalities. When backwardness is taken to include backwardness in either accuracy or comprehension or both (as there was a great deal of overlap) the corresponding figures increase to 10·1 per cent, 14·5 per cent and 27·0 per cent. Details of this and also of the extent of borderline backwardness are shown in Table 7.10 below.

These figures can be compared with the figures for specific reading retardation found in the Isle of Wight survey, which were 5·4 per cent for the general population, 14·0 per cent for the physical dis-

TABLE 7.10. *Backward and borderline readers (reading accuracy and/
or reading comprehension)*

	Controls No. = 148		PH children without neurological abnormalities No. = 44		PH children with neurological abnormalities No. = 26	
	No.	%	No.	%	No.	%
Backward readers (including non-readers in brackets)	15 (8)	10·1	7 (3)	14·5	7 (2)	27·0
Borderline backward readers	13	8·8	4	8·3	7	27·0

order but no brain disorder group and 26·5 per cent for the brain disorder group. In the Isle of Wight study, however, the effect of WISC IQ has been partialled out whereas the figures shown in Table 7.10 do not take IQ into account. Certainly, as far as the control group and the PH children without neurological abnormalities were concerned, the non-verbal IQ scores of the backward or 'borderline backward' readers tended, in about half the cases, to fall into the range 80–90, but clearly factors other than intelligence must also have been contributing to their difficulties. Findings from other studies where intelligence was not partialled out include, among ordinary 8 year olds, a reading backwardness rate of 14 per cent in the Kent study (Morris, 1966) and 15·3 per cent in the Dunbarton-shire study (Clark, 1970) although different tests were used in these.

When the neurologically abnormal group is considered it must first be remembered that lower intelligence was undoubtedly an important element in some cases. The fact remains that over one-quarter of this group were backward by twenty-eight months or more and a further quarter by between nineteen and twenty-eight months (and thus probably 'at risk' of falling further behind and becoming truly backward). This finding is in line with other studies, for example that of Barsch and Ruddell (1962) who looked at reading development in seventy-seven cerebral-palsied children (thirty-two of whom attended ordinary schools) and found that only 31 per cent were average or above in reading, the results being similar for children in ordinary and special schools, and it does seem very likely, as was the conclusion in the Isle of Wight study, that the poor reading of this group was in part due to the direct effects of brain dysfunction.

(b) Other factors associated with reading backwardness

Apart from intelligence level and the existence of some degree of brain dysfunction, what other factors appeared to have been associated with the rather high rates of reading backwardness found in this study? (It must be emphasized that the establishment of significant associations does not of course allow conclusions to be drawn as to causality and the very small number involved made it very unlikely that even significant associations would be found.)

An obvious factor, which applied particularly to the handicapped children, was that of absence from school. The effects of absence on primary school performance have been discussed in detail by Douglas and Ross (1965) who looked at 3,273 children and found that during the first three years of junior school the absence rate was relatively constant, averaging between 2·4 to 2·7 weeks a year. While the amount of absence or the age distribution of the absence had little effect (in terms of performance at 11 years old) on children from the upper middle classes,

> in all other social classes considerable effects are recorded, children who are consistently absent or often absent in the last two years of primary school making lower scores at eleven years and showing a relative deterioration in scores between eight and eleven years. On the whole, children who are away often in the first two years but make good attendances in subsequent years catch up, but not if they come from the lower manual working class or go to primary schools that have a poor academic record.

In the Isle of Wight study (Rutter et al., 1970) it was found that the handicapped groups (including those with and without brain disorders) had been absent significantly more often than the controls, and absence rates were also looked at in this study (Table 7.11 below).

The differences between the groups are marked: 27·0 per cent of the handicapped group have missed more than two full weeks of

TABLE 7.II. *School absences: comparison of control and handicapped groups*

Number of half-day absences during the school term (autumn term 1969 or 1970)	Handicapped group No. = 74		Controls No. = 148	
	No.	%	No.	%
No absences	8	10·8	32	21·6
1–10 absences	24	32·4	67	45·2
11–20 absences	17	22·9	23	15·5
Over 20 absences	20	27·0	16	10·8
Not known	5	6·7	10	6·7

school but only 10·8 per cent of the controls, this difference being significant at the 5 per cent level. Within the handicapped group the highest absence rates were among the haemophiliacs and the thalidomide children. In each case three out of the four children missed more than two weeks' schooling in the term under consideration. The next highest rate was among the cerebral-palsied children, nearly half of whom were absent for over two weeks in the term, while most of the spina bifida and hydrocephalic children missed between one and two weeks of schooling. The absence rate was lowest among the group with congenital abnormalities.

In Table 7.12 the association between school absence in one selected term and reading backwardness in the handicapped group is looked at.

TABLE 7.12. *Reading backwardness and school absence in the handicapped group (percentages)*

	Absent for less than 2 weeks	Absent for more than 2 weeks	Not known
Backward and borderline readers No. = 25	56	32	12
Rest of handicapped group No. = 49	72	24	4

Although a somewhat greater proportion of the backward readers group had been absent for more than two weeks in the term selected, the difference is not statistically significant.

The effect of absences was also examined in terms of the amount of hospitalization children had experienced since the age of five, details being shown in appendix K.2. There appeared to be no association between the amount of hospitalization and school attainment, 26 per cent of the PH 'high attainers' having been in hospital for five or more weeks and only 17 per cent of the 'low attainers'. This may have been because most of the hospitalization took place when the children were still in infant classes, or in some cases during the school holidays.

Other factors which were considered likely to be related to reading skills were not, as was the case with school absence, confined largely to the handicapped group but applied to all the children in the study. Vernon (1968) has summarized such factors well, dividing them into 'environmental' or 'individual' factors, and she has pointed out that 'even when a genetically determined developmental or maturational lag or neurological abnormality has been demonstrated, social and psychiatric disorders are commonly present'. The number of possible associated factors is long and their relationship complex: only three are looked at briefly here, social class, size of family and the presence of behaviour disorders.

When the effects of social class are examined (appendix J.1) there is a tendency (as other studies have shown) for a higher proportion of the backward and borderline readers to come from social classes IV and V (37 per cent) than of children who are not backward (25 per cent) and a somewhat lower proportion to come from social classes I and II, although the numbers are too small to be statistically significant.

Family size was considered next (appendix J.2), Douglas (1964), Clark (1970) and others having found some association between backwardness and membership of a family of four or more children. In the case of the backward group there is only a very slight tendency for the children to come from larger families but over half of the 'borderline' readers come from large families compared to only a third of the children without reading problems.

Finally the association between backwardness and behaviour disorders was examined. This is an area about which a great deal has been written. Recent work includes that of Rutter et al. (1970) who have discussed the association at some length in their Isle of Wight study and Clark (1970) who, like Rutter, found firstly an association between reading backwardness and the existence of a behaviour disorder in general (47·4 per cent of her 8 year old backward readers being 'deviant' on the teachers' scale) and between reading backwardness and antisocial (rather than neurotic) disorders in particular. Such an association was not, however, found in this study. Of the backward readers 6·8 per cent showed neurotic disorders and 17·2 per cent antisocial disorders, while the figures for the borderline group were 8·3 per cent and 20·8 per cent (on either the teacher or parent scales). These rates were very similar to those for the children without reading problems.

(v) OVERALL ACADEMIC ATTAINMENT

(a) Measures

In addition to looking separately at ability in arithmetic, reading fluency and comprehension, it was decided that an overall assessment of attainment should be made for each child, on the basis of which children would be assigned to either a 'high attainers' or 'low attainers' group. Four measures were used to obtain the overall score, each child being rated on a 1 (high) to 5 (low) scale on each measure. The following measures made up the composite score:

1 Arithmetical ability (already described)
2 Reading accuracy
3 Reading comprehension
4 Parental assessment of attainment level.

To obtain the ratings for two and three, the children's accuracy or comprehension ages were compared with their chronological ages (CA) and ratings were assigned as follows:

Rating	Reading accuracy or comprehension in relation to CA
1	Over twenty-four months above CA
2	Fifteen to twenty-four months above CA
3	Zero to twelve months above or below CA
4	Thirteen to twenty-four months below CA
5	Over twenty-four months below CA

The fourth measure was introduced in an attempt to utilize the mother's knowledge of the child's ability in the child's overall level of attainment in school in relation to his peers on a five-point scale, 1 being superior, 2 above average, 3 average, 4 below average and 5 very poor, these ratings being obtained during the parental interviews. Before a decision was taken to include this measure, these ratings were compared with the reading and arithmetic ratings and also with teachers' ratings of overall attainment which were obtained for the PH children only. Such comparisons indicated that the mother's appraisal of the child's attainment level was a realistic one and should be included in the final assessment.

To obtain the overall assessment score the children's scores (from 1–5) on each measure were summed and an average score calculated for each child. These could range from a 'high' of 1·0 to a 'low' of 5·0.

(b) Findings for overall attainment

The distribution of scores for the different groups is shown in Figure 7.1 below.

FIGURE 7.1. *Distribution of overall academic attainment scores*

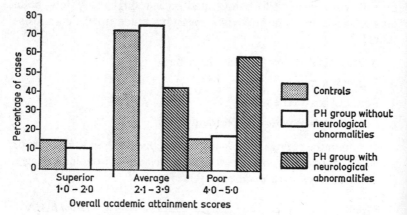

The proportion of controls and PH children scoring in the superior, average and poor range is very similar. None of the children with neurological abnormalities, however, score in the superior range, under half in the average range and over half in the poor range.

The mean scores for the different groups are shown in Table 7.13 below.

TABLE 7.13. *Mean overall academic attainment scores*

Groups	Size of group	Mean overall academic attainment score	SD
Controls	148	3·02	0·81
Total PH group	74	3·44*	0·72
PH without neurological abnormalities	48	3·13†	0·78
PH with neurological abnormalities	26	3·96*	0·54

* Difference from controls significant at the 0·1 per cent level
† Difference from group with neurological abnormalities significant at the 0·1 per cent level

Once again, there is no significant difference between the mean scores for the controls (3·02) and the group without neurological abnormalities (3·13) whereas those with neurological abnormalities are much poorer (3·96), the difference between them and the other groups being highly significant ($p < 0.001$). As in the case of arithmetic and reading, an analysis of co-variance was used to partial out the effects of intelligence, the results being shown below. (The slightly different mean scores in Table 7.14 below result from the different size of the groups, IQ scores not being available for all the children.)

TABLE 7.14. *Mean academic attainment score before and after adjustment of scores according to non-verbal IQ*

Group (mean CA months)	No.	Mean non-verbal IQ	Mean academic attainment score (months)	Adjusted mean attainment score (months)
Controls (107·16)	121	104·7	2·99	3·10
PH group without neurological abnormalities (106·7)	44	102·2	3·11	3·13
PH group with neurological abnormalities (106·08)	23	83·3	3·98	3·32

Once again, after I Q has been taken into account there is no significant difference between the scores of the three groups (F = 0·874 [df 2, 184] not significant at the 5 per cent level).

A more useful way of looking at the results is in terms of the proportion of children in each group who were high attainers or low attainers (in terms of actual performance, without intelligence being taken into account). To obtain the dichotomy the mean score for all the controls (3·02) plus one standard deviation (0·86) (i.e. a score of 3·88) was taken as the cut-off point, children with scores greater than this being regarded as low attainers and the others as high attainers. The results are shown in Table 7.15.

TABLE 7.15. *Proportion of high and low attainers in the different groups*

	High attainers No.	High attainers %	Low attainers No.	Low attainers %
Controls (No. = 148)	109	73·6	39	26·3
Handicapped without neurological abnormalities (No. = 48)	32	66·7	16	33·3
Handicapped with neurological abnormalities (No. = 26)	6	23·0	20	76·9

Nearly three-quarters (73·6 per cent) of the controls fall into the 'high attainers' group and two-thirds of the PH children without neurological abnormalities, an insignificant difference. The position is reversed for the children with neurological abnormalities, three-quarters of whom are poor attainers, the difference between this group and the other PH children being significant at the 0·1 per cent level ($x^2 = 11·14$, df 1). This is not to say that these children are necessarily wrongly placed in ordinary schools, since it has been shown that most were performing adequately when attainment was related to I Q. Within each group a small number of children were doing very poorly indeed (i.e. with scores greater than 4·74, more than two standard deviations below the mean of the controls). In the neurologically abnormal group there were three such children (11·5 per cent), in the PH group without neurological abnormalities two (4·4 per cent) and in the control group five (3·4 per cent). All these children clearly required more extra help than was at present available for them.

(c) Factors related to overall attainment level

One of the aims of this research inquiry was to attempt to elucidate some of the main factors which affect the academic success of physically handicapped children, and to assess their relative import-ance. Factors of potential importance fall into two main groups, firstly those related to the presence or absence of a physical handi-cap, with or without additional neurological abnormalities, and secondly those which may affect non-handicapped children also. The first category includes such factors as the type and severity of handicap, while the latter would include intelligence, sex, age, social class and family factors. Not all the factors are independent of one another; intelligence level for example is generally related to the extent and nature of neurological impairment.

The importance of these factors taken separately has been dis-cussed earlier in this chapter. Can we come to any conclusions about their relative importance? To explore this, an analysis of the findings was carried out by computer (NCHS, 1964). Details of the pro-gramme are given in appendix L. Basically this analysis enables us to look at a number of different independent variables (which could be different factors of the kind discussed above) at the same time, and to decide which of these has the strongest correlation with the depen-dent variable (in this case overall social adjustment). The sample is then dichotomized into two groups which embody this variable.

For example (a purely imaginary one), if the most important inde-pendent variable had been found to be eye colour the programme might have split the sample into two groups with, let us say, in group 1 children with green or blue eyes (these colours being correlated with better adjustment) and in group 2 children with eyes of all other colours. The same process would then be carried out again. Group 1 (the green- and blue-eyed children) would be examined to see which of the remaining independent variables correlated best with academic attainment, and sex (for example) might be found to be most important. The group would then be split into groups 3 and 4 according to sex. The same process would be carried out for group 2, this splitting continuing until the specified minimum size of group or some other criterion was reached.

The best results are obtained from this programme when the sample is much larger than the present one (a sample of at least 1,000 cases being most desirable). This and other constraints meant that it was not entirely suitable for this study. However, the results are included here since firstly the programme provides an interesting and not very well-known tool for studies of this kind, and secondly the results, although not statistically significant because of the small size of the sample, do give a useful indication of the relative importance of some of the factors discussed above.

Only a limited number of factors can be examined at any one time and the following six were selected as independent variables and their relative importance as regards overall social adjustment (the dependent variable) investigated. These were:

1 Broad nature of the disorder (no disorder [controls]; physical handicap alone; physical handicap with neurological abnormalities).

2 Type of handicap (i.e. cerebral palsy, spina bifida, etc.)

3 Social class

4 Size of family

5 Sex

6 Size of school class

Intelligence level has already been shown to be of great importance; unfortunately it could not be included here as the scores were not available for all the children. Consideration was also given as to whether age should be included, as there was a possibility that handicapped children might do comparatively well in their first year of junior school and might then fall behind. In fact similar proportions of high and low attainers were found in each age group (appendix K.1). Figure 7.2 below shows the results of the computer analysis.

The most important split is of course the first one (A). The result confirms what has already been suggested several times, that in this study the presence or absence of a neurological abnormality played a major part in determining academic success. Next in importance was the type of handicap, with cerebral-palsied and spina bifida children tending to do poorly (these of course making up most of the neurologically impaired group) and the other children and the controls better. Table 7.16 gives more details.

One point that should be mentioned here concerns severity of handicap. As Table 7.17 shows, this had little effect on attainment level.

Next in importance to the factors described above were social class

FIGURE 7.2. *Factors affecting academic attainment: results of computer analysis*

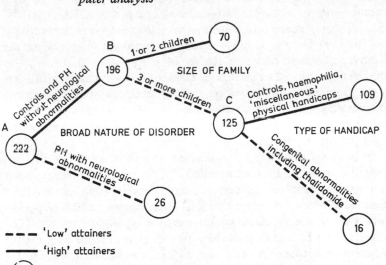

TABLE 7.16. *Category of handicap and academic attainment*

Category of handicap	High attainment No.	High attainment %	Low attainment No.	Low attainment %
No handicap	109	73·6	39	26·3
Congenital abnormalities including thalidomide	13	59·1	9	40·9
Spina bifida	4	33·3	8	66·6
Cerebral palsy	5	31·3	11	68·7
'Other' including haemophilia	16	66·6	8	33·3

TABLE 7.17. *Overall academic attainment and severity of handicap*

	Mildly handicapped (No. = 13)	Moderately handicapped (No. = 45)	Severely handicapped (No. = 16)
High attainment	6	24	8
Low attainment	7	21	8

and size of family which were of almost equal importance, 'high' attainment being associated with social classes I and II or with membership of a one- or two-child as opposed to a larger family. Size of school class and sex were of very little importance compared to the other factors. There was only a very slight tendency for the better performers to be in classes of 31–5 rather than of 36–40 children, and in fact children in classes of 26–30 children did less well, possibly because poorer ability children were sometimes deliberately placed in smaller classes. Boys were very slightly superior to girls, 69 per cent of the boys being high attainers and 63·5 per cent of the girls.

Split B on the diagram shows that after the neurologically impaired group had been channelled off, the most important factor determining academic success was size of family (one- or two-child families superior), followed by social class (classes I and II superior) and size of school class, which were of equal importance. The crucial point here is that all these factors carried more weight than whether or not, and in what way, a child was handicapped. In fact the factor carrying least weight was whether the child did or did not have a physical disorder *per se*.

At point C on the diagram the group contains only control and physical disorder children from families with three or more children. Once again the relative weight of all the factors was considered and the most important was shown to be the type of handicap, with the congenital abnormalities and thalidomide group performing slightly worse than the controls, the children with haemophilia and those with 'miscellaneous' physical disorders. Following this in importance was sex, boys doing better than girls. Again, the least important factor was whether the child did or did not have a physical handicap.

In summing up, the results of this study suggest that the following factors are of paramount importance in determining the likelihood of academic success for a PH child in an ordinary school:

1 Whether or not he has a neurological impairment.

2 His intelligence level, which is likely to be closely associated with the extent and nature of intellectual impairment.

3 His social class membership.

4 The number of children in his family.

In comparison with these factors, the size of class in which he is placed is of little importance and also carrying little weight are the exact nature of the physical disorder (provided there is no neurological impairment) and the severity of the handicap.

The relative importance of these different factors can be illustrated if the characteristics of the seventeen PH children with the highest overall attainment scores are compared with those whose attainment level was poorest. Details are given in appendix K.3, but the main features of the very successful children were firstly that none were neurologically impaired and secondly that only one child had a non-verbal IQ score of below 100. Many came from professional families and few from large families. Their handicaps varied considerably in their nature and severity.

The characteristics of the eighteen children with the lowest academic attainment scores were very different (appendix K.4). 68 per cent of the children had neurological abnormalities and 50 per cent of those tested had non-verbal IQ scores below 85. A relatively small proportion of children came from small families and a high proportion from social classes III (manual), IV and V. The other point to notice here is that quite a high proportion of the children with the best academic attainment scores tended also to be the children with the best social adjustment scores, and there was a similar association between low attainment and poor adjustment. In the group as a whole (PH children and controls) there was a correlation of +0·368 between academic attainment and social adjustment.

To end this section, and to illustrate the educational problems of a child with a brain disorder in an excellent ordinary school whose staff could not be more sympathetic, the case of Martin is presented.

At a year old, Martin fractured his skull after a fall. Complete paralysis coupled with epilepsy followed. Gradually the use of his left side was regained, the fits were brought under control and he was left with a right-sided flaccid hemiparesis. At 3 years old he made a score of 80 on the Stanford Binet test (no scatter) and the medical officer who assessed him thought that he would 'probably be able to attend an ordinary school'. Placement in an ordinary private nursery for nine months was then arranged. After he had been reassessed two months before his fifth birthday, ordinary infant school placement was recommended, 'provided that there is a minimum of stairs and that he is not roughly handled in the playground'. His distract-ability was noted, and regular checks on his progress recommended.

After two terms in the infant school Martin was referred to the school psychological service for 'lack of initiative and concentration'. His teacher reported that 'he usually just draws crosses or squiggles and seldom paints. He will talk to other children but never plays with them and allows them to take over his toys. When he loses interest he just sits until further activity is suggested. He finds great difficulty in carrying out simple instructions and lacks initiative.' The psychological assessment yielded a score of 98 on the Stanford Binet (L–M form). Auditory and visual memory seemed poor but apart from this an even spread of failures on the verbal and performance was noted. Sympathetic handling and gentle encouragement were recommended 'since it would be comparatively easy to overstress him' and he was to be kept under continuous review.

When the time came for a transfer to junior school, his class teacher expressed doubts as to whether he would cope owing to his paralysis and poor balance, but his parents were opposed to residential placement and he was placed in an ordinary junior school. At first progress was very slow and erratic. At the end of his first term, it was stated on his 3HP form (report on a backward child) that he could do little in the way of drawing, that he fluctuated in his ability to concentrate and that he did not mix easily. Two years later the picture was brighter. He had 'responded well to being part of an ordinary school', his coordination was better, he was making 'marked progress' in reading and enjoyed this and music, although his drawings were still at an infant level. He was 'very eager to please', was 'no longer solitary' and was 'slowly increasing his circle of friends'. Nine months later there was a fairly sudden and striking lapse in academic progress, behavioural problems appeared and a school phobia developed. This appears to have been temporary; two months later the head reported that he was 'his old happy self', but with only a year before he transfers to secondary school his parents are now considering whether they should then transfer him to a special school.

Martin's case illustrates well how even under the best circum-stances (in a school where the head and the class teacher and the child's classmates were exceptionally patient and understanding, and where psychological help was available) a child with neurological impairment may find it very difficult to hold his own, academically and socially, in an ordinary school. For such a child, placement in a special class in an ordinary school where he could get the individual help he clearly needs but is not getting now might be a better solution.

The infant group

This chapter has been largely concerned with the 7–10 year olds, and in conclusion a very brief account will be given of the findings for the twenty-five children at the infant stage. It must be re-emphasized that the infant group was highly selective; the majority of the children were heavily physically handicapped and seventeen had some degree of neurological impairment. Children with spina bifida and hydrocephalus comprised over half the group. While the classes they attended were of a normal size (ten were in classes of thirty-five or more, twelve in classes of twenty-five to thirty-four and only three in classes of under twenty-five, one being a special class), the arrangements made for them were in other ways (especially on the care side) often rather special and costly for the LEAs, and are considered in detail in chapter 8. The questions that were investigated on the educational side concerned firstly the level of intellectual and language development at which they were functioning and secondly whether they were making satisfactory progress as far as could be judged at such an early stage.

(i) INTELLECTUAL AND LANGUAGE DEVELOPMENT

Two tests were used to assess the general ability of the children. One, the English picture vocabulary test (EPVT) is designed for assessment of levels of listening vocabulary and can be interpreted as a measure of verbal ability (Brimer and Dunn, 1963) while the other, Raven's coloured progressive matrices (Raven, 1965) measures non-verbal intelligence. In addition, teachers were asked to rate the children on a simple four-point scale (superior, average, dull, ESN).

The mean test score on the EPVT was 105·7 and on Raven's matrices 103·0 and the distribution of scores on the tests, along with the teachers' assessments, are given in Table 7.18 below.

It is well established that neurologically impaired children tend to score more poorly on non-verbal tests (which usually involve perceptual and/or visuo-motor skills) than on verbal tests, and in view of the large number of cerebral-palsied and hydrocephalic children

TABLE 7.18. *Distribution of verbal and non-verbal intelligence in the infant group*

Test/assessment	IQ range				
	Very able 130+	Superior 115–29	Average 85–114	Dull 70–84	ESN below 70
English picture voca-bulary test	1	5	16	3	0
Raven's coloured matrices	1	5	14	5	0
Teachers' assessment	4		18	2	0

in the group it was surprising that the difference between the scores on the EPVT and the matrices was not greater. When the scores of the twelve children with spina bifida and hydrocephalus, for example, were looked at separately, means of 104·4 on the EPVT and 100·8 on the matrices were obtained; the difference is very small, and the average score on the matrices suggests that these children were not severely handicapped by purely perceptual problems, although this test does not, of course, involve visuo-motor ability. Several neuro-logically impaired children in fact did better on the matrices, as Table 7.19 below shows.

TABLE 7.19. *Comparison of scores on the English picture vocabulary test and on Raven's matrices: infant group*

	No. of children	
	With neurological abnorma-lities	Without neurological abnorma-lities
Scores on EPVT and matrices similar (within 5 IQ points of each other)	4	3
EPVT score higher by 6+ points	7	3
Raven's matrices score higher by 6+ points	5	3
TOTALS	16	9

Apart from this unexpected finding, the main feature of the children's scores is the normality of the distribution. Some of the children had been formally tested prior to placement in an ordinary school, and in the other cases an important criterion which medical officers or parents had used in judging the appropriateness of such a placement for a heavily handicapped child was the apparent 'normality' of intelligence. The great majority of the children in this group were thus of good average intelligence and the findings do not offer evidence as to whether less able children could be similarly placed.

(ii) EDUCATIONAL ATTAINMENTS

As Kellmer Pringle and Fiddes (1970) point out in their study of thalidomide children, at the infant level 'normal' children are only just making a beginning with formal measurable attainment. Too much weight cannot therefore be given to the findings for the infant group, fewer than half of whom were in their last year of infant school. Two means of assessment were used, firstly the Southgate group reading test and secondly the class teacher's assessment of the child's overall educational level with particular reference to reading and arithmetic.

Although the Southgate group reading test is standardized on children aged from 5·8 to 8·1 years, Southgate (1959) suggests that testing of reading ability is best left until most children are at least 6 years old, the test being particularly useful for children aged six to seven and a half and for older children who have been slow in learning to read. The test is a word selection test and in each school it was given to a small group of children comprising the handicapped child and from two to four other children whom the teacher selected as being at roughly the same stage. The latter were not used as controls but were simply included to put the handicapped child at ease by being tested with his friends. The results are summarized below.

Of the nine non-readers, five were under 6½ years old and could hardly have been expected to have achieved much; four were in fact described by teachers as 'almost' able to read. The four others were, however, over 7 years old. One child with genito-urinary abnormalities had missed a great deal of schooling; the other three were children with spina bifida and hydrocephalus, one of whom was in a special class, while teachers felt that the other two needed more individual help than they were actually getting.

TABLE 7.20. *Reading level of handicapped infants (Southgate group reading test)*

Reading level	Number of children
Non-readers	9
Reading age below CA	4
Reading age equal to or above CA	12
TOTAL	25

The other way in which educational attainment was assessed was through the class teacher's ratings, taking into account both reading and arithmetic. In an attempt to discover how realistic the parental assessment of their children's abilities was, the mothers were also asked to rate the children on a similar scale. The results are shown below (Table 7.21).

TABLE 7.21. *Overall attainment: teacher and parent assessments: infant group*

	No. of children	
Rating	Teacher assessment	Parental assessment
Exceptionally good	3	1
Above average	3	3
Average	8	12
Below average	6	7
Very poor	5	2
TOTALS	25	25

There was a close correspondence in the teacher and mother ratings, the same children being picked out by both as above or below average although mothers were slightly less likely to give their children a very high or a very low rating. Teachers were also asked how satisfied they were with the children's progress: fourteen were 'satisfied' and five 'fairly satisfied'. In six other cases (which have already been discussed in chapter 3) the teachers were concerned about the slow rate of progress.

In summing up, the children can be thought of as falling into three groups. In the largest group (comprising about 60 per cent of the children) progress was satisfactory; in a second group the children were still too young to have any measurable formal attainments but had shown no signs of specific difficulties. Finally, there were six children (24 per cent) about whose progress teachers were definitely worried and who would clearly have benefited from more individual attention. Most were children whose I Q scores, at least on one of the tests, fell into the dull (i.e. below 85) range. As noted in chapter 3, five of these children were being transferred to special schools at the junior level.

REFERENCES

ABERCROMBIE, M. L. T. (1960) 'Perception and eye movements; some speculations on disorders in cerebral palsy', *Cerebral Palsy Bulletin*, 2, pp. 142–8.

ABERCROMBIE, M. L. T. (1964) *Perceptual and Visuo-motor Disorders in Cerebral Palsy*, Little Club Clinics in Developmental Medicine, 11, Spastics Society/Heinemann, London.

ANDERSON, E. M. (1973) 'Cognitive defects and behavioural disorders in children with spina bifida and hydrocephalus', *British Journal of Educational Psychology* (in press).

ASCHER, P. and SCHONELL, F. E. (1950) 'A survey of 400 cases of cerebral palsy in childhood', *Archives of Diseases in Childhood*, 25, p. 360.

BADELL-RIBERA, A., SHULMAN, K. and PADDOCK, N. (1966) 'The relationship of non-progressive hydrocephalus to intellectual functioning in children with spina bifida cystica', *Paediatrics*, 37, pp. 787–93.

BARSCH, R. H. and RUDDELL, B. (1962) 'A study of reading development among 77 children with cerebral palsy', *Cerebral Palsy Review*, 23 (2), pp. 3–10.

BRIMER, M. A. and DUNN, L. M. (1963) *Manual for the English Picture Vocabulary Tests*, NFER, London.

CLARK, M. M. (1970) *Reading Difficulties in Schools*, Penguin Books, Harmondsworth, Middlesex.

DAVIE, R., BUTLER, N. and GOLDSTEIN, H. (1972) *From Birth to Seven: The Second Report of the National Child Development Study (1958 Cohort)*, Longmans, London.

DOUGLAS, J. W. B. (1964) *The Home and the School*, MacGibbon and Kee, London.

DOUGLAS, J. W. B. and ROSS, J. M. (1965) 'The effects of absence on school performance', *British Journal of Educational Psychology*, 35, pp. 28–40.

FLOYER, E. B. (1965) *A Psychological Study of a City's Cerebral-Palsied Children*, British Council for the Welfare of Spastics, London.

HASKELL, S. H. (1972) *Arithmetical Disabilities in Programmed Instruction, A Remedial Approach*, C. C. Thomas, Illinois.

JOHNSON, J. C. (1962) *Educating Hearing-Impaired Children in Ordinary Schools*, University of Manchester Press.

LAURENCE, K. M. and TEW, B. J. (1967) 'Follow-up of sixty-five survivors from the four hundred and twenty-five cases of spina bifida born in South Wales between 1956 and 1962', *Developmental Medicine and Child Neurology*, Supplement 13, pp. 1–3.

LORBER, J. (1971) 'Results of treatment of myelomeningocele', *Developmental Medicine and Child Neurology*, 13 (3), pp. 279–303.

MILLER, E. and SETHI, L. (1971a) 'The effects of hydrocephalus on perception', *Developmental Medicine and Child Neurology*, Supplement 25, pp. 77–81.

MILLER, E. and SETHI, L. (1971b) 'Tactile matching in children with hydrocephalus', *Neuropaediatrie*, 3, pp. 191–4.

MORRIS, J. M. (1966) *Standards and Progress in Reading*, NFER, Slough, Bucks.

National Centre for Health Statistics (University of Pennsylvania) (1964), 'Automatic interaction detection programme', in chapters 2 and 4 in Sonquist, J. A. and Morgan, J. N. (eds.) *The Detection of Interaction Effects*, Monograph 35, Survey Research Centre, Institute for Social Research, University of Michigan, Ann Arbor.

NEALE, M. (1966) *Analysis of Reading Ability*, Macmillan, London.

PERLSTEIN, M. A. and HOOD, P. N. (1956) 'Infantile spastic hemiplegia. progress among cerebral palsied children', *Developmental Medicine and Centre de l'Enfance*, 6, p. 567.

PHILLIPS, C. J. and WHITE, R. R. (1964) 'The prediction of educational progress among cerebral palsied children', *Development Medicine and Child Neurology*, 6, pp. 167–74.

PRINGLE, M. L. KELLMER, BUTLER, N. R. and DAVIE, R. (1966) *11,000 Seven Year Olds*, Longmans, London.

PRINGLE, M. L. KELLMER and FIDDES, D. O. (1970) *The Challenge of Thalidomide*, National Bureau for Co-operation in Child Care, London.

PIDGEON, D. A. (1968) *Manual of Instructions for Non-Verbal Test 5*, NFER, Slough, Bucks.

RAVEN, J. C. (1965) *Guide to Using the Coloured Progressive Matrices*, H. J. Lewis, London.

RUTTER, M., TIZARD, J. and WHITMORE, K. (eds.) (1970) *Education, Health and Behaviour*, Longmans, London.

SCHONELL, F. J. and SCHONELL, F. E. (1957) *Diagnosis and Remedial Teaching in Arithmetic*, Oliver and Boyd, Edinburgh.

SOUTHGATE, V. (1959) *Southgate Group Reading Tests – Manual of Instructions*, University of London Press.

SPAIN, B. (1970) 'Spina bifida survey', GLC Research and Intelligence Unit, *Quarterly Bulletin*, 12, pp. 5–12.

VERNON, M. D. (1968) *Backward Readers*, College of Special Education, London.

WEDELL, K. (1964) 'Some aspects of perceptual motor development in young children', in Loring, J. (ed.) *Learning Problems of the Cerebral Palsied*, Spastics Society/Heinemann, London.

III Making Ordinary Schools Special

Chapter 8 · Special Arrangements in Ordinary Schools

Introduction

The findings presented in the preceding chapters suggest that the majority of PH children in this study, particularly those with purely physical disorders, were well placed in ordinary schools. This was true as regards both their academic and their social development. A minority, most of them children with neurological abnormalities, were only just 'getting by' academically, and would clearly have benefited from more individual and/or specialized help than they were given, although teachers nearly always thought that such help should be given within the framework of the ordinary school.

The overlap (in terms of type and severity of handicap) between children in ordinary and special schools has already been referred to and it has been pointed out that this study included severely handicapped children for whom special school had been a real possibility. A reasonable inference which could be drawn from these findings would therefore be that a substantial proportion of children at present in special schools (particularly those without neurological abnormalities) would be likely to do well in ordinary schools. A second inference which might be made, however, is that many children who have neurological abnormalities in addition to the physical handicap (whether they are at present in ordinary or special schools) are likely to need more specialized help than is given in an ordinary class. This means that some kind of alternative type of provision within the ordinary school must be considered if such children are to attend them.

Whatever type of arrangements are made the quality of provision must be good. Among those hesitant about seeing a larger proportion of PH children placed in ordinary schools there exists a real fear that this would deprive the children of the quality of medical care and treatment and specialized educational help that they would be given in a special school. Unfortunately such a fear tends to be self-fulfilling. If administrators and others are afraid that special provision in ordinary schools will be of an inferior quality, they tend to go on placing children in special schools, and to go on expanding provision there. In this way the energy, the constructive thought, the expertise and the money which might have gone into the improvement or expansion of provisions in ordinary schools continues to be mainly channelled into the special schools. There are exceptions and their number is growing, but until there is a much greater commitment to ordinary school placement, special provisions there are likely to remain inferior.

One of the signs of the general lack of interest in making special provisions in ordinary schools is that little has been written about the present state of affairs and how it could be improved, a recent exception being the survey of PH children in ordinary schools carried out by the Department of Education and Science. The main aim of this section of the book has been, therefore, to examine this whole question.

In this chapter the different forms which special provisions may take and the special arrangements needed in each case are discussed. The two main forms are firstly, provision for children placed individually in ordinary classes in their local (or nearest suitable) schools and secondly, the provision of special classes for PH children in ordinary schools. A third form of special provision which is becoming more popular is the modification of one primary school in each area so that all the suitable PH children in the area can be accommodated there in ordinary classes. The excellent arrangements which are being made in some areas show what can be done, although the general situation is far from satisfactory. For this reason I have included in the following chapter an account of practice in Scandinavia (particularly Sweden) where there is a much greater commitment to integration at both the national and local level.

1 Individual placement in ordinary classes

In the following section, the special provisions needed and the existing situation are discussed under the headings of transport, school design and special aids, personal assistance, physiotherapy and speech therapy, remedial teaching and the provision of information and advice, in particular to class teachers.

(i) TRANSPORT

PH children may require special transport to and from their local schools. This only applied to about a quarter of the junior group, six of whom came in wheelchairs, four by private car, one in a welfare department van, two by LEA buses and seven by taxis paid for by the LEA. Among the infants, one-third of the children came by taxi, four by private car and the remainder in wheelchairs or on foot. Taxi transport provided by the LEA is the most common form of special transport, costs being reduced if two or three children attend the same or neighbouring schools. Some taxi firms insist on the child being accompanied by an adult, but otherwise few problems other than cost exist.

(ii) SCHOOL DESIGN AND SPECIAL AIDS

In this study class teachers were asked to list all the modifications which had been made, or were wanted, and all the special aids in use or required. Great variations were found in the extent to which physical modifications were needed but often minor adaptations were sufficient.

The greatest problems are those created by (i) poor mobility and (ii) special toileting needs. In the junior group 40·5 per cent of the children had impaired mobility. Six were virtually confined to wheelchairs and four others used wheelchairs for at least part of their time in school. The problems of the infant group were greater. Only three of the twenty-five children were fully mobile: ten others had severe problems and could not manage steps on their own (five used wheelchairs for most of the time) and seven more had considerable problems. Sixteen out of the twenty-five used walking aids. (Comparable figures for children in England and Wales as a whole are shown in appendix C.I.) In the junior schools ramps had been provided in only three cases (once by a parent). In four other cases they were badly needed; two of the schools were waiting for replies for a request to the LEA, while in the other two no request had been made. These were all one-level schools but there were nearly always a few steps up and down which a busy teacher might have to haul a wheelchair several times a day. Ramps had been provided in four of the infant schools and in two other cases were needed. Local authorities did seem ready to provide ramps when these were requested but one problem seemed to be that teachers were unaware that they would do so.

The other major difficulty concerned toileting. The problem might take the form of getting a wheelchair into the toilet, or of a child with a walking aid getting in and out easily, or space might be needed for a welfare assistant to change or express a child, or for the child to manœuvre in to empty his appliance. The main needs were for space and privacy, while minor modifications such as the provision of hand rails or holding springs on the doors were sometimes useful. The problem is a considerable one. 16 per cent of the junior group were incontinent and sixteen of the twenty-five infants. Six of them wore appliances, the others pads or nappies and twelve needed complete toilet assistance.

Advance planning when a new school is being designed is really required if adequate space and privacy are to be provided, especially since increasing numbers of incontinent spina bifida children are reaching school age. This is still only an ideal and at present schools have to cope in a variety of *ad hoc* ways. In one school, two toilets were to be knocked into one, in others children were changed in the medical room, or the handicapped child was allowed to use the more spacious staff toilets. In a very few cases a hand rail or holding spring or a lock on the door had been provided and in one case, a bidet. In one area the local deputy medical officer of health had made a survey of ordinary schools where there were spina bifida children to see what sorts of modifications were required.

Frequently modifications which would have been useful had not been requested simply because the staff, unused to coping with P H children, had not thought of them. In particular there was a lack of awareness of the child's need for privacy. This was partly because parents sometimes felt that they had been lucky to get their child into an ordinary school and did not wish to 'cause trouble' or 'draw attention to him' by making it known that he was very sensitive about the lack of such privacy. It was also the case that the children were rarely asked directly about what minor modifications would be helpful.

When it came to the provision of special furniture or aids in the classroom very little had been done. In special schools, great care is taken to ensure that the furniture used by the P H child is tailor-made and the physiotherapist is nearly always consulted. Among the juniors however, only three children had specially designed chairs or desks and among the infants only five. When teachers were asked whether anything was required, the only requests were in one case for a table that a wheelchair could go under and in the other for a special table for a child who stood most of the time. Only rarely had the child's needs been discussed with a physiotherapist.

Impaired hand control was a common problem, affecting one-third of the children in each group. In most cases the impairment was a minor one, but in the case of certain children with cerebral palsy, thalidomide deformities, peripheral neuritis, rheumatoid arthritis and arthrogryposis, it was considerable. Little in the way of special equipment was being used. Two of the children had electric typewriters provided by the LEA and in another case this has been suggested, but otherwise, apart from a few simple aids such as thicker pencils, the children were using normal equipment. Again it appeared to be a case of teachers not knowing what was available or where to obtain it.

To sum up, local authorities were generally willing to make modifications or to provide special aids but were rarely requested to do so. There appeared to be several reasons for this. Firstly, many children in the study were able to use normal equipment satisfactorily and some had rejected efforts to provide anything 'special'. Secondly, teachers were unaware that a problem existed (for example the need for toilet privacy). Thirdly, the child's needs were obvious (for instance poor hand control) but the teacher did not know what special equipment was available or who to approach for advice. Fourthly, teachers knew exactly what they wanted (for example ramps, or a special chair) but once again did not know who to approach or were too busy to find out.

Two things seem essential. Firstly, before the PH child arrives in the school, both the head and the class teacher should meet the person who assessed him and recommended his placement there, as well as the parents, to discuss any special arrangements which may be needed. Secondly, after the child has been in school for a few weeks, the class teacher should be visited and asked whether there are any problems relating to the general management or education of the child which she or he would like to discuss. The actual ways in which such information and advice might be provided are discussed later in this chapter but the need for direct contact between the class teacher and a supportive 'expert' (whoever this may be) cannot be overemphasized. In Sweden and Denmark the problem of the provision of technical aids has been at least partly met by the establishment of state-run regional centres to which ordinary teachers can apply for advice and equipment. It might be possible for local authorities, either separately or in combination, to set up similar centres here, and in some cases these might be linked to special schools. In London an aids centre has been set up by the Disabled Living Foundation, where aids of all kinds can be examined and demonstrated.

(iii) PERSONAL ASSISTANCE

In Sweden, a PH child in an ordinary school is entitled, where necessary, to a full-time personal assistant. This system is practised by a few LEAs here, such staff being known variously as 'welfare assistants', infant or junior 'helpers' and so on. Five of the juniors in this study and sixteen of the infants had such assistants. In the case of four of the juniors and five of the infants a full-time assistant had been allocated to one child. In seven further cases, two children in a school shared a full-time helper, while the other children had part-time helpers. A few examples are given below of the duties of such assistants, as the system, which is still confined to certain LEAs, should be more widely known.

Peter is a child with severe internal congenital deformities which have resulted in bowel incontinence. He was placed in an ordinary school with a full-time welfare assistant, appointed initially for a trial period. In this case, the assistant was well informed about his difficulties. She has met the local assistant education officer for handicapped children, and with the head visited Peter's infant school, to talk with his previous assistant, and also visited a school for spina bifida children. Her main duties are to ensure that he goes to the toilet frequently to prevent accidents, to 'be around' all the time, but especially during PE and games in case accidents occur, and to change him. She also supervises his intake of roughage at mealtimes. For the rest of her time she helps in the school in other ways. Ultimately Peter will be able to cope with his own management, but in the meantime the presence of a sensible adult who understands his problems is very reassuring and Peter was one of the best-adjusted children in the study.

Another example is provided by James and Robin, two fairly heavily handicapped children with spina bifida and hydrocephalus whose parents were very anxious for ordinary school placement. They share a welfare assistant who previously worked as a district nurse. Her experience also included rehabilitation work with children in hospital and she was invited by the education department to take on this job. Her duties keep her almost fully occupied. Both children are incontinent and require complete toilet assistance; both spend at least part of the time in wheelchairs and need much assistance in moving around the school; while the other children do PE she does daily individual exercises with them which their physiotherapist has taught her. Otherwise she helps generally in the classroom at the class teacher's request.

Welfare assistants are not only employed to help with incontinent children. Mark, for example, has severe haemophilia and at 5 years old needs full-time supervision from a welfare assistant who also takes him from school to his nearby home and back at lunchtime. Paul has relapsing peripheral neuritis and his muscle power can vary enormously. His assistant's duties are to supervise him generally, to ensure that he takes his steroid tablets, to stay with him in the classroom at morning break and to go for a walk with him at lunchtime as the playground is not felt to be safe for him. During PE lessons she gives him (and a few classmates) specially planned exercises which his mother has shown her. Eventually, if his condition improves, the amount of time she spends with him may be phased out and she may take on more general duties in the school.

The duties of welfare assistants are thus very varied. They include general supervision, help on the care side (with toileting, moving, dressing and feeding) and individual help during physical activities such as music and movement, PE, games, nature walks and longer expeditions. Sometimes they include responsibility for doing special exercises with the children. Welfare assistants may also (if the teacher requests this and under her supervision) give individual help in the classroom, particularly with the basic skills. It had been expected that teachers might feel uneasy about the presence of another adult in the classroom. In fact only one teacher expressed such a reservation and on the contrary teachers frequently commented on how helpful the assistants were. Clearly the more skilled the teacher, the better able she was to utilize to the full this extra help both inside and outside the classroom. In some cases welfare assistants spent part of their time helping with other children in the same or different classes, an arrangement which reduced the danger that the PH child would become overdependent on his helper.

In only two (out of twenty-one) cases had the personal assistant system not worked well. In one case (fortunately rare) the child and his assistant simply did not get on. In the other an assistant with two PH children to look after found the job 'boring' and requested a transfer. Part of the trouble had been her lack of information about the management of the children. For example in PE 'I never take him out of his chair, as I'm afraid the others will bump into him. I've never been told what limits I can go to with him . . . and I'm very worried about the valve.' It is at best an inefficient use of resources and at worst positively detrimental to a child to be provided with a full-time assistant who overprotects him to the extent that he stays in his chair all day, never joins in and reaches a state where he will do nothing on his own initiative either physically or academically. An assistant who has never been properly informed about the child's difficulties and about how to treat him cannot be blamed for this state of affairs. Generally the mothers had given sensible guidance to the assistant but cases did exist where the assistant had learned mainly by trial and error. In one local authority, the adviser for special education was hoping to set up courses for assistants in ordinary schools. For the time being, however, what is essential is that the assistant is at the outset given adequate guidance and support, particularly on the medical side.

(iv) THE PROVISION OF THERAPY

(a) Physiotherapy

A common argument in favour of special school placement is that only there can intensive physiotherapy be provided for those who need it. Certainly the provision of physiotherapy for children in ordinary schools is a major problem, but it will not be solved until a more constructive approach is taken, that is until we ask, 'How could physiotherapy best be provided for PH children in ordinary schools in areas of different kinds?' This may mean the setting up of a research project designed specifically to answer this question.

What was in fact happening in the ordinary schools? In the recent DES survey (*Health of the School Child*, 1972) it was found that 12 per cent of PH children in ordinary schools, in particular cerebral-palsied children, required physiotherapy. 90 per cent of these obtained it, in 66 per cent of cases in hospital and in only 3·5 per cent of cases in school. In this study, among the juniors a similar proportion (12 per cent) were having physiotherapy. In most cases this was provided once a week in the local hospital during or after school hours, although sometimes it was more often. One hemiplegic, for example, has physiotherapy three times a week at the local hospital school. He is picked up by ambulance at school during the afternoon and taken home by ambulance afterwards. Altogether he misses about two hours of schooling a week. It appeared to be only rarely that a child who needed physiotherapy was not getting any, but this does occur. The team placing one hemiplegic child (who transferred from a special school) had agreed that admission to an ordinary school was a 'first priority' but that 'continuity of physiotherapy was an objective of nearly as much importance'. In effect the two needs proved incompatible, as he was placed in his local village school and arrangements to transport him to the local town for physiotherapy proved so complicated that in the end this was never done.

In the infant group nearly half of the children required physiotherapy. In one village school the physiotherapist visited the cerebral-palsied child once a fortnight; for the rest of the time the welfare assistant did the exercises she had been taught with the child each day, while two of the older children did daily 'walking practice' with him. In the case of two spina bifida children, the school was visited weekly by a remedial gymnast. Each child had a twenty-minute individual session with her, and a thirty-minute session with a small group of fifteen other children who needed specialized help. Each day the welfare assistant carried out the walking and balancing exercises she had been taught, including work on parallel bars provided by the LEA and set up in the corridor. In both cases and in other cases where physiotherapists (for example from the spastics centres) occasionally visited the school, teachers were noticeably more confident that they were 'doing the right thing'.

In all the other cases the children had to travel for their physiotherapy, generally once a week and occasionally either more or less frequently. Three children went to local spastics centres and the others to hospitals. Usually an afternoon of schooling a week was missed. Occasionally physiotherapy was given after school hours but generally mothers had younger children to look after then, and

sometimes there were real difficulties. One child who had physiotherapy twice a week had to go to hospital in the mornings as this
was when the children's sessions were held. Delays in ambulance
transport meant that often two whole mornings a week of schooling,
a time when the basic skills were taught, were missed. The fact
that he was of above average intelligence and that his welfare
assistant gave him extra individual help eased the situation, but it
shows what can happen when frequent physiotherapy is felt to be
essential.

The ideal arrangement is for the therapist to visit the school and to
treat the child regularly there, but because of her limited time and of
the inadequate space and equipment this is rarely possible. The
whole issue really needs to be looked at much more systematically.
Could mobile physiotherapy units be developed, for example?
Could domiciliary physiotherapy services, already being used in a
few areas for pre-school children be expanded? Could more of the
welfare assistants be trained to carry out simple daily exercises with
the children during normal P E or games periods? Could more use
be made of facilities in special schools? Could the timing of visits to
local hospitals for physiotherapy be better planned? How can we
ensure that there is adequate liaison between the therapist and the
ordinary classroom teacher? Until constructive proposals are put
forward to answer questions such as these, the present situation is
unlikely to improve and there will continue to be children in ordinary schools getting no physiotherapy who would clearly benefit
from it, or getting insufficient physiotherapy or missing too much
school. There will also be children in special schools who, were
this question solved, could probably be transferred to ordinary
schools.

(b) *Speech therapy*

A much smaller proportion of PH children in ordinary schools will
require speech therapy than physiotherapy. Of those in the DES
survey 3·5 per cent needed it, but only two in three of these children
were having any. Although speech therapy is much more likely to be
available as part of the services for non-handicapped children, it is
unfortunately the case that in both ordinary and special schools
speech therapists are nearly always in short supply.

In the junior group five children (6·8 per cent) were thought to
need speech therapy but in only two cases was this provided, in one

case at school and in the other at a local health clinic. Four of the twenty-five infants also required speech therapy. One child spent an afternoon a week at a spastics centre where both speech therapy and physiotherapy were given, in two cases the speech therapist visited the school and in the fourth case no speech therapy was available. There are, it is clear, marked variations in the availability of speech therapy, but generally the situation is unsatisfactory and special arrangements would have to be made if, for example, more cerebral-palsied children were placed in ordinary schools.

(v) THE PROVISION OF REMEDIAL OR OTHER SPECIALIZED
    TEACHING HELP

Most PH children of normal intelligence placed in ordinary schools are unlikely to need a great deal more extra help on the teaching side than do their non-handicapped peers. This is especially true in the infant schools where, as Webb (1967) points out, 'the variable pace, and possibility of individual or small group work makes considera-tion of special needs less difficult than it might be in a more rigid situation', and teachers both here and in the junior schools often pointed out that PH children were much less of a problem than were emotionally disturbed children.

Having said this, however, a sizeable minority of the PH children did require extra help, in particular two groups, firstly children who had had long periods of hospitalization or were frequently absent and secondly children with neurological abnormalities who had specific learning difficulties or who learned slowly because of atten-tional problems.

For the first group, and for some of the second, the normal re-medial services provided in the school should be able to provide the kind of help needed although these vary markedly in their avail-ability and in their quality from one local authority to another. A primary school may have its own remedial teachers, or make use of peripatetic remedial staff, or remedial teachers may be attached to the school psychological service in centres to which the children are taken.

For children with specific learning disabilities the situation is much less satisfactory. To start with, their difficulties often go un-diagnosed; where they have been diagnosed little advice is at present available for teachers about how to cope. In a later section more is said about the provision of advice to teachers and about different ways of organizing special provision within the ordinary school for children such as these.

Table 8.1 below gives some idea of the needs of the children in this study. Teachers were asked 'Do you think X needs extra help in reading/arithmetic? and then whether and under what arrangements such help was being given. Unfortunately there was not time to interview teachers about the children in the control group as well, but as the proportions of handicapped children needing extra help were roughly equivalent to the proportions of low achievers in this group it was likely that teachers would have described approximately 26 per cent of the controls (this being the proportion of low achievers) as also needing help in reading and a somewhat higher proportion in arithmetic. As has been pointed out, it was the children with neurological abnormalities who were most in need of extra help, but it was not possible to judge the extent to which the existence of specific learning difficulties accounted for this need since few had been systematically assessed to see whether these existed.

TABLE 8.1. *Percentage of children needing extra teaching help: junior group*

| | Groups | | |
	Children with neurological abnormalities	Children without neurological abnormalities	Total PH group
Need extra help in reading	65·3	35·4	45·9
% of above group getting extra help in reading	64·7	58·8	61·7
Need extra help in arithmetic	80·7	31·2	48·6
% of above group getting extra help in arithmetic	25·0	20·0	23·0

The first obvious point is that large numbers of PH children who needed extra help were not getting it, especially in number work, a situation which reflects the general inadequacy of remedial services in ordinary schools. When extra help was given, the arrangements made were extremely varied. Overall, half the children receiving remedial help in reading had daily help, usually in a small group for from twenty minutes to an hour. The help might be given by a trained remedial teacher in the school, a peripatetic teacher or the class teacher, while two children were receiving such help in small classes for immigrants and four others in a 'remedial class'. In most other cases remedial help was given two or three times a week.

Arrangements for extra help in arithmetic were much less satisfactory and such help was usually only available if there was a remedial class in the school or if the class teacher herself was able to allocate a little of her time to giving extra help in this area.

In the infant group there were five children whom teachers considered particularly in need of extra help. In two cases this was because of the children's high absence rate while the other three were children with spina bifida and hydrocephalus. All these children had very poor concentration and 'did nothing' unless their teachers were 'standing over' them. In one case the spina bifida child had been placed in a reception class of thirty-six children, many of them immigrants. She spent her time 'socializing' with the other children, and although the welfare assistant was able to give some help, the class teacher was clearly too busy to do so. There were also two children with cerebral palsy in the infant group who needed more help than the teachers could give. Suggestions about what could be done to improve this situation are made in the following section.

(vi) THE PROVISION OF INFORMATION AND ADVICE

Up to this point the special needs of the children have been considered; equally important and often neglected are the needs of the staff, in particular the class teachers, for information and advice. As Webb (1967) points out, 'teachers can only be expected to give the right kind of help to the child who is their daily responsibility when they have full information about him, particularly from doctors and parents.'

In this section three aspects of this question are considered in the light of the findings in this study. Firstly the situation as it is now was investigated. Class teachers were asked whether they knew they were to have a PH child in their class, whether, and if so why, they were worried about this and what information about the child they had been provided with. Secondly the extent to which they were satisfied with the information they had been given was examined and they were asked what else they would like to have known. Finally, suggestions are made about how the present situation might be improved.

Eighty-eight of the teachers knew in advance that they were to have a PH child in their class, either because they had been informed by the head, or because the child was moving up from a lower class. However, one in six of the junior school teachers had not known the nature of the handicap in advance and there were occasional cases where the teacher did not know the real nature of the disorder until my visit to the school, while other teachers confessed they 'didn't really know' what (for example) spina bifida was.

All the teachers were asked whether they had felt worried on hearing there was to be a PH child in the class, and also whether they still felt worried, and their replies are shown in Table 8.2.

TABLE 8.2. *Class teachers' anxieties about having a PH child in the class*

Extent of anxiety	At the time of initial placement				After at least one term			
	Infant teachers		Junior teachers		Infant teachers		Junior teachers	
	No.	%	No.	%	No.	%	No.	%
Not worried	13	52	42	57	21	84	69	93
A little worried	8	32	19	26	3	12	3	4
Considerably worried	4	16	13	17	1	4	2	3
TOTALS	25		74		25		74	

Nearly half had been worried, the reasons for this generally being related to lack of information about what the child's physical condition would involve, in terms of daily management. There are probably a number of teachers who refuse to take PH children for this very reason, and this is particularly unfortunate in view of the fact that the proportion of worried teachers drops sharply after the child has been in the class for a few weeks, the worries which remain now tending to relate more to educational than to physical problems.

A number of studies have been carried out on the attitudes of teachers towards the placement of children with different types of physical or emotional disorders. It has been found that the two factors which are most important in producing favourable attitudes towards their integration are, on the one hand, the amount and quality of information teachers have about them, and on the other, contact factors, that is, experience with them. For this reason teachers in one school, who were not actually in contact with the PH children there, did not have more favourable attitudes than teachers in schools where there were no PH children. Haring and his colleagues (1958) also found that 'increased knowledge *per se* was not a significant factor in effecting modifications in teachers' attitudes' but that classroom experience with the children played a crucial role.

What were the main reasons which teachers in the present study gave for their initial anxieties? These are summarized in Table 8.3.

TABLE 8.3. *Reasons for class teachers' anxieties*

Nature of anxiety	No. of times mentioned
Coping generally	10
Fear of injury	19
What to do in PE/games	6
Coping with classmates' reactions	6
Being able to give enough attention	5
Personal feelings about the handicap	4
Coping with incontinence	3

Several teachers were simply worried about how they would cope generally. A teacher with two spina bifida children (although she had an assistant) had been worried 'about how they would fit in . . . whether everything would have to be geared to them . . . whether I'd be able to give them enough attention. It was the unknown quantity which bothered me.' For another teacher 'It was my first teaching post and I was on probation. I wasn't sure generally how I'd cope, or what the reactions of the other children would be.'

More than one in five teachers, however, were quite specific about the fact that it was the possibility of injury to the child which worried them. They were anxious not only about haemophiliac children but also about children in wheelchairs and in fact about most children with impaired mobility. Paradoxically, the better integrated the child, the more a teacher may have to worry about. A child who is taken out of his wheelchair and encouraged to crawl in an infant classroom, to pull himself up on the furniture, to propel himself through the corridors on a trolley and to participate in PE will obviously need more careful supervision than one who sits in a wheelchair all day. However, teachers who had encouraged the children to be as mobile as possible were not, after a few weeks, any more anxious than those who had been more cautious. Once they had seen the child in action, knew exactly what the dangers were and had spoken to the other children in the class about these, their fears about injuries generally disappeared.

A study of injuries at school carried out by the Department of Education and Science in 1965 (*Health of the School Child*, 1969) produced an overall accident rate, over three terms, of 11 per cent, the rate in secondary schools being rather higher and in primary schools lower. Fractured bones were most common, followed by cuts and abrasions, and accidents occurred most often in the playground, followed by playing fields, gymnasiums and classrooms. Is this rate higher among PH children in ordinary schools? This was not the case in this study. Teachers were asked whether the juniors had been injured at school during the previous term. Only four of the controls had been injured (two fractures, one cut requiring stitches and one black eye) and two of the PH children, giving an incidence of approximately 3 per cent per term for both groups. Both the PH children were haemophiliacs: one had fallen and cut himself slightly in the playground, the other in the classroom, internal bruising and bleeding resulting. However they were back in school after a few days. Almost all the absences of the haemophiliacs resulted from injuries sustained outside school. Certainly PH children in ordinary schools do require careful supervision, but this seems to be effective in preventing an above average injury rate.

The next point about which several teachers had been worried related to the child's participation in physical activities at school. How far could and should he participate, and how would he feel if he had to watch? Generally teachers had a talk with the parent, which resulted in their getting the child to tackle what he felt he could manage, but some were overcautious. Teachers do require much more specific information about the children's disabilities and also more practical suggestions about how physical activities could be modified to enable them to take part. A useful booklet has been published on physical education for PH children in special schools (DES, 1971); something similar but geared to ordinary schools is now needed.

Teachers were also worried about how they would cope with the other children's reactions to the PH child. This was discussed in chapter 4, but there is also the question of how they cope with their own reactions. No teacher should be forced to accept a child for whom she feels a physical aversion; however, only four of the ninety-nine teachers in the study confessed to having had such feelings (one felt 'squeamish', another 'dreaded' having the child) and only one still felt uneasy. In all four cases the children were handicapped by limb deficiencies. The sample was of course self-selected, that is, teachers with very strong feelings of aversion would already have had the chance to refuse to take such a child, but certainly among primary school teachers this seems to be a minor problem. Three teachers had also been rather worried about coping with incontinence (for example, accidents in the classroom or in PE) or with the welfare assistant's absence, but again this was largely because of their initial lack of practical information on the medical side.

Many of the worries described above spring from a lack of information. How much information did teachers possess, and who had supplied this? Firstly teachers were asked whether they had received any information about their PH pupil, and if so, who had provided this. The main findings are summarized in Tables 8.4 and 8.5 below.

TABLE 8.4. *Information provided to class teachers about the PH child*

	Infant teachers No. = 25		Junior teachers No. = 74	
No. of sources	No.	%	No.	%
No information	0	0	6	8
One person	2	8	24	32
Two people	15	60	22	30
More than two people	8	32	22	30

TABLE 8.5. *Class teachers' sources of information about the PH child*

Source	Infant teachers No.	%	Junior teachers No.	%
Head	18	72	33	45
Colleague	8	32	40	54
Parent	22	88	39	53
Welfare assistant	6	24	3	4
School nurse	1	4	4	5
School medical officer	1	4	1	1
Physiotherapist	3	12	1	1

In very rare cases other sources of information had been available, for example meetings with staff from the child's previous school, with a psychologist or speech therapist or health visitor, or visits to special schools, but generally the main source was the head (whose information was based usually on a brief letter from the school health department) and the mother. It was extremely rare for the class teacher to have met the school medical officer and only occasionally had she seen the medical records (which are not always kept in the school). In the infant schools teachers had found the mother the most valuable source of information and also the welfare assistant, while in junior schools colleagues tended to provide most information.

At this point it is worth saying a little more on the subject of parent–teacher contacts. Kellmer Pringle *et al.* (1966) and others have shown that parental interest and school performance are closely related. In this study, one measure of parental interest was the number of occasions during the last school year on which one or both of the parents had talked to the class teacher. This was rather a crude measure since a 'talk' with the teacher could range from a few words at the school gate or 'open day' to a long discussion about the child's progress. The main reason for asking mothers this question, however, was to find out whether any major differences existed between the control and the handicapped groups. Table 8.6 indicates that the amount of contact was very similar for both.

The close similarities may seem a little surprising but one factor which undoubtedly operates is that parents of handicapped children often make a point of 'not bothering' the class teacher more than is absolutely necessary. The table also conceals the fact that contacts

TABLE 8.6. *Contact between parents and teachers: comparison of handicapped and control groups*

No. of meetings with class teacher in the last year	Handicapped No. = 74 %	Controls No. = 98 %
Never	6·7	10·2
Once	27·0	28·5
2 or more times	66·2	61·2

with the teacher were in the case of the handicapped group more often initiated by the mother, whereas in the case of the controls mothers were more likely to leave it to the school to initiate contact. In the case of the infant group, contact with the class teacher was very frequent since many mothers brought their children to school.

In addition to being questioned about their sources of information regarding their PH pupils, teachers were also asked about the content of their training courses, and about prior contact with handicapped people. Some 32 per cent of the infant teachers and 41 per cent of the junior school teachers had, while at training college, attended lectures on handicapped children or visited special schools, but there had been little specifically about PH pupils and the general feeling was that the lectures and visits had helped them very little in coping with the present situation. About 57 per cent of the teachers had had some prior personal contact with handicapped children or adults and most felt that this had given them a better understanding of a handicapped person's problems. Several teachers had tried to obtain information about spina bifida from local libraries with little success, and the excellent booklets published by the Association for Spina Bifida and Hydrocephalus did not appear to be reaching the ordinary schools. Where visits to special schools had been arranged, this was usually entirely on the teachers' own initiative.

How satisfied had teachers been about the information they were given? Their feelings are summarized in Table 8.7 below.

Two in three junior teachers were satisfied with the information they had been given but only one in five of the infant teachers, this difference reflecting the fact that the infant group was much more heavily handicapped. Those who were 'satisfied' can be divided into three groups. Firstly, in many cases the child's handicap was an

TABLE 8.7. *Teacher satisfaction with information provided about their PH pupils*

	Infant teachers		Junior teachers	
	No.	%	No.	%
Satisfied	5	20	49	66
Not very satisfied	10	40	22	30
Very dissatisfied	10	40	3	4
TOTALS	25		74	

uncomplicated one (such as a limb deficiency) to which the child had adjusted well, and no real problems existed. Secondly, a very few teachers did not want to know more about the handicap: one teacher with a spina bifida child put it this way: 'He's very well-adjusted . . . and I'd only find it complicating to know what was going on inside his head.'

Thirdly, a small number of teachers were satisfied because they were getting all the information and support they wished for. Usually this was from the parent, and only occasionally from the local health authorities. In one area, for example, the school medical officer visited the school personally before a child was placed there, the medical records were fully available and, said the head, 'I can ring and ask the medical officer for advice or a visit at any time I want.' Possibly other doctors would do this were they asked to, but teachers had rarely been encouraged to approach them.

Why were so many teachers dissatisfied and what sort of information would they have liked? The great majority wanted more information on the medical side. Children were often placed in ordinary schools and a minimum amount of information provided by letter only. There were cases in which the schools had not been told the child was incontinent; the fact that he had hydrocephalus as well as spina bifida might be omitted, and if hydrocephalus was mentioned it rarely meant anything to the teachers. One head who had asked for more information about a spina bifida child was told that she could not have access to confidential medical records (she had never asked for these) and that the information she had been given was 'adequate'. She 'simply didn't know who to turn to for help'. This attitude that teachers should not see the medical records was not uncommon.

Another head who had shown great willingness to take PH children had

> never had a talk with anyone who really knew anything about spina bifida . . . all I know is what I've got from the library. Information about the children is never offered, I've always had to ask for it. I'm not grousing, but I feel that as we cope with the children all day it would be helpful if the health departments were more forthcoming. Once the doctor did come . . . but made no comments at all [about the two spina bifida children] and there was no chance of a chat.

The lack of information was not confined to spina bifida children. One teacher with a haemophiliac child 'would very much like to have met someone personally to discuss what sort of things are likely to go wrong, and what to do if this happens'. Another who had a severely handicapped haemophiliac in a wheelchair in her class would have 'loved to have met the doctor' and thought it a 'shame that the doctor never discusses things directly with the class teacher'. She did not know whether or when it was safe to take the child out of the chair, whether he would become 'grotesque' sitting there all day, or what could be done in the way of physiotherapy. A teacher with a child who suffered from relapsing peripheral neuritis had 'never been told anything officially about his condition . . . for instance if he's likely to collapse suddenly and what to do if this happens'. Teachers with cerebral-palsied children were often equally in the dark. In the case of a child with ataxic diplegia, the teacher had 'no medical information about what was involved, or what sort of behaviour to expect'.

Often teachers wanted straightforward technical details, for example about the ileal loop operation and how to cope with the child's appliance, about how much feeling a child had and how much pressure could be exerted (for example in PE), about what height a desk should be, what effect a fall would have on a child's valve and what physical activities he could and could not take part in. While it was a lack of information about the medical aspects of the child's condition which caused most dissatisfaction, some teachers also wanted to know more about the educational implications of the condition. If a child had been assessed by an educational psychologist or doctor it was very rare that details were made known to the class teacher. Teachers were also generally worried about how far they should 'push' PH children educationally, and had little idea of what standards to expect. Even when the child's difficulties had been diagnosed, teachers were given little practical advice. As one teacher put it, 'it's very frustrating to be told that a child has a particular problem which could be trained [in this case visuo-motor difficulties] and then not be told what to do'.

Considering the paucity of information and advice which class teachers, heads and often welfare assistants received, it was remarkable that their attitude to integration was still in almost all cases so positive. One teacher for instance was changing a doubly incontinent spina bifida child in her class two or three times a day, worrying in the meantime that it was 'not fair to the other children to be out of the classroom so much', yet was still convinced of the rightness of the placement. In this case the local authority was quick to provide a welfare assistant when the situation was brought to their notice. Another teacher, although she already had forty children in her class, offered to take two new children with spina bifida, although both were in wheelchairs. Heads often went to considerable trouble to make special arrangements to suit handicapped children, for example reorganizing the location of classes so that the PH child's room was accessible to a wheelchair. An experienced village head took on a very handicapped cerebral-palsied child before she had any promise of help because she was convinced of the social value of such placement and felt that 'If I'd been the mother I'd have wanted him to go to an ordinary school, at least until he's older.' There is a slight danger that heads known to be sympathetic towards taking very handicapped PH children may be overloaded with them, but most local authorities were aware of this. Once a school had had experience with one such child, an interest in taking more soon developed. There is, of course, the other danger that one unsuccessful placement may have the opposite effect, but only three heads out of all the schools visited expressed strong reservations in the light of actual experience with PH children.

Despite this, the situation as regards the provision of information and advice is most unsatisfactory and careful thought must be given to how it can be remedied. Ordinary teachers need help in two major areas, in coping firstly with the children's special educational needs and secondly with their physical condition and its management. As far as special educational needs are concerned, there were, as Rutter et al. (1970) found on the Isle of Wight, enormous inadequacies in the remedial services: as was stated among their conclusions, '[educationally backward] children were not getting what was needed'.

How much can actually be done by a teacher in a large ordinary class is debatable. Tyson (1970) describes experimental work being carried out in Chicago. The aim here is to help the classroom teacher to undertake some of the necessary remediation for children with learning disabilities. Initially the child is assessed by a team of psychologists and psychoeducational diagnosticians (teachers with an advanced training in diagnostic and remedial techniques). Next, a plan of remediation is decided on and the psychoeducational diagnostician starts this off herself in the school, all the time keeping the teacher informed of progress and gradually encouraging her to take on an increasing share of the specialized work. Tyson ends her description of this type of advisory service with the comment, 'whether teachers in primary schools in the UK with classes of up to forty would be capable of undertaking specialized remedial work for possibly 10 per cent of the children in their classroom is a matter for speculation'.

There can be no doubt that many teachers would like to be better equipped to meet the needs of such children. One local authority which recently set up short in-service training courses on learning difficulties of different kinds found them vastly oversubscribed. At the same time, as the authors of the Isle of Wight study point out (Rutter *et al.*, 1970), there are a fair number of people in most local authorities who should be able to fill the role of educational consultants; yet 'how best to make use of the specialist knowledge available in many areas has received remarkably little study'. There is also a mistaken feeling among some teachers that to have to ask for advice implies incompetence on their part.

This may be partly why the teachers in the study were more likely to draw attention to the lack of advice and information they had received about the child's physical needs than about his educational needs. There can be no doubt, however, that more liaison is needed between the school health service and the schools themselves. It is very desirable that a school should be visited by a local authority medical officer before a substantially handicapped child is placed there, that the medical records should be made available to the head and the class teacher concerned and that the class teacher should have the opportunity to discuss her anxieties on the medical side, both initially and after the child has been in the school for some weeks, with a well-informed person. Much rethinking is needed about how such liaison can be attained, especially when in 1974 the school health service (in its present form) disappears.

Many of the medical, educational and other problems which the placement of PH children in ordinary schools may give rise to could be met, and in some areas are being met to a limited extent, by the appointment of advisers in special education with particular responsibility for handicapped children in ordinary schools. The details of such a service (including the amount of specialization regarding the handicaps covered) need careful working out, but a short account of an American programme of this kind by Rogers, Haarer and Scandary (1969) may indicate the lines along which such a service might develop. The programme is known as the 'teacher counselor programme for the physically handicapped' and was devised by the Michigan department of public instruction specifically to meet the need created by the placement of larger numbers of handicapped children in ordinary classes. The children in question included those described in this country as physically handicapped, delicate, partially sighted and partially hearing children. One teacher counselor for the physically handicapped (TCPH) can be employed for every 2,500 school-age children: a recent survey in Michigan indicated that about 10 per cent of the children had special needs of these kinds so that such a person's caseload could be as many as 250 children, many of whom however would require little help.

The TCPH performs a variety of functions, all being designed to assist the PH child and/or his teacher in the ordinary class. Duties include eight main areas as follows:

1 Assisting in the discovery and placement of PH children suitable for ordinary classes.

2 Serving as a resource person for the ordinary class teacher. This may include giving the teacher background information about the handicap and the specific disability, supplementing information in the medical records which might be helpful in the learning situation, and contacting the local health services, the hospitals, the social agencies and any other sources which might provide useful information and help.

3 Working individually with a child who is having difficulty in keeping up with his work in cases where the teacher has not the necessary training and/or the time, or helping the teacher in

selecting suitable programmes, giving advice on what she could do in P E and other problem areas.

4 Assisting the teacher in acquiring special materials or equipment which will contribute to the child's education.

5 Acting as a referral agent to obtain treatment or diagnosis for the PH child.

6 Assisting the child's parents through home calls and contacts in understanding the child's educational needs.

7 Keeping the local school administration informed as to the progress and adjustment of P H children in ordinary schools.

8 Giving vocational guidance to P H children in high schools.

Many of these services reflect exactly the sort of help the ordinary teachers in this study said they required, particularly those outlined in 2, 3 and 4. Other duties not listed here include ensuring that information is passed on when a child moves from a special to an ordinary school or vice versa, or from one ordinary school to another, and also getting help for pre-school children. Certainly the time has come to recognize the need for such a service and the fact that a number of local authorities here have started experimenting with the provision of help of this kind is extremely encouraging.

THREE CASE HISTORIES

This chapter has been mainly concerned with deficiencies in the special arrangements made for P H children in ordinary schools. It is equally important to stress the fact that in many cases successful arrangements have been made for them, and three examples are given below. These cases were chosen since the children were all severely handicapped and between them illustrate three types of disability commonly found in ordinary schools, that is, cerebral palsy, spina bifida with hydrocephalus and severe congenital abnormalities affecting limb functions (in this case arthrogryposis).

Case 1

Mary is $7\frac{1}{2}$ years old and has cerebral palsy (mixed quadriplegia and athetosis). She has very poor hand control and difficulties in dressing, eating and writing. Both her legs are affected and although she can walk alone without aids she does so slowly and shakily and tires easily. She is shortsighted, has a slight high frequency hearing loss, and her speech is slow and slurred, and sometimes barely intelligible to her teacher. She attends the local spastics centre for physiotherapy once a week and has weekly speech therapy at school. She has recently begun to suffer from epilepsy (petit mal) but her fits are controlled by epanutin and rarely occur in school.

Although Mary has no welfare assistant and the head was initially worried about accepting her, both head and class teacher are now certain that this is the right placement for her. Mary's parents contacted the Spastics Society who arranged for them to go with the head and class teacher to the local special school to see how she might be helped in school. As a result an electric typewriter was provided by the LEA and modifications made to her desk and chair. At that time she was having occupational therapy at the local spastics centre and was given help there on how to type.

Academically Mary is slightly above average and socially she is very well accepted and happy. The children were told about her before her arrival and although they were at first curious this quickly wore off. Remarks are sometimes made in a friendly way about her 'shoogly' legs but this does not seem to upset her and she is a very well-adjusted child.

The success of her placement seems to be mainly attributable to an exceedingly supportive home on the one hand and on the other to a very sympathetic and cooperative school.

Case 2

Anne is an 8½ year old and has spina bifida and hydrocephalus. She is paraplegic and uses a wheelchair a great deal of the time although she can walk short distances with calipers and crutches. Her hand movements are slightly clumsy. She is doubly incontinent, wears pads and rubbers and needs complete toilet assistance, and she has a full-time welfare assistant at school. She wears glasses and has a slight stammer. Like Mary she suffers from petit mal epilepsy but this is well controlled and she has had no fits since she started at school.

She is of average ability, although she has a little difficulty in number work; her concentration is poor and she is 'slow in setting about things' but keeps up well with the rest of the class. Socially she is a very well-accepted 'normal' little girl and the other children show great consideration towards her. There are two particularly interesting features about her placement. One is that the class teacher and the welfare assistant have, largely by their own efforts, become very well informed both about her particular difficulties and about spina bifida in general. They were invited first by the head of her infant school to sit in on classes there to see how she functioned, and the head arranged for them to go to visit a local special school and obtained booklets on spina bifida from the Association for Spina Bifida and Hydrocephalus. The teacher and welfare assistant have also been to see Anne having physiotherapy in hospital to find out what exercises she can do in school.

A number of special arrangements have helped in the success of this placement. The welfare assistant plays a key part. She changes Anne three times a day in a small room to which Anne herself has a key, so that she feels quite secure, although no secret is made of the fact that she goes there 'to be changed'. The assistant is responsible for her medication and for assisting her in PE. She also helps her into the playground and dining room in her wheelchair but, once there, her friends have the responsibility for looking after her. Whenever possible the assistant helps in other classes so that Anne will not become overdependent. The school has assisted Anne's social adjustment in a number of other small ways. When she moved up into the juniors, care was taken to include her six closest friends in the same class. The head also talked to older children who were in danger of 'smothering' her with help and they have seen a film about a pre-school handicapped children's group and about their later integration in ordinary schools. The film excited many questions, one of the most positive being a suggestion that perhaps Anne could be doing even more for herself than was the case.

Case 3

The final example of a child whose integration has been very successful is that of Henry, a 10 year old who is severely handicapped by arthrogryposis. All Henry's limbs have been affected by this congenital disorder. His arms are only rudimentary; he can move only one finger of his left hand and even his shoulder movements are minimal. He cannot dress or toilet himself and at mealtimes has to use his mouth to manœuvre his cup and plate. He either writes with a pencil in his mouth or uses a headband with a stylus and an electric typewriter. Although he can walk short distances very slowly he cannot manage stairs on his own.

Despite these severe handicaps Henry, a boy of average intelligence, is making very satisfactory progress academically and is also extremely well adjusted. He tackles new situations well (for example, he has learned to swim a length of the school pool unaided) and has overcome his disability to a remarkable extent. He participates actively in all the school activities, tries apparatus work and kicks a football with the others in PE and joins his friends in the playground unless there is rain or snow. He is very well liked, and sees a great deal of his friends outside school hours.

The head and all the staff and assistants appeared to accept it as quite natural that a child as handicapped as this should be in an ordinary school and although he has had a full-time welfare assistant from the start (an essential factor in the success of this placement), he copes very well indeed even when she is absent, asking for help when he needs it in a matter-of-fact and cheerful way. As in the other cases selected here there was an excellent relationship between the school and the home.

2 Special arrangements for groups of PH children in ordinary schools

In the preceding section it was shown that provided the necessary special arrangements are made many PH children can be successfully placed in ordinary classes in their local schools. Two main drawbacks exist. On the one hand it may be very difficult and expensive to provide each child with the special physical facilities he needs; on the other there are a substantial number of children, some already in the ordinary schools, who clearly need more individual and specialized teaching than is usually available in an ordinary class. What kinds of arrangements can be made for such children?

There are two main possibilities. Firstly, one primary school in the area can be selected in which a special class or classes for PH children can be established. This system is widely used in Scandinavia and is described in some detail in chapter 9. Placement in a small special class of about eight to twelve children might be suitable for the following groups:

1 Children who have specific learning difficulties in addition to handicaps of varying degrees of severity. This would include many children with neurological abnormalities, particularly

those with cerebral palsy or spina bifida and hydrocephalus. Their abilities would tend to lie in the 'dull-average' range. Many would be likely to have perceptual and visuo-motor difficulties and almost all would have difficulties in concentration.

2 Children with 'minimal cerebral dysfunction'. Although they have no gross motor difficulties, their specific learning disabilities and often their disturbed behaviour make individual help, even if only for one or two years, a necessity, particularly at an early age.

3 Children with physical handicaps which are too severe to allow ordinary class placement even in an adapted school, for whom such classes might offer an alternative to a special school, at least at the primary stage. These might include children with severe speech defects for whom ordinary class placement would be particularly difficult.

A variant which is being tried in some areas is to set up small special classes which contain children with emotional and intellectual as well as physical handicaps. One of the conclusions of a DES survey of such 'units' carried out in 1967 and 1968 (DES, 1970) was that they

provided convincing evidence for the belief that for the great majority of handicapped children of nursery and infant school age there is little that can be provided in a highly specialized school which cannot equally well be provided in a unit catering for children with a wide range of disorders. By admitting children with different handicaps most authorities would have sufficient children to make at least one special class.

The authors also thought that there was 'much to be said for a close working relationship with a normal school'.

Such an arrangement may work well at this stage, but at the junior level PH children placed in such classes may receive neither the social benefits of ordinary class placement nor the educational benefits which can be given in a class set up specifically for PH children with learning difficulties. If such 'mixed' classes are established (and there is a case for doing so in rural areas where there are not enough PH children to form a special class on their own) they will need an exceptionally sympathetic host school, teachers of very high calibre and excellent supportive services, in particular from educational psychologists.

The alternative to the establishment of special classes is for one school in an area to be selected for special adaptations and other special provisions in the way of transport, therapy and so on, and for places to be made available there for all 'suitable' PH children living within the area. This is likely to mean from five to twelve children at any one time. The children would be fully integrated into the ordinary classes.

This arrangement is now being tried out in a number of areas. A possible difficulty is that although the physical needs of the children may be well catered for, those with specific learning disabilities are unlikely to get all the help they need. One school in the study had tried to anticipate this problem by appointing extra teaching staff so that or two small classes (of about fifteen to twenty children) could be set up, taking a mixture of handicapped and non-handicapped pupils. In this way more individual help could be given while the social benefits of integration were retained.

In another area careful plans were being made for the adaptation of a first and a middle school for PH children. In addition, however, a teacher with special qualifications was to be appointed to each school to be responsible for the PH pupils and for the 'help clinic' or 'resource room'. Children with learning difficulties would leave their ordinary classes as required for special help in the clinic from her. Part of her time would be spent teaching in the ordinary classes. This seems a particularly promising arrangement, although its success will depend to a large extent on the calibre of the special teachers. In this, as in all cases where only one 'special' teacher is appointed, there is a real danger of lack of continuity should she leave. For this reason the policy in one area has been to appoint at least two special teachers to any one unit.

(i) SURVEY FINDINGS

As part of this study visits were made to all the special 'units' in ordinary schools for PH children of nursery or primary school age known to the author, and a summary of the provision which was available in mid-1972 is shown in Table 8.8. Although the list is not a comprehensive one, it gives some idea of the variety of provision with which local authorities are experimenting. The term 'unit' is used for convenience only, to refer to a situation in which special provision was made for a group of PH children but in many cases the PH children were in fact integrated into the ordinary classes. In this,

TABLE 8.8. *Special arrangements for groups of PH children in ordinary schools*

Ages and handicaps catered for	No. of PH children	Main features
A Nursery group, mixed physical handicaps	15	Complete integration with non-handicapped children: no special class as such
B Nursery unit, mixed physical handicaps	13	Separate special class
C 'Spina bifida unit', nursery/ infant	10	Nursery class of PH and non-handicapped children: spina bifida children integrated in ordinary infant classes
D Infant unit, mixed physical handicaps	10	Separate special class
E Infant 'observation' class	6	Mixed special class, 6 PH and 9 with miscellaneous handicaps (ESN, socially deprived, maladjusted etc.)
F Infant 'unit', mixed physical handicaps	7	Mixed integrated class, 7 PH and 13 non-handicapped children
G Infant/junior unit, mixed physical handicaps	11	Separate special class, subdivided into an infant and junior group
H 'Spina bifida unit', juniors	6	All children integrated in ordinary classes
I Junior unit, mixed physical handicaps	10	Separate special class
J Thalidomide 'unit', juniors	12	All children integrated in ordinary classes

as in all cases where only one 'special' teacher is appointed, there is a real danger of lack of continuity should she leave. For this reason the policy in one area has been to appoint at least two special teachers to anyone unit.

Broadly speaking two main types of special arrangements were being made, (1) the setting up of special classes either for PH children (*B*, *D*, *G*, *I*) or children with 'mixed' handicaps (E), or (2) selection of a school for special modifications and the provision of extra services, with full integration of the children into ordinary classes of a normal (*A*, *C* [infants], *H*, and *J*) or somewhat reduced (*C* [primary class], *F*) size. In the remainder of this chapter a little will be said about the strengths and weaknesses of these arrangements, on the basis of visits to each 'unit' and of the questionnaires which the teachers in charge completed.

There are still very few special classes for PH children in ordinary schools in this country in contrast to Scandinavia, the situation there being described in detail in the following chapter. The four PH classes visited in England had from ten to thirteen children with an age range of about three years, while the class with 'mixed' handicaps included six PH children and nine others. The classes generally drew children from within a radius of about six miles from the school, taxi transport being used. Of the forty-four children in the PH classes, nineteen were cerebral-palsied and fifteen had spina bifida, generally with hydrocephalus, and the children tended to be low-average or ESN in ability. Although teachers could usually obtain any special furniture or equipment they wanted, the physical facilities were poor. None of the units had been purpose-built, and one had been waiting for a year for special adaptations (ramps, redesigned toilet, etc.) In two cases a room other than the classroom had been made available to the unit and in a third a room for physiotherapy was being built. One of the host schools was particularly unsuitable for PH children, with steps to the hall and library up which wheelchairs had to be lifted bodily, and all the second and third year classes on the first floor and therefore quite inaccessible.

The situation as regards staffing varied. Each of the classes had a full-time teacher and the infant/junior unit had also a part-timer. Two of the teachers had special qualifications and experience in the education of PH children, and one had had in-service training. Only two taught occasionally in the ordinary classes and none of the regular teachers taught in the special classes. While the special teachers would have liked more contacts with other professionals working with PH children, the two who had taught in special schools said they preferred the special class system and all but one discussed their problems with the regular staff. Each special class had one or two full-time helpers half of whom had had prior nursing experience, but in two cases the ancillary help was clearly insufficient.

Physiotherapy was provided in three units on a sessional basis: in the others the children had to attend a local health centre or hospital although attempts were being made to arrange for the therapist to come to the school. Children in one unit had speech therapy at the health centre, but otherwise none was available.

One of the main questions investigated was the extent to which integration with the rest of the children was actually taking place. All the teachers considered this important, and three of the five were satisfied with the amount of integration. What was happening varied greatly from one school to another. In some cases the PH children joined the others during assembly, breaks and at lunch, in others they were treated as a separate group. The extent to which they joined other classes for PE, music and movement, and project work also varied from one school to another. Only two children joined regular classes for work in the basic skills. In all cases non-handicapped children visited the units to play and no cases of teasing or 'unpleasantness' were reported, perhaps because heads had 'prepared' the other children for the establishment of the unit.

Two main suggestions were made by the teachers about why there was not more integration. One related to the design of the school: either the unit was in a separate wing and there was no need for non-handicapped children to go near it, or the host school was unsuitable for handicapped children, because of steps, small classrooms and so on. The other reason mentioned was that teachers in the regular classes had reservations about taking PH children into their classes or were too busy to take a real interest in the unit. Even when heads are enthusiastic, successful integration depends to a considerable extent on the special class teachers enlisting the support and enthusiasm of their colleagues, this being a point which was also emphasized in the DES survey of units for partially hearing children (DES, 1967, pp. 30–1; 33–4).

To sum up, the main difficulties of the units seemed to be as follows. Firstly, their physical facilities were inadequate. They had started off in a 'spare' hut or classroom and subsequent arrangements had been rather makeshift. Secondly, the unit was not always fully accepted as an integral part of the school by other members of staff, partly because they had not always been consulted about its establishment in the first place and partly because they lacked information about the children in it. Thirdly, the special class teachers were receiving inadequate supportive services from outside the school. In particular, they lacked adequate medical information about the children in their care. Fourthly, arrangements for the provision of physiotherapy and even more for speech therapy tended to be unsatisfactory. Finally, in all but one unit teachers were worried about what would happen to the children when they left, as no special provision in an ordinary school had as yet been planned at the next stage. Most of these difficulties are not insurmountable, and are not arguments against the system *per se*, but they do suggest that if special classes are to offer facilities which compare with those in the special schools an equal amount of care must go into their planning. Very similar conclusions were reached in a recent DES survey of special classes and units for handicapped children (DES, 1972b).

The other main type of arrangement investigated was the situation where the school had been adapted and special facilities provided but where the children were placed in the ordinary classes. In general this system was working very successfully and details of arrangements in three such schools, one a nursery school, one an infant school and one a junior school, are given below.

The nursery school group consisted of fifteen PH children, including a number with spina bifida and cerebral palsy. There is no 'unit' as such, since the children are fully integrated, but their presence at the school is recognized by the authority in terms of the provision of extra space and staffing. On the teaching and care side there are, for the whole school (which runs separate morning and afternoon sessions), two teachers and four full-time and two part-time nursery nurses. The teachers are exceptionally well qualified, since in addition to their normal qualifications the head has had extra training in child development and in the education of PH children, while her deputy has had prior experience with such children. Both have also attended in-service training courses, including one on spina bifida children.

Although the children have to go out of school for physiotherapy and speech therapy, the head makes personal contact with all therapists and others dealing with the children to ensure that their efforts are coordinated. No special furniture (apart from mobility aids) or equipment is used in school, the latter being improvised in the play situation as the need arises. The PH children participate actively in all indoor and outdoor activities and integration is total, the only real difficulty being with non-speaking children who may be left out unless the staff are watchful. All the parents are encouraged to visit the school and have become extremely interested in the progress of the handicapped children and all the staff are consulted about whether a child with a particular handicap (for instance, haemophilia) should be admitted.

Few of the problems which were found where there were special classes have arisen here: the only real difficulty lies in placing the children once they leave the school, since not all will be able to integrate into ordinary classes. Nevertheless, the school itself provides an outstanding example of how full integration can be achieved for this age group when the necessary expertise and commitment are present.

The next example shows what can be done for quite severely handicapped spina bifida children. In this case 'units' for spina bifida children were located in an infant school and the junior school which it 'feeds'. The schools themselves lay on the periphery of a northern industrial town with a population of about 131,000. In the infant school there are five spina bifida children in ordinary classes, as well as a small number of PH children in a nursery class which non-handicapped children also attend, and in the junior school six spina bifida children, four being in wheelchairs.

The same type of special arrangements have been made in both schools. The infant school has a large purpose-built 'changing-room' (an addition to the school) with three specially designed toilets and a sluice on one side, and two couches on the other. An old classroom has been divided and equipped as a physiotherapy/treatment room, and modifications (for example rails, low shelves) have been made in some of the classrooms. The physiotherapist (who is employed jointly by the health and education departments) treats the children twice a week and a speech therapist spends two and a half days a week in the school. Three part-time helpers (two are SRNs) are attached to the 'unit' and look after the children's physical needs.

One teacher (without special training) is in overall charge of the handicapped group, a post of special responsibility having been created for this purpose. The spina bifida children spend all their time in ordinary classes, the class size being very slightly reduced. The head and all the staff were clearly proud of the unit and felt that this form of placement was best suited to the children's social and educational needs. They stressed that such units should be kept fairly small because otherwise the handicapped children might become 'a group apart'.

A problem which the junior school was facing was that of two spina bifida children of very low ability. While ordinary schools can cope successfully with children who have severe physical handicaps, they are often unable to offer the necessary help to the child who is also educationally subnormal or who has specific learning difficulties, and by no means all spina bifida children can be catered for under the arrangements described here.

The last example of successful integration comes from a junior school which mainly serves a council estate some distance from the centre of a large city. All the city's thalidomide children were placed here. Originally the children attended a school for 'delicate' children. Parental pressure resulted in a 'unit' (again a misnomer) for them being set up in an ordinary school which was physically suitable and had a sympathetic head. Two extra teachers and an ancillary helper were seconded to the unit, one of the teachers who had special school experience being given a head of department post.

Preparations for the children's transfer were extremely careful. The teacher and helper were first seconded to the school to get to know the children and their abilities and the head made several visits as well. She then prepared both the ordinary children and their parents for the arrival of the thalidomide group. For two weeks, until they found their feet, the children were placed in two 'special' classes under the two new teachers. For the rest of the term they were joined by different groups of non-handicapped children to give them the opportunity of meeting the other children in the school, particularly those of their own age, and of moving about with large numbers of active children, and the following term were placed in ordinary classes according to their ages and ability, not more than two being assigned to any one class. As previously agreed, the 'special' teachers then became responsible for ordinary classes, which had the effect of reducing the size of each class to no more than thirty children. Integration at lessons, for PE, at mealtimes and in fact for all activities is now complete.

The arrangements were all carefully planned. A specially adapted and equipped toilet room was provided, and another room set aside for the fitting of prostheses. Ordinary desks have been adapted, wall brackets assist the children in getting up steps and, since many have rudimentary arms, electric typewriters are in use in most classrooms.

The school has been very well supported by specialists. All the children were assessed before entering the school and reassessed recently, the range of intelligence being from below 70 to well above average. During their first year an occupational therapist from the local hospital visited the school regularly to advise on equipment and independence training. One child is visited regularly in school by a physiotherapist who has trained the welfare worker in daily exercises; a nurse also visits regularly and liaises with the parents about the most suitable clothing for the children and a social worker is on hand.

The head and all her staff felt that integration had been 'tremendously and unexpectedly successful', even in the case of a limbless child, and another who had no speech and an IQ below 70 when he arrived. The children generally had 'blossomed academically', especially in their third and fourth years, and had become markedly more mature and independent. Teasing had simply not arisen; all the children had non-handicapped friends and were accepted in 'an entirely natural way' and the ordinary children were felt to have benefited greatly. The success of the experiment was confirmed when it was decided at a joint meeting of LEA officials, medical staff, parents and the head that all should go on to ordinary secondary schools and at the time of writing seven children had been transferred to the local comprehensive school.

Finally, it has to be asked why this experiment was so successful. Five reasons stand out. Firstly, everyone – head, staff, parents and children – was fully consulted and kept fully informed. Secondly, there was exceedingly careful planning at all stages of all the aspects of integration which had to be taken into account. Thirdly, the head and her staff had excellent support throughout the LEA, doctors, psychologists, therapists and others. Fourthly, all were aiming from the start at complete integration. Finally, the start which the children had in a special school may, for many, have been quite essential.

Undoubtedly, successful integration will be less easy to achieve when children because of their special educational needs have to be placed in special classes. However, if the same care is taken over the planning of such classes as in the example above, including discussions among all the staff about their exact aims regarding social integration and about the means by which this is to be achieved, then many of the difficulties raised earlier could be overcome. A final point concerns the exact form of special provision which is selected. It is difficult to generalize about this since a great deal will depend on factors such as whether the area is urban or rural, what sort of special services already exist in both special and ordinary schools, the incidence of certain types of physical handicaps in the area, the resources the local authority has available and current plans for school building. One local authority may decide to make minor modifications as required in several schools, while another may select particular schools for extensive adaptations. In one, a system of special classes for PH children may be established, while another may prefer to retain as many children as possible in ordinary classes while providing the specialized teaching needed through 'help clinics'. In yet other cases a combination of special classes, for instance for children with specific learning disabilities, and of help clinics may be used.

Whatever system is chosen, it is important that continuity of special provision from the nursery to the secondary level and beyond should be planned for. It is also important that the special arrangements made for any particular child should be kept constantly under review and that wherever possible the final goal should be full integration.

REFERENCES

DAVIE, R., BUTLER, N. and GOLDSTEIN, H. (1972) *From Birth to Seven: The Second Report of the National Child Development Study (1958 Cohort)*, Longmans, London.

Department of Education and Science (1967) *Units for Partially Hearing Children, Education Survey I*, HMSO, London.

Department of Education and Science (1969) *Health of the School Child*, HMSO, London.

Department of Education and Science (1970) *Diagnostic and Assessment Units, Education Survey 9*, HMSO, London.

Department of Education and Science (1971) *Physical Education for the Physically Handicapped*, HMSO, London.

Department of Education and Science (1972a) *Health of the School Child*, HMSO, London.

Department of Education and Science (1972b) *Aspects of Special Education. Schools for Delicate Children, Special Classes in Ordinary Schools. Education survey 17*, HMSO, London.

HARING, N. G., STERN, G. G. and CRUICKSHANK, W. M. (1958) *Attitudes of Educators Towards Exceptional Children*, Syracuse University Press, New York.

ROGERS, W., HAARER, D. and SCANDARY, J. (1969) *The Teacher Counselor Program for the Physically Handicapped*, Ingram Intermediate School District, Mason, Michigan.

RUTTER, M., TIZARD, J. and WHITMORE, K. (eds.) (1970) *Education, Health and Behaviour*, Longmans, London.

TYSON, M. (1970) 'The design of remedial programmes', chapter 22 in MITTLER, P. (ed.) *The Psychological Assessment of Mental and Physical Handicaps*, Methuen, London.

WEBB, L. (1967) *Children with Special Needs in the Infants' School*, Colin Smythe, London.

Chapter 9 · The Integration of Handicapped Children in Scandinavian Schools

Introduction

This chapter is an account of a four-week visit made in September 1970 to Sweden, Norway and Denmark. The purpose of the visit was to study the provisions made in Scandinavia for physically handicapped children either in special or in ordinary classes within the ordinary schools, and through discussion with a wide range of persons concerned with this field to evaluate the success of these provisions and to discover what the problems were, and how they were being met. Fuller details of this visit are given in a booklet published by the College of Special Education (Anderson, 1971).

Scandinavia was chosen for the study since all three countries, and in particular Sweden, are committed to a very active policy of educating physically handicapped children in ordinary schools in their home districts, and an extensive reorganization of special educational services is going on with this in mind. The desirability of increased integration is not questioned but the extent to which it is considered possible is a very lively current issue. Demographically this is an interesting area for such a study since within Scandinavia there is an enormous range of population densities, with very low densities and great communication problems throughout the north.

Previous personal contacts with teachers and administrators working in these countries made it possible to arrange an exceedingly varied programme of visits; particular emphasis was laid on meeting staff and handicapped pupils in special and ordinary classes within urban and rural schools of all sizes and levels.

This chapter begins with a short account of the ways in which services for physically handicapped children are being reorganized in each of the three countries, much of this reorganization, especially in Norway, being still at the planning stage. In following sections the foundations of successful integration, such as appropriate school design, provision of special aids and transport, personal assistance and supportive services for parents are looked at. Next, the strengths and weaknesses of the system of special classes for physically handicapped children in ordinary schools are discussed, while arrangements made for severely handicapped individuals in ordinary classes are illustrated by means of four case histories.

The organization of special education in Scandinavia

(i) SWEDEN

(a) The Swedish school system

In Sweden the central administration of education is in the hands of the National Board of Education, and the responsibility is shared between this board and the local authorities. Since the 1962 Education Act the school system has been based on nine years of compulsory education in a comprehensive school (*grundskolan*) which takes children from seven to sixteen, the junior stage comprising grades 1–3, the middle school grades 4–6 and the senior stage grades 7–9. The comprehensive school is organized in districts. Usually each district includes one school unit with all three departments, and smaller school units with either lower or middle departments or both. Each district is under the management of a headmaster and is called a 'headmaster's district': it includes the special classes in the district although there are also generally one or more 'headmasters for special education'. After grade 9 different types of more advanced schooling are available, but this report is mainly concerned with P H children in the compulsory school.

(b) Special education

The term 'special education' refers to special facilities made available within the ordinary school system, whether these are special classes or special provisions made in the ordinary classes, the responsibility for special education being that of each county and its

local school board. The latest estimate of the numbers of handicapped children in Sweden is given in Table 9.1 below.

TABLE 9.1. *Handicapped children in Sweden, 1968–9*

Handicap	Incidence per 1 000	Total children
Mentally retarded	10·0	15 000
Epilepsy	10·0	15 000
Cerebral palsy	1·7	2 500
Polio	0·0	800
Blind	0·4	600
Deaf	0·7	1 050
Heart	4·0	6 000
Asthma	10·0	15 000
Accidents	7·0	10 500
Others	2·0	3 000
TOTAL		69 450

In 1967–8 out of a total of nearly 900,000 children in ordinary
schools in Sweden, there were 38,120 children in 3,720 special
classes, and almost as many (29,300 in 1965–6) in ordinary classes
receiving supplementary lessons. Approximately two-thirds of the
special class children are in classes for slow learners, while other
types of special classes include 'school maturity' classes for those
considered too immature for school, observation classes (for maladjusted pupils), classes for children with reading and writing disorders, for those whose sight or hearing is impaired and for the
motor-handicapped.

For children who cannot be educated in the ordinary schools
'special schools' still exist, but their numbers are being rapidly
reduced, especially in the case of physically handicapped children
since an increasing number of such pupils are being integrated into
ordinary classes. The most significant trends in the education of
handicapped children in Sweden are thus, in the words of the
National Board of Education (1967), 'integration, adaptation,
individualization and flexibility'. The board states that its aim is to
present a flexible system of possibilities where parents and children
can choose between alternatives, and where every effort is made to
find out what is best for the individual child and his development.

The three major alternatives for physically handicapped children are:

1 The child attends school in an ordinary class with remedial teaching where necessary, technical aids, transport to and from school, personal assistance, etc.

2 He attends a special class for the motor-handicapped within the ordinary school, with additional remedial teaching, personal assistance, treatment facilities, etc., living either at home or in a hostel for motor-handicapped pupils.

3 He receives schooling, medical care, etc., and boarding facilities if necessary, in an institution for the severely motor-handicapped.

Thus in 1969 the placement of thalidomide schoolchildren was 75 per cent in (1), 12 per cent in (2) and 13 per cent in (3). Figures for the total number of physically handicapped children in each of these groups were not available, since it is not known exactly how many are attending ordinary schools, and also because the situation is changing so rapidly, but in February 1970 there was a total of 666 'motor-handicapped' (i.e. P H) children in 105 special classes, less than half of these classes being in a few special institutions for handicapped children, and over 50 per cent in ordinary schools, any one ordinary school having between one and five special classes. About 65 per cent of this group were cerebral-palsied children. Some 386 of the 666 children were boarders, the great majority of these living in one of three special centres for P H children in Stockholm, Uppsala and Gothenburg. It should also be pointed out that a number of P H children attend other special classes (for example, for slow learners and for children with reading and writing disorders). A final point to note is that in Sweden parents have the right to refuse to send their children to special schools, but this right is rarely invoked since the facilities which can be made available in ordinary schools ensure that an alternative to special school placement usually exists. Schools do also have the right to refuse to take handicapped children (although public opinion acts as a deterrent), and difficulties in arranging suitable placement were reported by a number of parents.

(c) *Decentralization*

At present, a move for decentralization of the special institutions for P H children is under way. To replace these the board aims to establish seven regional centres for their medical and educational care, the largest of these being Stockholm (population 800,000) and the smallest Umea (53,000). Eventually, the only special school will be a 'gymnasial school' containing all three forms of voluntary upper secondary education (85 per cent of pupils opt to stay on after compulsory school), i.e. gymnasium, continuation school and vocational school. This school will be in Stockholm and will probably have a completely separate boarding section. Apart from this there will generally be in each region a pattern of classes for PH children in ordinary schools (with hostels if necessary for children from outlying areas). Specialist medical care will be available probably in the paediatric department of the regional hospital, with in addition a special centre for physiotherapy and occupational therapy, and probably provision for observation and assessment. Each region will eventually have its own team of special staff, including a consultant for special education for PH children, based at the centre and going out as needed, although there are only three such consultants at present. The central board will look after the regional centres only in so far as they ask for help.

There will be considerable variety in the actual patterns established in each region, partly depending upon what sort of centres already exist, each region being required to send its plans to the board for approval. In this way simple replication of old patterns of institutional care is prevented. The Association of Parents of Handicapped Children is playing a very active role in Sweden, and has been consulted by the board on the plans for the new centres.

(ii) NORWAY

(a) The present system

Major changes in the present organization of special educational services have been planned, with increased emphasis on keeping children where possible in their local schools. In a country with a population of only 3,500,000 and with very difficult communications it is particularly hard to provide a comprehensive range of advisory services on a local basis.

At present the special schools are run directly by the state while special education in ordinary schools is the responsibility of the local boards of education; a third category exists, of state-run social and/or medical centres for severely handicapped children with special educational services being provided by the local authority.

(b) Plans for reorganization

One of the main aims of the reorganization of services is to simplify this confusing situation and to do away with the old categories of handicapped children, replacing these with two main concepts: firstly the provision of special education within the ordinary schools, and secondly its provision outside them. The other major aim is decentralization: the municipalities are to be responsible for most special education, with the special schools run by the state (mainly for blind, deaf and mentally retarded children and those with social problems) being reduced to a relatively small number. These schools will have boarding facilities and will also be used as long-term observation centres.

Under the new system a board or council for special education is to be set up in each county with responsibility for planning services and for ensuring cooperation between the medical, social and educational staff. Locally, special education is to be provided at two levels: (1) within a group of several municipalities and (2) within the county as a whole. At this second level, the traditional pattern of special schools or classes may sometimes be needed, although it is hoped that these will be day schools, with the children coming by taxi, and that where weekly boarding accommodation is required, it can be provided in a hostel which is quite separate from the school.

(c) Local guidance centres

The most interesting feature of planning in Norway, however, is the idea of providing special education facilities within a group of municipalities. What is envisaged is the establishment of local guidance centres, each having a radius of about one hour's travelling time (rather than being based on population) and serving several municipalities. It is hoped that each centre will have a full-time professional team including a school psychologist, a social worker, a physiotherapist, a speech therapist and three to five consultant teachers (including at least one pre-school teacher) with experience of working with children with different types of handicaps. Members of the team will go out from the centre to ordinary schools and special classes, both to give treatment and as consultants. Little treatment will be carried out at the centre itself apart from short-term observation and assessment. Paediatricians and other medical specialists will serve several centres. The main obstacle to the success of such a programme is staffing, as specially trained teachers, psychologists and therapists are all in short supply and reluctant to leave the main towns.

There will in addition to the smaller centres be five or six larger ones, in towns such as Oslo, Bergen, Trondheim, Tromso and Stavanger, serving much wider areas and with greatly expanded professional teams.

In recent years the director and other members of the Norwegian Council for Special Education have travelled through all the counties consulting local opinion, discussing the problems in the establishment of such a system and asking them to produce their own plans for special education. Several pilot schemes are now under way, the best developed being that based on Haugesund (population 18,000) under the direction of a school psychologist.

This project is one of a number being carried out by the Norwegian State Council of Experiments and Research in Schools and concerns 'the integrating of handicapped persons in the ordinary local society, whatever this society may be . . .' It has these widely formulated goals:

1 To give special education to handicapped children, young people and adults in the neighbourhood of their homes and as far as possible in connection with an ordinary environment.

2 To coordinate/integrate all local social/health offices, schools etc. which are dealing with the welfare, treatment and education of the handicapped.

3 To register handicapped children and treat them as early as possible.

4 To participate in the plan of district services for the handicapped.

5 To create a stimulating educational-psychological local centre in order to give inspiration to the staff and provide the best possible diagnosis and treatment for handicapped people.

6 To work out new methods in the treatment of the handicapped.

The project started in July 1969, the emphasis being on integrating handicapped children in ordinary local schools. Most of these children were mentally retarded, hearing-impaired and emotionally disturbed and the full-time team at Haugesund centre consisted in 1970 of four psychologists, six special teachers and two social workers. The psychologist in charge reports that

> our main aim in the initial year has been to make the teachers in ordinary schools better equipped to do their work in the classes and to pay special attention to handicapped children, to plan out special programmes for the handicapped and supervise their teachers, and to change the attitudes toward the handicapped in schools and society in a more positive and desirable direction. We look on our project as a complex social psychological process which will last for years.

(iii) DENMARK

(a) Policy in special education

Like Sweden, Denmark is (from 1974) to have a nine-year compulsory course of education for children from 7–16 years old and the main aim is that special education should be provided by the LEAs within this framework, although government boarding schools for handicapped children also exist. The inspector for special education has stated (Jorgensen, 1970) that

> the most important factor in special education is that it should interfere as little as possible with the pupil's normal schooling . . . the possibilities open to the handicapped child, listed in the order in which they should be resorted to, are:
>
> 1 To remain in normal classes with extra coaching and suitable aids.
>
> 2 To attend a special class in an ordinary school or if necessary one of the primary education centres for severely handicapped children.
>
> 3 To enter a special school or, in case of need, a special boarding school.

The aim of the Danish system of special education is thus to integrate handicapped children into the general education system. As part of an inquiry into the number of PH pupils attending primary (i.e. compulsory) schools, the Inspectorate of Special Education sent, in 1966, a questionnaire to the school psychological services. Areas with a total of 388,000 pupils reported 388 PH children or 1 per

1,000. These children were being taught under the arrangements outlined in Table 9.2 below.

TABLE 9.2. *Educational arrangements for PH pupils in Denmark, 1966*

Type of placement	No. of pupils	% of total
Ordinary classes	255	} 51·3
Ordinary classes and supplementary teaching	49	
Special classes at ordinary schools	88	16·5
Special schools for ESN pupils	10	1·9
Special boarding schools for PH pupils	150	28·1
Lessons at home	7	1·3
No information	5	0·9
TOTAL	564	100

(b) *Special education centres*

The most interesting organizational feature of the Danish special education system is the existence of the special education centres, which were set up to enable handicapped children to live at home while receiving primary school education at a school adapted to meet the demands of their particular handicaps. Two groups of children attend the centres: those who would previously have had to attend a state institution, and those with a considerable handicap who would have been unable to derive sufficient benefit from education in a normal class, transport by school buses being provided.

In Denmark eleven or twelve such centres are planned and it is recommended that each should draw on an area with at least 50,000 school-age pupils if the handicapped children are to be suitably grouped according to age and handicap. These classes are to 'form a natural part of the school so that both teachers and children can become fully integrated' which is 'best achieved by keeping the handicapped groups small'. The most practical arrangement having regard to special equipment, qualified staff etc. is that 'there should be no more than a single category of handicapped children at one school. Integration would then be required at a maximum of four schools, with classes for speech and reading, for the hearing-handicapped, the physically handicapped and the visually-handicapped' (Jorgensen, 1970).

The first special class for PH children was set up at Herning, the oldest of these centres, in 1961. By 1968 there were twenty such classes at education centres with a total of 130 pupils. Children are admitted to the education centre's classes for the handicapped on the recommendation of the school psychologist after discussion with the home, the medical authorities and the child's local school.

The PH classes are often called 'cerebral-palsied classes', although they contain a few children with other handicaps. It is recommended that they should not exceed six children, that 'the instruction should aim at the possible transfer of the child to ordinary classes' and that if possible the children should have a few of their lessons in ordinary classes. Teachers in special classes should have taken a one-year course in special education (although this is not always the case), and are advised to continue to teach in ordinary classes. They are entitled to an assistant on the care side. The medical consultant of the local orthopaedic hospital usually acts as a consultant, and physiotherapy and speech therapy are provided. Each centre has attached to it a school psychologist (if possible specializing in a particular category of disability) who is concerned especially with the assessment and placement of handicapped children. Centres may also have education advisers who are expert consultants (for instance in the field of hearing impairment) with particular responsibility for the special classes in the centre. Finally at the Ministry of Education level there is an inspector of special education aided by six consultants for the different groups of handicapped children, one of these being the physically handicapped.

The bases of increased integration

Increased integration is only desirable if a number of basic special facilities can be provided for handicapped pupils in ordinary schools and in this section those to which particular attention has been paid in Scandinavia are examined. Several of these formed the subject matter of the report of a working party set up in 1966 by the Swedish National Board of Education to look at ways in which they could forward integration.

(i) SCHOOL BUILDINGS AND DESIGN

In 1967 the National Swedish Board of Urban Planning published its *Regulations for Access for the Disabled to Buildings*, their gist being that 'those spaces in a building which are open to the public shall, to a reasonable extent, be constructed and designed so that they may be accessible to and used by persons whose capacity for locomotion is reduced in consequence of age, infirmity or illness'. These regulations make it obligatory for one means of approach to the public buildings to be so designed and constructed that it can be used by the disabled on adjacent premises and in the interior and also for at least one clothes rack and toilet room in each public building to be designed for such a purpose.

Of more direct importance are the regulations about school buildings which state that in each 'headmaster area' (an area with about 1,000–2,000 school-age children) at least one school building must be specially adapted for the handicapped. This means that schools of more than one storey will have a lift which like the entrances and corridors will be wide enough for wheelchairs, as well as ramps, special toilets, doors without thresholds and so on. While this applies to new schools, old schools are required to make appropriate adaptations where necessary, even if they have only one handicapped pupil, these being paid for by the local school board which gets back about one-third of the costs from a state grant. The Association of Parents of Handicapped Children has appointed a full-time *ombudsman*, one of whose duties is to look after legal matters pertaining to school buildings. The working party also made recommendations on how school hostels could be modified to take handicapped children.

(ii) TRANSPORT

Physically handicapped children in ordinary schools are entitled to special transport to and from school if they need it, costs being paid by the home community. The working party recommended that if costs were above about £1.50 per day per pupil, the state (and after two years the county boards) should pay a contribution to the community.

Taxi transport is most frequently used in Norway and Sweden, although where there are enough special classes there is a school bus. In certain areas the local community owns a small bus equipped to transport handicapped people which can be booked by whoever needs it. In Denmark most centres of special instruction plan and operate a number of school bus or taxi routes from the central office of the school psychologist, although they encourage pupils to make use of public transport where possible.

In general the Scandinavians seem prepared to pay high transport costs to enable children to live at home and to attend ordinary schools; it is the distances involved rather than the cost which is the most worrying problem.

(iii) EDUCATIONAL AIDS

Handicapped children are entitled to free provision of any special educational aids they need, these generally being paid for by the local communities, and the system for providing such aids to children in ordinary schools is particularly well organized in Sweden and Denmark where rather similar national centres exist.

In Sweden the 1966 working party recommended that a centre for teaching aids for the whole country should be set up near a special school in which there was a team of specialists and children of various ages and handicaps. Such a centre was to have four main tasks:

1 The testing out and assessment of the suitability of different aids.

2 The setting-up of an exhibition centre and the provision of information about the aids available to teachers in ordinary and special schools.

3 The lending of such aids to children in ordinary schools.

4 The development of new aids.

The first such centre was set up at a school for PH children in Gothenburg, its director having previously been a special school head. It consists of a permanent exhibition, workshops and offices, and catalogues of aids are available. Its director handles a steady flow of requests for help from heads, class teachers, occupational therapists, physiotherapists and others working both in special and in ordinary classes. Sometimes these requests are simply for specific aids, but more often the director must visit the school concerned to observe the child in the classroom setting and discuss his needs for special furniture or equipment with the class teacher and perhaps the parents and local physiotherapist. This entails much time spent travelling but it has meant that very practical help is provided remarkably rapidly. It has, of course, been difficult to ensure that all teachers in ordinary schools who may have handicapped pupils know of the existence of the centres (several of which now exist); this has generally been done by sending leaflets to the county boards to pass on to all school heads.

A similar centre exists in Denmark at the Herning centre of special instruction (the Herning centre laboratory for the provision of technical aids for special education). Information about it is sent to all school psychologists and special classes, and a teacher with a handicapped child in an ordinary class can contact the centre via the school psychologist. In addition to the collection of aids there is a special educational publishing department here which, for example, has facilities for enlarging textbooks for partially-sighted pupils; there are technicians to look after the electrical equipment including closed-circuit TV. In general expenses for special aids are met by the local communities, but where there are expenses which greatly exceed those for the usual educational materials a special subsidy is granted. Material which is needed for only a short period is available on loan.

(iv) PERSONAL ASSISTANTS

In Sweden, handicapped children in ordinary schools can automatically be provided with help from a personal assistant, the municipality receiving a state grant for such a person who might be requested by the team placing the child, the parent, the class teacher or the psychologist. There appears to be great variety in the methods of recruiting such people, in the total hours they work and in the actual timetabling of their hours with the child. Generally it is the head who decides what sort of assistant to recruit and for how long, after discussion with the class teacher and doctor, and parents have also stressed the importance of their participating in the choice of assistant.

The Swedish working party made a distinction between assistants on (1) the teaching side and (2) the care side (i.e. meals/transport/toileting/dressing, etc.) An individual child in an ordinary class is entitled to one assistant, while a special class of eight to ten children is entitled to one assistant on the care side and another on the teaching side, but special classes tend to have only one full-time assistant (i.e. on the care side only) and in Norway and Denmark two classes sometimes share an assistant.

(v) ADVISORY SERVICES FOR TEACHERS

The teacher of a handicapped child in an ordinary or special class is in greater need of support than a special school teacher, and in all the Scandinavian countries attempts are being made to increase the number of advisory or consultant staff, both at the national and local levels.

In Sweden it is planned that each of the regional centres should have its own full-time consultant for P H children, but at present there are only three of these. Two are based in Stockholm; one (acting for P H children and also for those with reading difficulties and those who are maladjusted) works halftime as a consultant and halftime as a head of a number of special classes; the other for the rest of the country. At the local level the picture differs from one area to another. In Malmo, for example, the head of the special P H classes has been assigned five hours weekly in which to visit ordinary schools with P H pupils while in other centres staff in the special institutions may receive frequent calls for advice without having extra time allocated for this. In several places pre-school teachers with experience in the education of P H children have been appointed as peripatetic advisers.

(vi) THE SCHOOL CLINIC

Children with learning difficulties in ordinary schools have available well-organized supplementary help through the school clinic system, especially in Sweden where the present trend is to increase the number of children in ordinary classes receiving such help while cutting down special classes. In most schools it is possible for children to have supplementary lessons for from two to five hours per week. If a teacher is giving this individual aid to single children or to very small groups of children during his total weekly service, he is said in Sweden to be teaching in a school clinic, this system being used to prevent or remedy difficulties in reading, writing, arithmetic and speech.

A typical example of such a clinic is that at Alunda school, a comprehensive central school for 800 pupils in grades 1–9 which is located in a village in central Sweden and serves a large country district. All grade 1 children are given group tests, and those with reading, writing or arithmetic difficulties (as well as those with behaviour problems) selected in this way are then given special tests to analyse their difficulties. The head and the parents are informed of these difficulties and the school doctor may also be called in. Next follows a meeting of all the teachers concerned with the child to make an individual programme of extra help for him involving from two to five hours of individual or small group work in the clinic.

Care is taken to motivate the child to want to go to the clinic by making sure, for example, that he does not miss any of his favourite subjects by going there; in this way children look forward to the extra help the clinic can provide. This clinic was housed in a separate building consisting of an office/testing room and two classrooms which were very well equipped with tape recorders, programmed tapes for children with reading difficulties and so on. The head of the clinic (who was also the district adviser on special education) worked part-time in the clinic, and there was one other full-time teacher who was experienced but not trained in this work. Apparently in Sweden about 40 per cent of clinic teachers have had special training. The clinic system can, of course, be used to help PH children who are in danger of falling behind in their ordinary classes; in this school one child with minor hemiplegia and an IQ within the normal range was having four hours' weekly extra help in reading and arithmetic.

The clinic system is also used in very small schools: in a village school several miles away with 200 children in grades 1–6 and a staff of ten, there were two 'help' classes for ESN children in grades 4 and 6 (five children in each) but for children in grades 1–3 with difficulties the clinic system was used. Here again a PH child with severe diplegia was using the clinic for four hours' weekly help in reading, writing and arithmetic.

(vii) PERIPATETIC THERAPISTS

While the special classes in ordinary schools often have a physiotherapy department in the school, this is not always the case, and no such service exists for children who are individually integrated and who may have to visit a special school or centre or regional hospital for physiotherapy. In one or two areas, however, where there is an increasing emphasis on home care, peripatetic physiotherapy services are being developed and two examples, both Swedish, are outlined below, one an urban and the other a rural service.

In Stockholm, one of the major functions of the bureau for PH children has been to organize free physiotherapy for all the children registered there. Of nearly 1,000 children and adolescents registered there in 1968, 655 received physiotherapy treatment within the framework of 'open' treatment, that is either at a physiotherapy institution or at home. This is carried out to a large extent by private physiotherapists. The bureau has appointed a head therapist who advises less experienced therapists on treatment and also handles all the business concerning technical aids and is responsible for the contact with technical experts who, together with the therapists, visit the children's homes to see what aids are necessary. Five full-time peripatetic physiotherapists are also employed by the bureau. A peripatetic nursery school teacher visits some of the children at home and brings toys which the child may borrow. These are chosen in cooperation with the physiotherapist.

Parents appear to like this system; one parent with a severely handicapped athetoid/hearing-impaired child in a school for the hearing-impaired where no therapy was available could in this way meet the physiotherapist at home three times weekly, while others commented on how valuable it was for the physiotherapist to see the home and what toys were available and to discuss the exercises and the child's progress in a familiar setting. Parents did not appear to feel that it was too tiring for their children to have physiotherapy after school, either at home or elsewhere.

A city of course is a relatively easy place in which to set up a peripatetic physiotherapy service but the greatest need is likely to be in rural areas such as Jönköping county which has a widely dispersed population of about 300,000. As the number of handicapped children in ordinary schools increases, the Jönköping rehabilitation clinic (which is used as an assessment centre for the whole district and which also has the only pre-school group in the district for P H children) has tried to expand its peripatetic services. Three full-time and one part-time physiotherapists are employed here and at the nearby children's hospital and each is peripatetic for one day a week, giving treatment and advice to children up to 100 miles from the centre. Generally children in ordinary schools have their treatment from local therapists in private practice and the main task of the rehabilitation clinic staff is to act as consultants to those with less experience, as well as visiting the local schools which have P H pupils.

In Denmark the question of a peripetetic physiotherapy service was discussed with the chief nursing executive officer in a rural county. Her view was that the shortage of and inexperience of physiotherapists would make this difficult. In her county a new development (to supplement intensive physiotherapy treatment at local centres) was to encourage the public health nurses to be present when the physiotherapist trained the mother in what exercises to give at home, so that they would be able to give the mother informed help and support.

(viii) IMPROVED SUPPORTIVE SERVICES FOR PARENTS

The commitment to integration in Sweden is paralleled by an awareness among teachers, therapists, social workers and others that if handicapped children are to attend local schools, instead of residential institutions, their parents need increased support, a view which has been put forward very clearly in Britain in *Living with Handicap* (Younghusband *et al.*, 1970).

In this section no attempt is made to give a general account of supportive services in Scandinavia but instead two completely different ways of approaching this question (one in Stockholm, the other in a rural area of Denmark) are outlined.

(a) Stockholm's bureau for PH children and adolescents

Although not primarily concerned with supportive services to parents, the bureau does in fact carry out this function by providing, through one rather than many agencies, a fairly comprehensive and long-term service for handicapped children.

Since 1953 the Stockholm city child welfare committee has led and developed certain activities for PH children under the age of twenty-one living in the city or county of Stockholm. The bureau itself provides a centre to replace the previous uncoordinated work done by hospitals, nursery schools, speech centres etc. At present about 1,100 PH children are registered (roughly 30 per cent being in the 7–11 year old age group). The centre is staffed by a senior social worker and four other social workers, each responsible for one section of the city. It has four nursery schools for PH children, one at the centre and the others in the city; in addition to the teaching staff and their assistants two full-time physiotherapists work at the centre and five peripatetic physiotherapists are based there. A full-time psychologist, a part-time speech therapist and a consultant paediatrician are also members of the centre's team which carries out assessment for school placement, the social workers having previously met the parents to discuss this with them, as well as doing follow-up work in the ordinary schools usually by means of case conferences at which the teachers concerned join the team.

At present the bureau is also planning to arrange lectures (in conjunction with the Board of Education and the Parents' Association) for class teachers in ordinary schools with physically handicapped pupils.

An example of how the bureau operates can be seen in the case of a very severely handicapped athetoid child now 7 years old and one of six children who have been trained there for two years by a modified version of the Peto method. Although this child has no speech, cannot walk, sits up only with difficulty and has very poor hand control she is very intelligent and her mother has secured her future placement in an ordinary school. Before she starts, the bureau's social worker will arrange for mother and child to make several visits to the school and will, with the head, recruit a full-time assistant, while her physiotherapist will have discussions with the class teacher and the director of the special aids centre on class management, seating and provision of various aids; the bureau's psychologist will meet the school psychologist to discuss test findings and possible difficulties. These members of the team will follow up and support the mother and child in this way through the child's school career.

(b) Denmark: a rural area's plans for supportive services

Quite a different pattern of supportive services is at present being established in the county of Ringkøping, Denmark, and some of the developments there were described to me by the county's chief nursing executive officer. These aim at giving improved and more comprehensive long-term supportive services to handicapped children and their families through, in particular, the public health nurses and county team.

(1) The role of the public health nurse

The public health nurse is to be the key figure in the family support and follow-up system, bringing in other professionals only where necessary. She has been chosen for this role since she, with the family doctor, often decides initially whether the child is to go on the 'at risk' register and is the first professional the mother gets to know well. In later dealings which the mother has with the health, welfare and education services, she is also often trusted as a 'neutral' person. She usually has the medical information the mother wishes and the opportunity and time to discuss with the mother long-term problems of care, anxieties about schooling and so on. She is also trained to prepare the family for meetings with other specialists and to keep them informed about arrangements which are being made for the child, and she sometimes helps the mother to carry out the programme of exercises planned by the physiotherapist. Overall, it is hoped that she will be able to provide the family with long-term support throughout the child's pre-school and school career.

The public health nurses are being prepared for this demanding role partly through in-service training, including attendance at case conferences and partly through the support of a team of specialists whom they know, the county team.

(2) *The county team*

The main function of the county team is to discuss at case conferences any particularly difficult problems of handicapped children and their families which cannot be solved by the public health nurses or by other local staff. The team has a permanent nucleus of specialists which includes the chief medical officer, other medical specialists, the family doctor, a representative from the rehabilitation clinic, a lawyer, the chief school psychologist, the chief nursing executive officer, social workers, public health nurses and a representative from the Mother's Aid Association. Others, such as the head of the child's school and the school doctor, are called in as required. The county is divided into three team areas with different social workers and nurses belonging to the team in each area. The team provides strong support for the public health nurses who are in direct contact with the family, and it is often decided at the team meetings who should help the mother on a particular problem. Another function of the team is that of a pressure group, in matters such as the establishment of more pre-schools, and it also takes seriously the responsibility for keeping the public informed about and receptive to new developments.

Special classes in ordinary schools

In this section a more detailed account is given of how the trend towards integration is actually working out in the special class system, while in the following section major problems in this area are examined. The illustrations given below are all taken from twelve schools with special classes for motor-handicapped and brain-damaged children in ordinary schools but include as well one class for hearing-impaired, one for speech-retarded and one for mentally handicapped children, and three classes for brain-injured children in an E S N school.

(i) GENERAL ORGANIZATION

The schools in which these classes were located ranged in size from a new Danish comprehensive school with over 1,000 children in grades 1–10 to a village school with only 200 in central Sweden; the number of special classes in any one school varied from six (with a total of thirty-eight pupils) to one (with six pupils). The largest class visited had nine children and the smallest, a grade 1 class with very severely handicapped cerebral-palsied children, had four, the usual figure being from six to eight children. Although the majority of children in these classes were moderately or severely handicapped cerebral-palsied children with perhaps half in each class using wheel-chairs, they included a small number of children with other handi-caps such as spina bifida or muscular dystrophy. The classes were known by a variety of names such as 'help' classes or 'CP classes' or just by a number or letter, such as 'C' classes.

The age range of each class varied; it was quite common for two grades to be combined but not usually more than two. Generally grade 1 children began on their own, going on to spend perhaps the next two years in a combined grade 1/ grade 2 class and thus having an extra year in which to consolidate the basic skills.

(ii) SCHOOL DESIGN

The premises occupied by the special classes varied a great deal, and in only one case were they totally inadequate. Most were located in ordinary schools designed for this purpose and so had such features as ramps, wide doors and corridors, low level switches, special toilets and a lift if necessary. Where there were three or more classes the layout was rather similar to that of a small special school with large purpose-built classrooms with adjoining toilets, physiotherapy and speech therapy rooms and medical rooms which served both the PH and the ordinary children. Other specialist rooms such as those for woodwork and metalwork and domestic science were also shared. In three schools the PH children had their own playground but normally their classes opened onto a communal one.

In Sweden I visited a comprehensive school into which three special classes, at present organized as a small special school on a nearby site, are to be moved. The ground floor of the school had been gutted and rebuilt, and a lift is being installed. Most of the classrooms and treatment rooms used by the PH children will be on the ground floor but the children will go to other floors for practical subjects and to the library, while the ordinary children will come to the ground floor for speech therapy, for metalwork and woodwork and to the school health centre. The common staffroom will be on the first floor. Staff of the two local special schools were closely consulted on the design and a guiding principle was to plan the rooms to encourage the greatest possible amount of contact between PH and non-handicapped children.

The same principle has been followed in the plans for a new Danish comprehensive for over 2,000 children in grades 1–10 which is to incorporate five or more special classes for PH children (since the school is in one of the centres of special instruction). A key feature here is that the school will be laid out in a number of blocks radiating from a central area, each block containing all the classes of a particular grade (for instance all grade 2 classes, including the special class) and in addition a room for small group work, a covered play area and a rest room for the PH children. Toilets are to be attached to each classroom. In a central area will be the specialist treatment room and next to the school swimming pool a small pool for hydrotherapy. A lift will give access to all parts of the school for the PH children.

(iii) EQUIPMENT

Generally the special classes were well equipped with specially adapted furniture and up-to-date educational aids and the staff were able to get advice about equipment fairly easily. It is probably true to say that, particularly in Sweden, the aids available for handicapped children in special classes are at least as comprehensive and as advanced as those in special schools here.

(iv) STAFFING

In Sweden the special classes were generally well staffed. In Stockholm, for example, one ordinary school for children in grades 1–6 had five special classes with six teachers (most of whom had had extra training), each aided by two assistants. There were also two full-time physiotherapists and one part-time, an occupational therapist and a part-time speech therapist. More commonly the class teacher had one assistant who might also help handicapped children in the ordinary class.

Among the regular school staff a post peculiar to Sweden is that of the school hostess, a person employed for a varying but usually short period each day in a number of schools although by no means in all. Her task is to make the children, especially the younger ones, feel at home in school, to help them in small matters and simply to be there as a non-teaching adult to whom they can turn for help. In several cases the hostesses had been especially valuable where there were PH children.

There is, as elsewhere, a shortage of trained teaching and paramedical staff and in view of this the few remaining special schools are being increasingly turned to for advice. There is a widespread feeling among special class teachers in Sweden that the special schools are in the best position to provide important advisory services and it is hoped that, as the number of children in special schools decreases, more experienced staff will be available as travelling consultants.

(v) RELATIONSHIPS BETWEEN THE SPECIAL CLASS AND ORDINARY CLASS TEACHERS

Most of the heads in whose schools special classes had been placed were enthusiastic about them and took a keen interest in what was going on, while allowing the special class teachers considerable autonomy. Prerequisites for good staff relationships appeared to be:

1 A head who was interested but not necessarily experienced in the education of the PH pupils.

2 A common staffroom.

3 A willingness on the part of the special staff to keep the ordinary teachers well informed about what they were doing.

4 A timetable and staffing ratio which allowed the special teachers to do some teaching in the ordinary classes and those of the ordinary staff who were interested to do some special class work.

It was suggested that when the ordinary children know the special teachers, and are also aware that their own teachers work in the special classes, they are more willing to accept the handicapped children on an equal basis.

At a school in Denmark with one PH class which contained five

K

12–14 year old severely handicapped CP children (three of whom had considerable hearing impairment, two very little speech and all severe motor difficulties), the class teacher (a trained speech therapist/teacher of hearing-impaired children) spent part of his time working with ordinary children who had reading or speech difficulties, while the specialists in the ordinary staff took the special class for English, biology, geography and history. At a meeting with the deputy head and all the teachers concerned, it was very clear that the ordinary staff were very interested in the special class and convinced that its location here was of benefit to the non-handicapped children.

(vi) INTEGRATION BETWEEN CHILDREN IN SPECIAL AND ORDINARY CLASSES

Both the amount of time which PH children spend with ordinary pupils and the quality of the interaction between them are important. The first of these varied enormously from one school to another, and seemed to depend less on the severity of the handicap than on the extent to which special teachers had thought about their practical aims in this area and how they might be achieved.

In one school, which has now had special classes for eight years, the head teacher was most imaginative about encouraging contacts, despite the location of her classes in one wing of a U-shaped school. Last year, of the thirty children in four special classes, about 40 per cent were participating in ordinary classes for at least part of the time. Certain children from ordinary classes had also, during their breaks, found interesting play going on in the special classroom, and were encouraged to join the PH children there.

It was common to find children, especially those in the upper grades, going to ordinary classes three or four times a week for subjects such as English, geography, history, biology, civics, singing and even PE. Several teachers stressed the need to integrate gradually, and thought it was more important to place a PH child in a class where he was good at something rather than worrying about whether he was the same age. Where failures to integrate were reported, this was nearly always because the child had been transferred full-time to an ordinary class without adequate preparation. One great potential advantage, especially at the pre-school level, in having special and ordinary classes within the same school is that children can be tried out for increasingly longer periods in the ordinary classes.

Apart from classroom integration other opportunities for the children to meet occur in the playground (usually shared) and at meals (although severely handicapped children usually had their own small dining-room), and one of the most useful pointers as to whether the child would fit in socially in the ordinary school appeared to be the extent to which he joined or was joined by children from the ordinary classes in the dining-room and the playground. In some schools ordinary pupils would come to the special classes during break to take their friends into the playground and to a considerable extent this reflected the amount of trouble which the special class teacher had taken to inform the ordinary pupils and staff about the handicapped children.

(vii) INFORMING PUPILS, TEACHERS AND PARENTS ABOUT THE HANDICAPPED CHILDREN

In Scandinavia there appeared to be more awareness of the importance of giving the ordinary pupils, their teachers and their parents information about the handicapped children than there is in this country, and a greater realization that getting information to the right people could affect to a considerable degree both the academic success and even more the social adjustment of the handicapped group. Although little research has been done in this important area, the empirical evidence suggests that careful preparation in the ordinary classes can do much to minimize the problem of teasing and, to a lesser extent, of social isolation. Several illustrations of what is being done are given below.

(viii) INFORMING THE CHILDREN

In one Swedish secondary school (ages thirteen to fifteen) where there are three classes for severely handicapped pupils the head holds a special assembly for all the new children. He calls the register so that the children are aware from the start that there are handicapped children among them, but since this first encounter is in the presence of a calm adult the non-handicapped group are given some cues about how to treat the other children. When the classes leave the hall, the handicapped group go out first, and the head then tells the other children a little about them. At the end of the first or during the second year the children are shown a film about cerebral palsy. (The handicapped group are consulted on this and also asked if they wish to be present when the film is shown, which they have always chosen to be.) At this school the problem of teasing has not arisen.

Another interesting example comes from a town in central Sweden where cerebral palsy was widely used as a term of mockery in all the schools. One of the special class teachers prepared, with the CP children, a tape which had a simple medical introduction and then recorded the children explaining how they did certain things, why their behaviour might sometimes seem odd and how it felt to be spastic. This tape was sent around all the schools in the district with the teachers giving time for discussion, and a great improvement in attitudes was reported.

Another common practice is for teachers in special classes (whether for PH, hearing-impaired or speech-retarded children) to go around the ordinary classes with some of the special equipment, such as deaf aids, explaining the difficulties of the handicapped pupils and how the equipment helps them. In several cases children in ordinary classes have been taken around the special classes and treatment rooms where it is explained to them what goes on there and where the use of the equipment is demonstrated to them. These methods are probably more effective than simply getting the ordinary class teacher to talk to her pupils.

A most successful example of such an approach comes from an experienced teacher of Danish speech-retarded children whose present class of seven children aged 6–8 years old includes four who are brain-injured, three being hyperactive. This class is situated on the second floor of a large, oldfashioned, noisy school where the classrooms open on to stairs leading to a central area through which the handicapped children must pass to reach their classroom. The class teacher secured for herself an invitation to one of the meetings of the school council, which includes representatives from each class. At the meeting she told the children about the special class, explaining the difficulties of the children (which she illustrated with a tape) and also explaining how the ordinary children should help by keeping a friendly eye on them during break, by being patient when they seemed to behave oddly and by not overexciting them. The school council representatives were then shown how all the equipment in the special classroom worked. Each class representative was then asked to explain to his own class the difficulties of the handicapped children and how they could help. This teacher felt that it was important for her group to retain normal contacts but at the same time realized that their behaviour could be disturbing to normal children; by such careful preparation she appeared to have ensured that the children were well accepted in the normal school. She also takes great care when placing these children in normal classes (usually after one or two years) to ensure that they will have very quick successes by being a little ahead of the other children.

As part of an advanced course in special education, three Swedish teachers have carried out a small research study into the effects of 'being prepared' upon ordinary primary school children's reactions to new handicapped classmates. The number of children in the study was too small for the results to be statistically significant, but the study did suggest strongly that the ordinary children found it much more difficult to accept handicapped children if not prepared in advance (Birgitta Clarin, personal communication). Research of this kind on a large scale would be valuable, particularly research into the type of information which is most effective.

(ix) INFORMING THE PARENTS

It has also been found advisable to give the ordinary children's parents information about the handicapped children, partly as a matter of public education and partly so that they can answer their own children's questions correctly without perpetuating mistaken beliefs. In one school all new parents are invited to visit the school, and the head, as he takes them around, explains as a matter of course the purpose of the ramps and the lift, and so can introduce the special classes in a natural way. In other cases experts from special schools and hospitals are called in to speak at parents' meetings.

(x) INFORMING THE TEACHERS

Various methods are used to inform the members of the regular staff about the PH groups' problems. In one school a paediatrician comes in to talk to all teachers and assistants who will be involved with these children, and to any others interested. In others this function is carried out by the special class teachers. The Swedish National Board of Education also tries to keep ordinary teachers informed, by means of booklets distributed to most schools, about how they can help handicapped children in their classes. Generally speaking there is, in Sweden in particular where it is aided by the press and television and by a strong Association of Parents of Handicapped Children, a climate of public opinion which tends to encourage teachers to take a positive attitude towards having handicapped pupils in ordinary schools.

Major problems in the special class system

In all the special classes I visited and in my talks with administrators I tried to get information about the actual problems which were being encountered as the special schools were gradually replaced by special classes. These seemed to be of two distinct kinds, firstly problems which are 'built into' the system and which can be minimized but not completely solved, and secondly those which are not inevitable but which at present frequently occur.

The only problem of the first kind appeared to be that of the time it took children living in sparsely populated areas to travel to the special classes. In Denmark, for example, where communications are easy and a fairly comprehensive coverage of 'centres of special instruction' exists, a few children were travelling for up to one and a half hours each way by bus, while even in Stockholm, where at present the only secondary level special classes are situated in a school south of the city, children travelling from northern suburbs have a two-hour journey each way. The consequences of such a situation are threefold. It is very tiring for the child; he does not know children in his home area and has little opportunity for after school visits to his friends; and the system is expensive to operate especially since taxis are often used.

One of the major problems of the second kind is that a number of special class teachers are either untrained or inadequately trained. On several occasions special class teachers admitted that they were unsure of the methods they should use to teach CP children, and it was fairly common to find that of three special class teachers only one had had appropriate training.

Closely related to the previous problem is that of the provision of advisory services for teachers of PH children in ordinary schools. One senior pre-school teacher in a special school described how each day she receives two or three phone calls from teachers all over the country asking for advice. Many teachers in special classes expressed the wish that experienced staff visit them, or that they could have time to visit the special institutions. There was a widespread feeling that it would be valuable if experienced staff from the special schools and classes were allocated some time for going out to the ordinary schools in an advisory capacity.

Relationships with the 'ordinary' part of the school

(i) PUPIL RELATIONSHIPS

In some cases there was so little contact between the handicapped and the other pupils that 'integration' meant almost nothing. The children arrived at different times, went in by different entrances, had separate breaks, ate, with few exceptions, in different dining-rooms or in the same one but without mixing at all since they were required to sit in classes. In one school where the situation was particularly bad no child from a special class had any lessons in ordinary classes. In most of these cases administrative arrangements and the failure to think beyond placement of handicapped and normal children in the same school were at fault. The problem of teasing was not one which appeared at all frequently, although both special and ordinary staff, parents and even a few handicapped teenagers were questioned about this. The two groups of children who are least well accepted are mentally retarded children and children with minor brain damage whose actual physical handicap is hardly apparent. As regards most PH children, however, though there may be some initial curiosity shown about them there is little teasing and few appeared to be socially isolated. This may be because in Scandinavia the public is generally very well informed about the problems of the handicapped. One mother with a diplegic son told me how surprised and dismayed she was when she took him on holiday to England to find people staring at him all the time.

(ii) RELATIONSHIPS BETWEEN THE SPECIAL AND THE ORDINARY STAFF

This can be a difficult area: in one school the situation had become so bad that for this and other reasons the special classes had been given the status of a special school, and the head of the ordinary school stated that he felt they were now quite 'divorced' from his part of the school. In another, teachers in the ordinary classes were reluctant to accept handicapped pupils, despite the existence of a large supporting special staff. In both cases a great deal of misunderstanding existed, not helped by the fact that the special classes were located in their own wing, and that in one of the schools there were even separate staffrooms, the special staff having decided the ordinary staffroom was 'too far' from their classes. In neither of these cases did the special staff teach in the ordinary classes or vice versa.

There is no need for such a situation to arise and it was exceptional to find such clearcut difficulties. They appeared to arise from a combination of factors including unfortunate location of the special classes, lack of information among the ordinary teachers about what the special staff were trying to do, personal difficulties partly due to insecurity about roles and also jealousy on the part of the ordinary teachers of the apparently privileged position – such as slightly shorter hours, smaller classes and ease in obtaining equipment – of the special staff.

Handicapped children in ordinary classes: four case histories

In this final section four short case histories are presented. They concern severely handicapped Swedish children for whom special arrangements were made in ordinary schools. Although in some cases there are unsolved problems it was my strong impression, after seeing these and other PH children in their classrooms and in the playground and after talking to head teachers, class teachers, consultants and parents, that integration of even severely handicapped children can and does work well, provided that it is properly prepared for.

A¹l the children were boys, aged ten, eleven, twelve and fourteen. Two were of superior intelligence and the others within the normal range. One had muscular dystrophy, while the others were cerebral-palsied, one being diagnosed as athetoid, one as diplegic and one as quadriplegic.

CASE I ANDERS, A IO YEAR OLD WITH MUSCULAR DYSTROPHY

Anders suffers from a progressive form of muscular dystrophy which causes wasting of the muscles and increasing weakness with great vulnerability to infections. He spends all his time in a wheelchair but is able to write slowly and to use an electric typewriter. It was against her doctor's advice but with the support of a physiotherapist that his mother was able to have him placed in an ordinary school. The head was initially very worried as to whether to accept Anders, but consulted and obtained the agreement of his staff and is now sure that he did the right thing and that it is 'quite natural' for the child to be there.

The school is a very large new one with grades 1–9, but with separate classroom and playground areas for children in grades 1–3, 4–6 and 7–9, and has been designed so that handicapped children can attend, being on one level with wide corridors and doors, and gently sloping approaches. Anders has a full-time assistant on the care side and his aids include a wheelchair, an electric typewriter and a specially adapted desk. He leaves school an hour early as he gets tired and has physiotherapy after school once a week at the local habilitation clinic a few miles away; he travels there, and to and from school, in a community-owned minibus especially equipped for the handicapped. While the other children have PE he catches up on the work he has missed by going home early.

This appears to be a most successful placement. Anders is keeping up with his school work and is popular, indeed a leader in the class. At home he has an electric 'car' in which he gets around the house and neighbourhood on his own, and he visits and is visited by many schoolfriends.

CASE 2 BENGT, A SEVERELY HANDICAPPED 11 YEAR OLD ATHETOID

This 11 year old athetoid boy is now fully integrated in an ordinary class in a school which takes children from grades 1–6 and which also has four special classes, mainly for cerebral-palsied children. He is extremely unsteady, cannot walk without support, makes gross involuntary movements with his arms and facial muscles and his speech is barely intelligible to a stranger.

After spending the first four years in the special classes, he was transferred to an ordinary class, only returning to the special class for physiotherapy while his own class has PE. He has a special desk and other technical aids and an assistant who helps him during certain lessons and the breaks and spends the rest of her time in the special classes. She noted that although his classmates look after him during break they like her to be there in the background as a responsible adult.

At first Bengt found an ordinary class tiring but this is no longer a problem. Academically he is near the top of the class, and even more striking is the fact that despite his severe difficulties and his very abnormal movements and appearance he is not only accepted by the rest of the class but obviously very popular. His entry into an ordinary class was carefully prepared. Firstly the matter was thoroughly discussed by the two class teachers concerned; his ordinary class teacher was at first worried but is now enthusiastic about having him. Secondly, after Bengt himself had agreed to this, his special class teacher spoke to his new class and their teacher herself (while the child waited outside with his father) explained his difficulties, introduced his assistant and asked for questions (which were in fact put to the assistant later on). He was made to feel welcome in the class and the problem of teasing has never arisen.

CASE 3 LARS, A 12 YEAR OLD DIPLEGIC

Lars, a goodlooking 12 year old in the same class as Bengt was very keen to transfer to an ordinary class at the same time, but since the teacher felt she could not cope with two severely handicapped pupils, it was arranged that he should go to the school nearest his home.

He is a diplegic, who walks slowly with crutches, rides a three-wheeled cycle and uses a wheelchair much of the time. His hand control is poor, he speaks slowly owing to difficulties in breathing, and he has marked perceptual problems.

For these reasons his teacher decided he should first be given a trial period in an ordinary class. He went to arithmetic lessons only and was observed and tested (in arithmetic) at the end of the trial period, went to English in the same way and finally had a full-time week in the class. As his teachers felt he could cope and he was still keen to be transferred, at the beginning of the following term he was moved to his local school, which is brand new, partially open plan, carpeted and built to take handicapped pupils, with two lifts, ramps and wide corridors.

Lars was introduced to his class in the same way as Bengt and has already made friends and is very happy there. Since he travels by taxi to the special school for physiotherapy, his whole new class have been taken there to look at the special classes and the physiotherapy department and to see one of his sessions in progress. He has also shown his class a film made of the physiotherapy there. He has an electric typewriter and special desk, and an assistant whose time-table is arranged so that she is with him for certain lessons only. When asked about how much help she gave him, he commented that it was mainly 'my friends who help me, but I help them too'. From observations in the classroom and in the playground when, accompanied by two friends (who gave the minimum of help necessary), he strapped his crutches on his cycle rack and rode over to where his mother always waits to see him cross the road, it seems that because of the preliminary care that has been taken he is likely to succeed in an ordinary school. At the end of this year when he moves into the 'secondary' part of the school, new difficulties will arise but these are already being anticipated and planned for.

CASE 4 MICHAEL, A 14 YEAR OLD SPASTIC QUADRIPLEGIC AT GRAMMAR SCHOOL

Michael's case history is given in some detail since, as he has attended at different times a wide variety of special and ordinary schools and classes, it illustrates a number of interesting points.

Michael is of superior intelligence but severely physically handicapped. His hands are worst affected; he cannot use them to write, dress or feed. Although he walks unsupported, his gait is slow and unsteady. He began school at 4 years old in an ordinary pre-school in the USA where his parents were on an extended visit. On returning to Sweden at five, the shortage of pre-schools there meant that he was out of school for a year and then, after considerable difficulties, was admitted to the local pre-school for a year. The head of the local primary school (an old building with steep stairs) would not accept him and he was admitted as one of a small number of day pupils to a special PH school.

Later some of the classes from this school were moved as a special unit into an ordinary school and during this period it was noticed that he came home with torn clothes and scratches on his face, that he had frequent nightmares and spoke little of school, while many people noted a change in his behaviour. After it had been discovered that a hyperactive classmate had been constantly teasing him and that two mentally handicapped children from another special class had been frequently knocking him down, it was decided that he should be placed in an ordinary class in another school, and his mother could not emphasize enough the enormous relief her son showed and the marked improvement in his behaviour which resulted from this. (Later on, when asked if he was ever teased in the ordinary school he answered 'No, why should they? There's nothing wrong with them.') This experience has also led his mother to stress the need to discuss with PH children regularly where they would prefer to go to school, at the same time pointing out the possible advantages and disadvantages of different kinds of schools.

Michael spent his last two years of 'compulsory school' in an ordinary class, and has just now started in the local grammar school to which he travels by taxi. When first transferred to an ordinary school he had an assistant for thirty-five hours a week: there was a reduction to twenty-five and then the teacher decided that by making a number of special arrangements she and Michael could cope without an assistant. His special aids include a specially designed desk and a tape recorder for making notes and doing exams. (He uses a sensitive microphone and a special booth has been erected in the classroom in which he sits during exams, as the class were listening in to and lipreading the answers he was recording.) He does his homework on a Possum typewriter. When he has to write, one of the school secretaries comes into the class to help, but generally his friends make carbon copies of their notes for him. It was his classmates who decided with him that an assistant on the care side was not necessary; they arranged to feed him themselves at school lunches on a rota basis while the school nurse helped with toileting.

Michael has just moved into the *gymnasium* where a lift has been installed for his benefit. He appears to have had no difficulty at all in settling in. Before he started there his mother arranged to meet all the staff and discussed the question of integration with them. Later she met each of the subject teachers in turn to discuss any special problems which might arise.

These case histories are not exceptional. The colleagues who arranged them all told me they know of many other children, similarly placed, whom they could have taken me to see. These children were chosen to fit in with my request to see pupils with severe handicaps of a kind which would make it difficult for them to be integrated within ordinary classes. They offer clear evidence that even severely disabled children can succeed academically and socially in many different kinds of ordinary schools, but very careful planning and a well-organized use of advisory staff with expert knowledge are necessary. For some children, especially those with cerebral palsy, initial placement in a special school may be a prerequisite, as it appears to have been in the case of Bengt and Lars. Arrangements of this kind are now being made, not just in a few particularly progressive areas, but increasingly throughout Sweden.

REFERENCES

ANDERSON, E. M. (1971) *Making Ordinary Schools Special: Guide Lines for Teachers No. 10.*, College of Special Education, London.

CLARIN, B. (1970) Personal communication.

JORGENSEN, I. SKOV (ed.) (1970) *Special Education in Denmark*, Det Danske Selskab, Copenhagen.

RUTTER, M., TIZARD, J., WHITMORE, K. (ed.) (1970) *Education, Health and Behaviour*, Longmans, London.

Swedish National Board of Education (1967) *Special Education in Sweden*, mimeographed information sheet, Section for Special Education UAI:I, Swedish National Board of Education, Stockholm.

YOUNGHUSBAND, E., BIRCHALL, D., DAVIE, R., PRINGLE, M. L. KELLMER (eds.) (1970) *Living with Handicap*, National Bureau for Co-operation in Child Care, London.

Chapter 10 · Concluding Comments

In our view the focus should be on the child and his family in their community and on his developmental needs as a child rather than primarily on a handicapping condition. The physical, emotional and social aspects of the child with special needs must be kept in constant balance with each other. The majority of such children grow up, and will continue to live, in a local community amongst ordinary people. They should be saved as far as possible from isolation and helped towards independence. (*Living with Handicap*, Younghusband *et al.*, 1970).

At the end of a recent meeting attended mainly by teachers, psychologists and parents of disabled children who had come together to hear about this research study, the chairman asked for a final question. It was put by a psychologist. He had, he said, found the study very interesting, but he was left with the question, 'What does it all prove?'

Now, as then, my answer must be that it does not 'prove' anything. I am not here referring primarily to statistical 'proof'. I have already pointed out that in the case of a sample which was small, and not truly random, even statistically significant results (or their absence) must be treated with caution. I mean rather that whether ordinary school placement is 'right' for any particular child is a question which is so individual and which often has so many different aspects that it would be misleading to claim that a study like this offered 'proofs' on which a decision could be based.

In essence, this study has been exploratory rather than experimental. The value of its end products, the findings, lies in pointing directions rather than in providing 'evidence' that one way is right, another wrong. Overall I hope that the information provided by this study will, when interpreted within the context of experience and prior research, be helpful in three ways. Firstly it may aid those who have to make decisions about the placement and the management in school of individual children. Secondly by pointing to gaps and inadequacies in existing provision it may indicate how the quality of such provision could be improved. Thirdly through an examination of the merits and drawbacks of different ways of organizing special educational treatment it may help to guide the planning of future services for disabled children.

My aims in this final chapter are twofold. Firstly I have tried to present as succinctly as possible the major findings which have been discussed in detail in the earlier chapters. Secondly I have at the same time tried to interpret their significance, and to tease out the implications for future policy. Among the readers of this book there will be some who disagree with the conclusions I have drawn. Their experience may suggest different interpretations, different solutions. This will be healthy because what is needed above all is that we should in this, as in other fields of education, constantly monitor, evaluate and modify what we are doing in the light of current knowledge.

The way in which I have presented the findings and their implications is in the form of answers to twelve questions. They cover those aspects of integration with which this study was concerned and which discussions with professionals of all kinds suggested were of major interest.

1 What sort of difficulties do the parents of disabled children of normal intelligence have in obtaining the type of school placement they would like?

There can be little doubt that the majority of parents in my sample preferred ordinary school placement. Of the seventy-four mothers with junior school children 4 per cent were in favour of special school placement, 13·5 per cent uncommitted and the others opposed in varying degrees; this pattern was similar for the infant group. The main reasons for these attitudes were firstly the belief that the child would obtain a better education in an ordinary school and secondly that he would benefit socially.

Special school placement had been suggested at some stage for two thirds of the 99 children in the study but only 8·1 per cent had actually attended special schools or units. Among the juniors the proportion of children with 'high' attainments and the proportion who were 'well-adjusted' were similar among those children for whom a special school had been suggested and among those for whom such placement had never been considered. This suggests that many parents were justified in insisting on ordinary school placement.

Commonly occurring problems connected with placement were that advice had come very late (when the child was well into his fourth year); that information about the alternatives available was often absent or inadequate; that the advice given by different professionals was sometimes contradictory; that placement decisions sometimes appeared to be made on the basis of a brief visit by a medical officer to the child's home; that it was sometimes necessary to be extremely persistent in order to obtain a recommendation for ordinary school placement. In a few cases ordinary schools had refused or had been unable to accept disabled pupils.

It is certainly the case that many local authority officials go to great trouble to meet the parents' wishes, and parents can on occasion be unrealistic about the ability of ordinary schools to cope with their child's physical or educational difficulties. Nevertheless, since the success of a child's placement depends to a considerable degree on how the parents feel about it, the importance of consulting them early on, and fully, about their wishes and of involving them in the final decision cannot be overestimated.

2 Are disabled children in ordinary schools really accepted by their non-handicapped classmates?

The overall impression given by this study was that at the primary school level the amount and quality of social integration between handicapped and non-handicapped children both inside and outside school was very encouraging. Nine in every ten parents of handicapped children (and eight in ten of the control group parents) considered that their children were happy at school, a view which was largely confirmed by teachers' reports and by my own observations.

This is not to deny the existence of problems in social relationships. The sociometric test results and other data showed that handicapped children were chosen less often as friends than the controls. There were considerable differences according to the nature of the disability, cerebral-palsied children followed by children with spina bifida tending to be the least popular whereas those with congenital abnormalities had almost as many friends as the controls. On the other hand, friendship choices did not appear to be affected by the severity of the handicap or by the actual functions which were impaired. Incontinent children were as likely to be chosen as friends as those with impaired mobility.

When individual friendship patterns were examined, a considerably smaller proportion of neurologically abnormal children were selected as 'best friends' or had their choice of friends reciprocated than was true of children with purely physical disorders who were more like the control group. This was also the case when the number of isolates (children receiving no friendship choices) was investigated. Only 3·4 per cent of the controls and 6·3 per cent of the handicapped children without neurological abnormalities were isolates, compared to 15·3 per cent of the neurologically abnormal group. Among the controls, sex and social isolation were unrelated whereas all the handicapped isolates but one were boys. Disabled children most 'at risk' of social isolation were of below average ability and attainment level; they tended to come from deprived or overprotective homes; finally, three out of the seven were cerebral-palsied.

Teasing was only a minor problem, although parent reports indicated that more was going on than teachers were aware of. Most children were only teased 'occasionally', namecalling being the most common form. Teasing was virtually confined to schools in London and a nearby industrial area, as were the few cases of bullying reported. Generally, once teasing had been reported it was dealt with effectively by the staff.

In many cases, teachers can do a great deal to further the social acceptance of handicapped children by preparing the class, or the school, for their arrival. This is only possible when the staff have adequate advance information. Preferably the head and class teacher should meet the child and his parents to discuss this beforehand.

The handicapped children had a good deal of contact with their classmates outside school hours. Although more of the controls (about two-thirds) than of the handicapped children (about half) saw their schoolfriends 'frequently' after school and at weekends, the amount of visiting between homes was comparable. Most parents were satisfied with the contacts their children had with neighbourhood friends, although sometimes this was restricted by the severity of the handicap.

3 Is social independence encouraged by ordinary school placement?

Findings on the Manchester scales of social adaptation suggested that social knowledge scores were related to intelligence level rather than to the severity or type of the handicap. Scores on the self-direction subscales, on the other hand, were clearly related to the severity of the handicap, the controls doing best, followed by the mildly, moderately and severely handicapped children in that order. Among the infants the fact that the social quotients (Vineland scale) were in all cases but one lower than the intelligence quotients was a reflection of the general severity of the handicaps.

In addition the presence or absence of a neurological abnormality also seemed to affect social independence. When twenty-four items on the Manchester self-direction scales measuring different aspects of independence were analysed separately, the controls were superior to the handicapped children without neurological abnormalities on ten items, but superior to the neurologically abnormal group on eighteen items. The cerebral-palsied children in particular were, although often mildly handicapped, less independent on many items than other handicapped children, especially on items reflecting within-the-home activities. There may be a tendency for this group to be overprotected at home.

On the whole the children's actual scores, with the exception of some of the neurologically abnormal group, suggested that they were as independent as their handicaps allowed. The rather long interview with the children which this test demands certainly suggested that the majority were keen to be as independent as their peers and were sensitive to the implications about independence of the questions put to them. Comparison of similarly handicapped children in special schools would be illuminating but for the majority of children ordinary school placement appeared to act as a stimulus to social independence.

4 Do disabled children in ordinary primary schools show a higher rate of different kinds of emotional and behavioural problems than their classmates?

Roughly 80 per cent of the infants and 73 per cent of the juniors in this study appeared to be making a good adjustment to their disabilities. Those anxieties which were expressed related mainly to appearance, to incontinence or to the inability to join in. The children who accepted their handicaps least well were more likely to have mothers whom teachers described as overprotective or overdemanding than were the other children.

The main measures used to investigate the extent and nature of behaviour disorders were the Rutter-Graham scales. The parent scale showed few differences in the rate of disorders among the controls (11·5 per cent) and the handicapped group (11·9 per cent), although when the latter group was subdivided the children with neurological abnormalities showed a higher rate of disorders (16·7 per cent) than did those without (9·0 per cent). The teacher scale showed an overall higher rate of disorder, 19 per cent among the controls and 14 per cent among the handicapped children. Once again there was a higher rate of deviant behaviour (25·0 per cent) in the neurologically abnormal group than among the other handicapped children (9·0 per cent). There was no evidence of any association between on the one hand the severity or visibility of the handicap, or the actual functions impaired, and on the other the presence of a behaviour disorder.

These findings suggest that most children without neurological disorders are well able to cope, emotionally, with the environment of an ordinary primary school. Certainly the rate of disorder in the control group especially among the girls was unexpectedly high, but even if it had been considerably lower the controls and children with purely physical disorders would still have been comparable. On the other hand the fact that one in four of the neurologically abnormal children were rated as 'deviant' on the teacher scale bears out what has already been said about this group being most 'at risk' in ordinary schools.

The children without neurological abnormalities also resembled the controls in that the disorder was generally expressed in antisocial rather than neurotic behaviour. The neurologically abnormal children on the other hand were as likely to show a neurotic as an antisocial type of disorder. Among the infants (two-thirds of whom had neurological abnormalities) the type of disturbed behaviour shown varied from marked aggression to almost complete withdrawal.

When individual items of behaviour were considered, the most striking finding was the short concentration span which teachers reported in 88 per cent of the cerebral-palsied and of the hydrocephalic juniors, but in only 43 per cent of the other handicapped children and 35 per cent of the controls. In the infant group as a whole, 76 per cent of the children had poor concentration compared to 23 per cent in a large group of non-handicapped infants.

5 Overall, how well were the disabled children coping with the social and emotional aspects of ordinary school placement?

All the children were rated as 'well adjusted' or 'less well adjusted' on the basis of their scores on a ten-item scale which took into account all the main aspects of social and emotional adjustment considered in the study. Some 72 per cent of the controls and 66·6 per cent of the PH children without neurological abnormalities were 'well adjusted'. In contrast, only one in three of the neurologically abnormal children fell into the well-adjusted group.

Factors which were unrelated to overall social adjustment included the age of the child, the severity of the handicap and the presence of a purely physical disorder *per se*. Factors which did affect social adjustment were intelligence level and also the presence of a neurological abnormality. A significantly higher proportion of children with congenital abnormalities than of those with cerebral palsy were well adjusted. In addition there was a tendency for the less well-adjusted children in both the handicapped and control groups to come from large families and from social classes IV and V. Among the handicapped children but not among the controls there was a tendency for the less well-adjusted children to be boys and to come from London schools rather than from urban schools outside London.

These findings do suggest which handicapped children are likely to be most vulnerable socially and emotionally in ordinary schools, a vulnerability which, because many are relatively mildly handicapped, may go unnoticed. Teachers need to be aware of the sort of difficulties (particularly in concentration) which these children may have, and should be assisted by their initial training courses, by in-service training and by advisory help in coping with their needs.

6 Do the educational attainments of disabled children in ordinary schools suggest that such placement is appropriate?

This study was mainly concerned with children of junior school age, but an attempt was also made to assess the educational progress of a small group of rather severely handicapped infants. Some of these had only started school recently and measurable attainments were not yet expected. Although almost half of the infants were handicapped quite severely by spina bifida and hydrocephalus no child scored below 70 on either the English picture vocabulary test (where the mean I Q was 105·7) or on Raven's coloured matrices (mean I Q 103·0, a surprisingly high figure in view of the children's handicaps).

Teachers rated six children as above average in their attainments, eight as average and eleven as below, and these ratings were confirmed by results on the Southgate reading test. In five cases the child's progress was so slow and his difficulties such that transfer to a special school at the junior level had been arranged, the only alternative available being placement in a large ordinary class. It was quite clear that it was the children's learning problems rather than their physical problems which made placement in a large ordinary class difficult.

In the case of the junior school children, only non-verbal intelligence was tested (NFER non-verbal test 5), no difference being found in the range of scores or in the mean I Q of the controls (104·7) and the PH children without neurological abnormalities (102·2). Among the neurologically abnormal group the mean I Q was only 83·3 (for which perceptual difficulties may have been partly responsible) and the scores clustered in the range 75–90, 48 per cent of the group having scores below 85. These differences must be remembered when the children's attainments are considered. No differences were found in the mean scores of the mildly, moderately and severely handicapped children.

For number work ability, 30·8 per cent of the controls and 29·5 per cent of the PH children without neurological abnormalities were given below average ratings compared to 78·1 per cent of the neurologically abnormal group. It seems unlikely that it was solely differences in intelligence level which were responsible for this disparity. Few children who needed extra help in arithmetic were getting it.

A similar pattern of results was found for reading, where two-thirds of the neurologically abnormal group were rated as 'below average'. The Neale analysis of reading ability test showed that, on average, the controls and PH children without neurological disorders were reading at an accuracy level a month below their chronological age (CA) whereas the neurologically abnormal children were on average fifteen months below. For comprehension the pattern was similar, the average comprehension age of the first two groups being two months below the CA but in the case of the neurologically abnormal group nineteen months below. Again, although these differences can be partly explained by IQ level differences, the IQ level of the neurologically abnormal child was such that a greater degree at least of reading fluency could have been expected.

The rate of reading backwardness (defined as a reading age at least twenty-eight months below the CA) was 10·1 per cent among the controls, 14·5 per cent among the PH children without neurological abnormalities and 27·0 per cent among the neurologically abnormal group. More remedial help was available for reading than for arithmetic but it was still often inadequate for handicapped and non-handicapped pupils alike.

When the different attainment measures used were combined to give an overall academic attainment score, and the children divided into high or low attainers, 26·3 per cent of the controls were low attainers, 33·3 per cent of the PH group without neurological abnormalities and 76·9 per cent of the group with such abnormalities. As in the case of social adjustment, the factors most closely related to attainment level were intelligence and the presence of a neurological abnormality. Children from small professional families were also more likely to do well. The size of the school class, the severity of the handicap, age and the presence of a purely physical disorder did not appear to be related to attainment level.

What conclusions do these findings suggest? Firstly, most of the children with purely physical disorders were well able to cope with and to benefit from the normal curriculum of an ordinary school. Secondly, I think it would be wrong to jump to the conclusion that the majority of children with neurological abnormalities were incorrectly placed in ordinary schools. Of the eight children whom teachers considered would be better placed elsewhere (either in a smaller class or a special school) only four were children with neuro-logical abnormalities (i.e. about 15 per cent of the neurologically abnormal group).

What was clear, however, was that a much larger proportion of this group than of the other PH children or the controls required extra help within the ordinary school and a number of possible ways of providing this, through 'help' clinics, peripatetic teachers, special classes and in-service training for regular class teachers have been suggested in this book.

A third point which these findings suggest is that in view of the differences found between the children with and without neuro-logical abnormalities, the blanket category 'physically handicapped' may be misleading. As was noted in *Living with Handicap* (Young-husband *et al.*, 1970), 'delineating a category helps to focus attention on it and promotes the provision of necessary resources. Reformulat-ing categories from time to time in \the light of experience and research is more than changing labels: it involves a re-thinking of the nature of special educational needs.'

These and other findings suggest that it is not the physical handi-cap *per se* but the existence of learning disorders which is important. The category physically handicapped might usefully be replaced by the two categories of motor- (or orthopaedically) handicapped and neurologically handicapped. Or, as Mittler (1970) has suggested, all the official categories might be replaced by the wider category of 'learning disorder'. This, he says, 'would have the advantage of stressing the educational and developmental aspects of the problem as distinct from primarily medical and administrative considera-tions'. Whatever reformulation is adopted it should be one which helps the ordinary teacher to identify those children in greatest need of help.

7 Are the needs of teachers with disabled children in their classes being met?

Most of the heads and class teachers in this study showed an encour-aging willingness to assume responsibility for children who were in some way 'different', and were coping with their daily needs sensibly and sensitively. At the same time their natural sympathy towards handicapped children may be traded on in the sense that once a school has agreed to accept a child it is unlikely that any further advice, support or even encouragement will be forthcoming from anyone outside the school other than the parents and sometimes the school medical officer.

Nearly half of the junior school teachers had had initial anxieties about coping with a disabled child. In particular, injuries were feared. One in six did not even know the nature of the handicap before the child arrived. The main source of information about the child was, for the infant teachers, the child's mother and for the junior school teachers, their colleagues. About 80 per cent of the former and 33 per cent of the latter were dissatisfied with the amount of information they had been given about the child, particularly on the medical side. It was exceedingly rare for the class teacher to have met either the medical officer who recommended the placement or the school medical officer (or indeed any other informed person) to discuss the physical condition and its management. Teachers would certainly welcome more information and advice, and this is needed both initially and in the form of a follow-up visit or letter during the first term, and in some cases at regular intervals afterwards.

On the educational side little advice was available either. A wide range of problems may be encountered and it is strongly recommended that local authorities consider establishing or extending a system of advisers for special education with special responsibility for children in ordinary schools. The amount of specialization among advisers will differ from one authority to another but there is no doubt that such a service would meet a need which already exists and which is likely to increase. At the same time the colleges of education should be preparing teachers to cope with a wide variety of handicapping conditions in ordinary schools.

8 How adequate are the arrangements made for the physical care and treatment of disabled children in ordinary schools?

The special provisions made in ordinary schools vary enormously from one local authority to another. Adaptations to the buildings are sometimes made before a child arrives and sometimes later on, on an *ad hoc* basis. In some cases they are clearly needed but have never been requested. Outstanding needs were for adaptations to help children with problems either of mobility or of toileting, and the need for toilet privacy was often not realized.

Few special educational aids were being used. Teachers were not always aware that a need existed, or of what equipment was available or how it could be obtained. It may be preferable for the adviser for special education and/or a medical officer to approach the school to find out what modifications or aids are needed, rather than waiting for a request to be made.

Some local authorities were very successfully meeting the daily physical needs of severely handicapped children through the appointment of personal assistants. This is often essential as without such a helper an impossible burden would be placed on the class teacher, and the extension of this system is recommended.

Roughly 12 per cent of the children needed physiotherapy and 7 per cent speech therapy. Facilities varied from one area to another. Speech therapists were in short supply. In the case of physiotherapy it was sometimes the case that a weekly session at the local hospital (the most common arrangement) met the child's needs. For children requiring daily exercises the situation was much less satisfactory. One interesting solution which might be worth extending was for a physiotherapist or remedial gymnast to visit the school regularly while leaving the daily exercises to the child's assistant under their supervision. This system was rare and the liaison between the school and the therapist often poor. Certainly, the present situation does not encourage ordinary school placement for children requiring intensive physiotherapy. Overall it would be extremely valuable if a small research scheme could be set up to explore the most effective ways of providing physiotherapy for children in ordinary schools in both rural and urban areas.

9 Is there a case for setting up more special classes for disabled children in ordinary schools?

In Scandinavia the special class system is increasingly being used as an alternative to the special school. In England the situation is quite different since special classes are at present only available for a minute proportion of physically handicapped children. Scandinavian experience suggests that such classes could, for many children, provide a satisfactory alternative (and one which parents would prefer) to day or residential PH school placement, particularly for those with severe physical handicaps, with specific learning disabilities in addition to a physical handicap or with minimal cerebral dysfunction.

While an extension of the special class system is advocated, two provisos must be made. The first is that if special classes are to offer facilities equal in quality to those of special schools – and there is no reason why they should not do so – then comparable resources must be allocated to them. The siting of the classes, the consultation with staff of the 'parent' school, the designing and equipping of the unit and the quality of the staffing are all immensely important factors. This is stressed by the Association for Special Education who, in the evidence they presented to the commission on children with special needs (Younghusband *et al.*, 1970) recommended that 'special education in ordinary schools should be special in fact as well as in name. The curriculum, methods, staffing and facilities should be very similar to those in special schools.' They added that 'special classes in ordinary schools should be planned and organized as part of the special education service, with a mutual interchange of information, methods and personnel'.

The second proviso which must be made is that the results of this and other studies suggest that real integration is more difficult to achieve if a child is placed in a special class than if the same child were placed individually in an ordinary class. While special classes offer much greater potential for integration than does the special school, this potential will only be realized if all the staff are convinced of the value of integration and plan carefully how it is to be achieved.

10 Is it possible to provide for the needs of several disabled children in an ordinary school without setting up a special class?

Once the decision has been taken to place several physically handicapped children in the same school, there are a number of ways in which special provision can be organized. A common alternative to the special class is to make extensive adaptations in a school, to appoint extra staff on the care side, to provide special transport and then to place the children individually in ordinary classes.

While this arrangement is satisfactory for children with purely physical disorders, it may not meet the needs of children with learning disorders or those who for other reasons need extra individual help. One way of getting around this is to appoint an extra teacher or teachers to the staff so that the size of the classes in which the handicapped children are placed can be substantially reduced, giving the class teacher more chance to provide individual help.

While this may work well, especially at the infant level, there is another possibility. This is to establish within the adapted school a 'help clinic' or 'resource room' and to appoint to the staff a teacher especially qualified or experienced in work with children with learning disorders, with a post of special responsibility for the handicapped children. While they will be placed in ordinary classes, they will go to the 'clinic' for specialized help as required. The teacher will spend part of her time teaching in the ordinary classes, and part in the clinic. The advantage of this system is that by remaining in the ordinary classes the children are more likely to be integrated socially, yet at the same time can get the specialized help they need. This system is now being tried out in one or two areas. Very careful planning is needed, and a great deal will depend on the calibre of the staff, but it seems an extremely promising approach.

11 How much does it cost to make special provisions of these kinds for disabled children in ordinary schools?

Nothing has yet been said about the comparative cost of different types of special provision. This question does not seem to have been officially investigated, the assumption usually being that ordinary school placement will be cheaper. With the help of figures provided by the Institute of Municipal Treasurers and Accountants (IMTA, 1972) and by three LEAs, appendix M was compiled. It is intended as no more than a rough guide, since some of the figures were only estimates and are likely to vary considerably from one authority to another. The costs per child shown in the appendix can be compared with the IMTA figure of £102.23 for the total cost (including debt charges) per ordinary primary school pupil per annum (1970–1, all authorities).

As appendix M shows, the cost per annum for a physically handicapped child will be roughly £571 in a day PH school, £532 in a special class and £655 in an ordinary class where three children are sharing taxi transport and a welfare assistant. For one child alone, the latter costs would be likely to rise to a total of over £1,000. While comparatively few disabled pupils will require full-time assistants and while two or three such pupils can usually be placed in the same school (except in rural areas), it has to be stressed that adequate help for severely handicapped children in ordinary schools cannot be provided cheaply. However, the average cost per PH pupil in an ordinary school would probably be substantially less than this.

12 If increasing numbers of disabled children are placed in ordinary schools, what will be the role of the special schools?

If more disabled children are placed in ordinary schools under the different kinds of arrangements described in this book, the situation here is likely to come to resemble that in Scandinavia, where there has been a reduction in the number of special schools and a rethinking of the functions of those that remain. As the pattern of handicaps has changed so markedly over the last two decades it would in any case be disturbing if the special schools were not rethinking their functions.

For certain children special schools may always be needed, but as the provision of special educational treatment within ordinary schools increases, this need is likely to be smaller than at present. Discussions in Sweden, where integration has already gone quite far, suggested three main functions for the special schools – all, I think, of relevance for us. The first is that they should be used increasingly as observation and assessment centres. Secondly they should provide children (from as early an age as possible) with an initial period of skilled and intensive training by teachers and therapists working closely together. Initial training in the use of special educational aids may be included. Children with neurological abnormalities are particularly likely to benefit from such a start. After this period, which might for some children last from one to four years, many children would be ready for transfer to a special or ordinary class. Ideally the special school would be sited close to an ordinary infant school so that for at least part of the time handicapped and non-handicapped children could be taught in mixed groups.

Thirdly special schools could act as advisory centres from which, as part of their duties, experienced teachers and therapists could travel as consultants to teachers in special and ordinary classes who needed help. We should certainly be considering ways in which the experience available in special schools can be made more readily available to those working outside them.

*　　　*　　　*　　　*　　　*

As a postscript, three last comments.

The first concerns handicapped teenagers. The present study was restricted to children in primary schools. Since little work had been done on integration it seemed logical to start by looking at children in this age group. However, it is the teenagers who are likely to have the greater problems. Kellmer Pringle and Fiddes (1970) in their study of thalidomide children pointed out that adolescence 'would bring new and serious problems which should be anticipated now by setting up a psychological counselling service for both parents and children'. In *Living with Handicap* (Younghusband et al., 1970) the authors comment on 'the surprising failure to recognize the acute problem of isolation from their peers that confronts many of the more seriously handicapped adolescents. We think it urgent that (their) needs should receive more systematic study and that greater efforts should be made to meet them as far as possible.' Some 20 per cent of the junior school teachers I interviewed anticipated problems of varying kinds, social, educational and physical, once their pupils had to transfer to secondary schools. It is certainly my own belief that research into the situation of the disabled teenager in ordinary schools is a matter of the first importance.

My second comment refers to the answer I was given when I asked the head of a nursery school in which total integration had been achieved what she considered to be essential if integration was really going to work. Her reply was that all those involved must *believe* in it. Such a belief was necessary but not sufficient. It must be backed up by the provision of the resources of the kind described in this book. Successful integration cannot be achieved on a shoestring.

I should like to end on a personal note. The most rewarding aspect of the many visits I made was that they gave me a new and first-hand appreciation of what is *possible*. Given special provisions of the kind I have described, it is possible to offer even severely handicapped children a satisfactory education in an ordinary school. Given imagination, backed up by expertise and by financial resources, it is possible to provide for children with additional specific learning difficulties without segregating them. Given commitment to the idea of integration it is possible, as Scandinavian experience has shown, to increase substantially the proportion of disabled children being educated in ordinary schools and to offer them facilities of the same quality as those at present provided in special schools. I was constantly surprised to discover how often the arrangements I have

304 · THE DISABLED SCHOOLCHILD

described opened up new possibilities to the parents, teachers, psychologists, doctors and others with whom I discussed them.

Many people feel strongly about the issues discussed in this book and it is difficult to achieve a balance between caution and optimism. I hope that I have drawn attention to the need for a very sober and down-to-earth assessment of the practical problems involved. I hope even more, however, that I have conveyed something of the exciting possibilities open to us for furthering the integration of disabled people in the community by making ordinary schools special.

REFERENCES

Institute of Municipal Treasurers and Accountants and Society of County Treasurers (1971) *Education Statistics, 1970–71*, IMTA/SCT, London.

MITTLER, P. (1970) *The Psychological Assessment of Mental and Physical Handicaps*, Methuen, London.

YOUNGHUSBAND, E., BIRCHALL, D., DAVIE, R., and PRINGLE, M. L. KELLMER (eds.) (1970) *Living with Handicap*, National Bureau for Co-operation in Child Care, London.

Appendices

Appendix A   List of tests and other assessment procedures

1. Intellectual and language development
(i)   English picture vocabulary test, Brimer and Dunn*
(ii) Raven's coloured matrices, a non-verbal test*
(iii) NFER non-verbal test 5, a group test†

2. Educational attainment
(i)   Southgate group reading test (Form 1A)*
(ii) Neale analysis of reading ability (Form A), giving accuracy and comprehension scores†
(iii) Teacher's assessment of child's achievement level in (a) reading and (b) arithmetic, made on a five-point scale
(iv) Teacher's assessment of child's overall achievement level made on a five-point scale
(v)   Parent's assessment of child's overall achievement level made on a five-point scale

3. Emotional and social adjustment
(i)   Sociometric test (see appendix F)†
(ii) Children's behaviour questionnaires (Rutter scales) completed by parents and teachers
(iii) Reports from parents and teachers obtained during the interviews
(iv) Manchester scales of social adaptation†
(v)   Vineland social maturity scale*
(vi) Observations of behaviour during group and individual testing sessions

* Infant group only
† Junior group only

Appendix B Assessment of disabilities

B.1. Notes on the ratings for the functional assessment of disabilities

The notes below summarize the criteria used in evaluating the children's functional disabilities on a four-point scale. As stated in chapter 2, they are derived mainly from the Pultibec system described by Lindon (1963) which was slightly modified for the purposes of this study.

PHYSICAL CAPACITY (HEALTH)

1 Physical capacity, general health, stature, body build, exercise tolerance and endurance, good average to exceptional. Capable of a full day's work. (No person with an overt defect can be placed in this grade.) (Note that children with functional difficulties but without any overt defect should be recorded under the appropriate quality only. P in these instances would remain grade 1.)

2 Physical capacity etc. low to average but within normal limits. If any one or more of these factors are affected or any defect such as scoliosis is present, even if they do not affect general health, the person should not be graded higher than P2.

3 Physical capacity less than in 2 but nevertheless capable of a full day's work if the environment is suitable. (Open employment likely.)

4 Physical capacity etc. reduced to an extent of rendering the person incapable of a full day's normal work or travelling without special facilities. (Probably sheltered employment.)

UPPER LIMBS

1 Normal

2 Slight loss of intricate skill due to loss of co-ordination but power and range normal for manual work – able to feed and wash.

3 Range and/or power limited as well as skill – not able to feed but can grasp objects.

4 Severe loss. Useless for all practical purposes (includes amputations).

LOCOMOTION

1 Able to use limb/limbs in a completely normal way.

2 Slight difficulty – able to run and walk but with less than usual dexterity and speed. May have some difficulty with stairs and crowds. Distance usually travelled in everyday life is not a problem.

3 Moderate difficulty. Able to walk only short to moderate distances (i.e. approximately 20–200 yards) without a rest at a slow pace and if necessary with aids. Tendency to fall rather easily. Running impractical but possible with one good limb. Stairs take time – some help may be needed.

4 May be able, with close supervision, to walk a few steps and to stand when holding on or supported. Stairs and gradients virtually impossible. Suitable building and transport necessary. Wheelchair needed when help not available, or all the time.

TOILET

1 Normal

2 Nocturnal enuresis – no special arrangement for day care.

3 Continent for practical purposes with, if necessary, aid of a urinary bag or catheter for bladder control or special training for bowel control. Special arrangements of width and space of toilet arrangements or hand rails etc. render child independent of further assistance. Able to attend to himself with special provisions.

4 As in 3, with additional problems such as manipulative difficulties, necessitating help in addition to, if necessary, special arrangements as in 3.

INTELLIGENCE-RATINGS

1 100+

2 85–99

3 70–84

4 below 70

BEHAVIOUR

1 Normal. Conscientious and persistent in any task. Well adjusted and unlikely to break down despite considerable provocation and difficulties even when considerably handicapped.

2 Normal – conscientious and persistent in tasks within his or her known capacity. Adjusted in normal circumstances.

3 Normal limits – conscientious, but lacks drive as compared with grades 1 and 2. Shows persistence and adjustment in favourable circumstances. Often emotionally immature or overexcitable and may be overprotected at home with a tendency to break down if this ceases. Needs close and kindly observation at school and later at work with advice and help to parents and employers.

4 Abnormal – overtly aggressive, withdrawn or other antisocial tendencies etc. beyond normal limits. Specialist medical evaluation and care usually necessary.

EYESIGHT

1 Normal visual acuity for near and distance vision.

2 Refractive error corrected by glasses for near and distance vision.

3 Strabismus, with or without suppression amblyopia – vision in used eye normal with or without glasses. Loss of binocular vision or latent squint if evaluated.

4 Visual impairment not completely corrected though visual acuity better than 6/24 with glasses.

COMMUNICATION

(a) *Hearing*

1 Normal hearing.

2 Borderline normal or variable hearing loss (eustachian catarrh). The former have slight loss of hearing for long distance conversation. Pure tone loss usually not over 60 dB except temporarily.

3 Partially deaf – satisfactory for person in normal school. Pure tone audiograph – loss over 30 dB but under 60 dB and usually aid from visiting peripatetic teacher of the deaf. Under care of audiology unit for full assessment and hearing aid evaluation.

4 Partially deaf – hearing loss similar to grade 3 but within region of 60 dB and above though largely below 85 dB. Needs special class for partially deaf. Under care of audiology unit.

(b) *Speech*

1 Speaks well at age level.

2 Mildly defective and some lack of clarity and/or fluency but intelligible to strangers.

3 Definite speech defects: consistently intelligible to children and adults who know child well, but not within normal time limits to all strangers, e.g. stammer, mild articulatory dyspraxias and dysarthrias.

4 Moderate speech defect intelligible to parents and siblings but not to others within normal time limits.

REFERENCES

LINDON, R. L. (1963), 'The Pultibcc system for the medical assessment of physically handicapped children', *Developmental Medicine and Child Neurology*, 5, pp. 125–45.

B.2. Functional assessment of disability - mildly handicapped child (example)

NAME OF CHILD ....

D.O.B. ....

HANDICAP ....R. Hemiplegia..

	A problems					B problems					
P	U		L		T	I	B	E		C	
	R	L	R	L				R	L	H	S

Grade
1 - no problem
2 - minor problem
3 - major problem
4 - major problem

P	Health good. Gait slightly abnormal, obvious flexion deformity of r. hand
U	Writes with l. hand. Slight loss of power r. arm and difficulty with fine finger movements of r. hand. Can't do shoelaces or tie, use scissors or cut up meat
L	Drags r. leg, but can run, climbs stairs slowly, participates in all physical activities
T	Normal
I	NFER non-verbal 5–86. Attainments poor, but improving steadily with remedial help. Teacher suspects child may have undiagnosed perceptual and visuo-motor difficulties
B	A scale -13 (antisocial disorder) Both parents and teacher B scale - 8 noted his restlessness, poor concentration and tendency to solitary play. A lonely child
E	Acuity normal
C	Hearing: normal Speech : slight dysarthria, difficulty in pronouncing words

Summary

Total problems : 6 (3 in A, 3 in B)

Major problems : 1 (in B)

Rating : mild handicap

B.3. Functional assessment of disability - severely handicapped child (example)

NAME OF CHILD..

D.O.B. ....

HANDICAP.........Spina bifida and hydrocephalus..................................

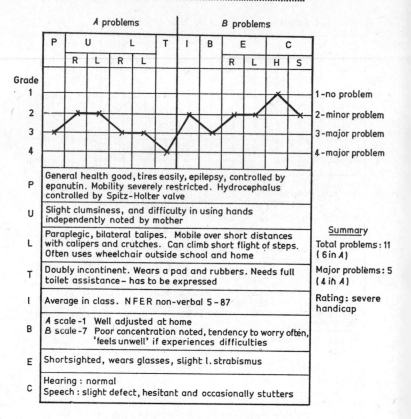

	A problems							B problems			
P	U		L		T	I	B	E		C	
	R	L	R	L				R	L	H	S

Grade
1 — 1-no problem
2 — 2-minor problem
3 — 3-major problem
4 — 4-major problem

P	General health good, tires easily, epilepsy, controlled by epanutin. Mobility severely restricted. Hydrocephalus controlled by Spitz-Holter valve
U	Slight clumsiness, and difficulty in using hands independently noted by mother
L	Paraplegic, bilateral talipes. Mobile over short distances with calipers and crutches. Can climb short flight of steps. Often uses wheelchair outside school and home
T	Doubly incontinent. Wears a pad and rubbers. Needs full toilet assistance – has to be expressed
I	Average in class. NFER non-verbal 5-87
B	A scale -1 Well adjusted at home B scale -7 Poor concentration noted, tendency to worry often, 'feels unwell' if experiences difficulties
E	Shortsighted, wears glasses, slight l. strabismus
C	Hearing : normal Speech : slight defect, hesitant and occasionally stutters

Summary
Total problems : 11
(6 in A)

Major problems : 5
(4 in A)

Rating : severe handicap

C.1. **Survey of physically handicapped children in ordinary schools (England) 1969-70: aids provided** (from *Health of the School Child*, 1972)

Disability	Number using wheel-chair	Number using walking aid (any)	Number using one or more pros-theses	Number using hearing aid	Number receiv-ing personal assis-tance	All children in survey
Cerebral palsy	47	161	17	28	403	1 468
Spina bifida	56	125	19	4	122	437
Myelomeningocele with Spitz-Holter valve	62	81	9	—	94	124
Myelomeningocele without Spitz-Holter valve	39	99	9	2	93	231
Hydrocephalus without myelo-meningocele	12	26	1	1	56	246
Post poliomyelitis	13	260	14	—	61	532
Heart defects rheu-matic, congenital	11	15	16	12	106	2 112
Haemophilia and Christmas disease	11	18	2	—	16	244
Muscular dystrophy and atrophy	53	32	11	1	134	268
Limbs – upper, lower, talipes, dislocated hips	84	428	363	11	444	2 397
Amputation – upper and lower limbs	11	34	163	2	33	204
Perthe's disease	13	199	9	2	68	456
Rheumatoid arthritis	6	17	3	2	32	199
Achondroplasia and other types of dwarfing	2	7	3	3	44	255
Other	54	192	44	29	308	1 911
TOTAL CHILDREN	393	1 482	597	73	1 748	10 200

C.2. Survey of physically handicapped children in ordinary schools (England) 1969-70: incontinence (from *Health of the School Child*, 1972)

Age	Boys and girls				
	Bladder only	Bowel only	Both bladder and bowel	Total	Number wearing appliance
5 and under	36	5	48	89	25
6	51	11	54	116	45
7–10	141	27	100	258	110
11–15	88	18	37	163	71
16 and over	11	2	8	21	11
TOTAL	327	63	247	637	262

Appendix D The sample

D.1. Mean age of different groups

Groups	No.	Mean age (months)	SD (months)
Total PH group	74	105·93	10·18
Controls	148	105·43	10·28
PH children without neurological abnormalities	48	106·43	10·74
PH children with neurological abnormalities	26	105·0	9·19

D.2. Distribution of handicapped children by forms

	Boys	Girls	Total	%
Form I	21	12	33	44·5
Form II	8	12	20	27·0
Form III	13	8	21	28·3
TOTALS	42	32	74	100·0

D.3. Size of class

No. of pupils in class	% of junior group No. = 74	% of infant group No. = 25
25 or below	14·9	12·0
26–30	24·3	24·0
31–35	33·8	40·0
36–40	25·5	24·0
Over 40	1·4	0·0

D.4. Children with toileting problems: junior group

	Nature of difficulty			
Disorder	Incontinence of bladder	Incontinence of bowels	Doubly incontinent	Total
Spina bifida	1	0	7	8
Bilateral hydronephrosis and hydroureters	1	0	0	1
Spinal injury and paraplegia	1	0	0	1
Ectopic vesica	1	0	0	1
Absence of rectum	0	1	0	1
Absence of lower bowel	0	0	1	1
Nocturnal enuresis and some day-time incontinence	2	0	0	2
TOTALS	6	1	8	15

D.5. Severely handicapped children: junior group

Nature of handicap	Boys	Girls	Total
Cerebral palsy	1	0	1
Thalidomide	2	1	3
Spina bifida and hydrocephalus	3	3	6
Fragilitas ossium	0	1	1
Spinal injury and paraplegia	0	1	1
Diastrophic dwarfism	0	1	1
Achondroplasia	0	1	1
Amyotonia congenita	1	0	1
Arthrogryposis	1	0	1
TOTALS	8	8	16

D.6. Social class in children with and without neurological abnormalities

Social class	Children with neuro-logical abnormalities No.	%	Children without neuro-logical abnormalities No.	%
I and II	3	11·5	12	25·0
III (non-manual)	4	15·3	4	8·3
III (manual)	9	34·6	22	45·8
IV and V	10	38·4	10	20·8
TOTALS	26	100·0	48	100·0

D.7. Size of family in handicapped and control groups

No. of children	Children without neurological abnormalities No. = 48		Children with neurological abnormalities No. = 26		PH group as a whole No. = 74		Controls No. = 148	
1	2	4·1%	4	15·3%	6	8·1%	8	5·4%
2–3	33	68·7%	14	53·8%	47	63·5%	76	51·3%
4–6	11	} 27·0%	6	} 30·7%	17	} 28·3%	46	} 38·5%
7+	2		2		4		11	
Not known	0	00·0	0	00·0	0	00·0	7	4·7%

D.8. Ordinal position of children in different groups (percentages)

Ordinal position	Children without neurological abnormalities No. = 48	Children with neurological abnormalities No. = 26	All PH children No. = 74	Controls No. = 148
Eldest	25·0	34·7	28·3	24·2
Youngest	39·5	26·9	35·1	29·6
Twin	2·0	11·5	5·4	2·6
Other	33·2	26·8	31·0	38·9
Not known	00·0	00·0	00·0	4·7

D.9. Whether mothers go out to work (percentages)

Group	Don't work	Part-time	Full-time
Controls	50·7	36·2	13·0
All PH children	64·8	24·3	10·8
PH without neurological abnormalities	66·6	20·8	12·5
PH with neurological abnormalities	61·5	30·7	7·6

Appendix E Casenotes on children with neurological abnormalities above the brainstem: juniors

1. Cerebral-palsied children

Case 1: Girl, 7·5 years, r. hemiplegia, uses r. limb for support, unable to hop r. leg, abnormal gait. Slight hearing defect suspected. Speech retarded and some dysarthria. Has speech therapy. Average I Q.

Case 2: Boy, 7·6 years, l. hemiplegia, abnormal gait, r. splint and exercises for l. arm, poor control l. arm and hand. Normal range I Q.

Case 3: Boy, 7·6 years, mild r. hemiplegia, slight clumsiness using r. hand, drops r. foot and wears r. splint, slight stammer. Dull-average range I Q.

Case 4: Boy, 7·9 years, twin, mild l. hemiplegia and epilepsy, uses l. arm and hand fairly well, drags l. leg slightly but can run. Dull-normal range I Q.

Case 5: Boy, 8·0 years, mild diplegia, inversion of feet, flexion of hips and knees, l. leg worse, runs on toes, upper limbs normal, slight stammer, has physiotherapy. Dull-normal range I Q.

Case 6: Boy, 8·2 years, mild ataxic diplegia and petit mal, poor hand control, handedness poorly developed, unsteady gait, dysarthria, normal I Q.

Case 7: Boy, 8·7 years, r. hemiplegia, poor control of fine finger movements (r. hand), slightly abnormal gait but can run, very mild dysarthria. Dull-average range I Q.

Case 8: Girl, 8·9 years, mild r. hemiplegia, poor balance, falls often, stiff r. leg, has physiotherapy, hands appear normal, slightly defective speech. Borderline E S N.

Case 9: Boy, 9·1 years, mild r. hemiplegia, r. arm held in flexion and rarely used. Walks with limp, contractures hamstrings r. leg, bone shortening r. tibia, speech hesitant, asthmatic attacks. Dull-normal range I Q.

Case 10: Boy, 9·3 years, r. hemiplegia, ataxic gait, mild dysarthria. Has physiotherapy and speech therapy. Dull-normal range I Q.

Case 11: Girl, 9·3 years, r. hemiplegia and minimal involvement of l. side. Severe incoordination r. arm and hand, many involuntary movements. R. ankle valgus, in-turning r. hip, drags r. foot. Borderline E S N.

Case 12: Girl, 9·5 years, l. hemiplegia and epilepsy (post meningitis), l. hand badly affected, spasms, uses little, slight limp l. leg, frequent migraines, slight stutter. Dull-normal range I Q.

Case 13: Girl, 9·6 years, mild r. hemiplegia, loss of fine finger control in r. hand and loss of power in r. arm. Gait almost normal, squint r. eye, spatial difficulties suspected. Dull-average range I Q.

Case 14: Boy, 9·7 years, r. hemiplegia, slight limp but can run, marked spasticity r. hand and arm, can grasp but little power, r. squint, myopia. Normal I Q.

Case 15: Girl, 9·10 years, mild l. hemiplegia, l. hand used little, very slight limp, retarded speech. Dull-normal range I Q.

Case 16: Boy, 10·2 years, twin, mild diplegia, very small child, slight weakness in r. arm and leg, spasticity l. leg, slight limp, operated for strabismus at three years, wears glasses. Dull-average I Q.

2. Children with spina bifida and hydrocephalus

Case 17: Boy, 8·5 years, lumbar myelomeningocele, arrested hydrocephalus, Spitz-Holter valve, doubly incontinent, recent ileostomy. Spatial and visuo-motor difficulties suspected. Dull-normal range I Q.

Case 18: Girl, 8·5 years, myelomeningocele, arrested hydrocephalus, Spitz-Holter valve, severe paraplegia, mainly in wheelchair, occasionally uses rollator and single leg caliper. Doubly incontinent, r. ileostomy, strabismus, spatial and visuo-motor difficulties suspected. Borderline E S N.

Case 19: Boy, 8·7 years, myelomeningocele, arrested hydrocephalus, Spitz-Holter valve, some paralysis legs but walks slowly without aids. Doubly incontinent, wears bag, eye defect suspected in l. eye. Borderline E S N.

Case 20: Girl, 8·8 years, myelomeningocele, arrested hydrocephalus, Spitz-Holter valve, flaccid paralysis of legs and bilateral talipes, walks short distances with calipers and elbow crutches, stutter, wears glasses. Average I Q.

Case 21: Girl, 8·8 years, myelomeningocele, arrested hydrocephalus, Spitz-Holter valve. Paraplegic, walks short distances with calipers and crutches or uses wheelchair. Slightly clumsy, difficulty in using hands independently. Doubly incontinent, urine expressed, wears pad and rubbers. Myopia, wears glasses, slight stutter. Average I Q.

Case 22: Girl, 8·10 years, myelomeningocele, arrested hydrocephalus, Spitz-Holter valve, paraplegic, caliper r. leg, walks a little but uses wheelchair often. Doubly incontinent, but has had ileal loop operation and wears bag. Dull-average range I Q.

Case 23: Boy, 9·0 years, lumbar myelomeningocele, arrested hydrocephalus, Spitz-Holter valve, doubly incontinent, recent ileostomy. Spatial and visuo-motor difficulties suspected. Dull-normal range I Q.

Case 24: Boy, 9·9 years, myelomeningocele, arrested hydrocephalus, Spitz-Holter valve, feet amputated, wears prostheses, stands, learning to walk. Uses wheelchair, bilateral CDH, doubly incontinent, wears bag, slight r. internal strabismus, wears glasses. Dull normal range I Q.

3. Children with other neurological abnormalities

Case 25: Boy, 8·8 years, minimal cerebral dysfunction, laterality poorly established, general clumsiness, poor balance, falls often. Slight speech defect. Below average spatial ability. Dull-average I Q.

Case 26: Boy, 9·5 years, r. flaccid hemiparesis following fractured skull. Rarely uses r. hand and arm, walks but tires easily, cannot run or jump, poor balance. Dull-normal range I Q.

Appendix F The sociometric test

Generally the NFER non-verbal test 5 was given to the children between 9.40 and 10.40 a.m., and after play the sociometric test. A copy of the test was handed to each child: at the top was a space for the child's name, age and the class while below this were three questions with spaces for the child's choices. The children were told:

> The next thing I would like you to do for me is rather different. It isn't really a test this time, because there are no right or wrong answers. I'm going to read out to you some questions which are on this sheet. They ask you to write down the names of the boys and girls you like doing things with best. This will help your teachers if they want to make up groups of boys and girls to do things together. It will also help me to find out about the kind of choices made by boys and girls of different ages. Remember just to choose children from this class. You can choose children who are absent today if you want to. If you need help in spelling the names, you will find them all on the blackboard. Try to fill in the forms quietly without talking to your friends.

The children were then instructed to fill in their name, age and form and the questions were read out to them. After each question the children were given time to write down their choices.

The questions were as follows:

1 Write down here the names of the three boys and girls from this class you would like to play with most during break. Be sure to put down your first three choices, first the person you would like best to play with, then your second choice and then your third.

2 Write down now the names of the three boys and girls you would like best to sit next to you.

3 This time I want you to imagine you are going to move into another class. Which three boys and girls from this class would you like best to go with you? Write down your first three choices.

Appendix G Behavioural disorders

G.I. Comparison of behaviour disorders in boys and girls in the control and handicapped groups

	Handicapped boys No.	%	Control boys No.	%	Handicapped girls No.	%	Control girls No.	%	Total boys No.	%	Total girls No.	%
Parental questionnaire												
Total with score 13 or more	5	13·5	9	12·3	2	6·6	6	10·5	14	12·7	8	9·1
Neurotic	1	2·7	3	4·1	2	6·6	3	5·2	4	3·6	5	5·7
Antisocial	4	10·8	5	8·2	0	0·0	3	5·2	10	9·0	3	3·4
TOTAL CHILDREN FOR WHOM QUESTIONNAIRE OBTAINED	37		73		30		57		110		87	
Teacher's questionnaire												
Total with a score 9 or more	7	17·9	14	17·9	3	10·0	13	21·6	21	17·6	16	17·7
Neurotic	2	5·1	4	5·1	1	3·3	5	8·3	6	5·0	5	5·5
Antisocial	5	12·8	10	12·8	2	6·6	8	13·3	12	10·0	8	8·8
TOTAL CHILDREN FOR WHOM QUESTIONNAIRE OBTAINED	39		78		30		60		119		90	
OVERLAP: CHILDREN DISTURBED ON BOTH QUESTIONNAIRES	2		3		0		2		5		2	

G.2. Percentage of children showing deviant behaviour on individual items of the parental scale

Behaviour	Boys			Girls		
	PH group	Controls	IOW general population	PH group	Controls	IOW general population
Restless	48·6	45·9	34·8	27·5	30·5	26·8
Fidgety	24·3	16·2	12·6	13·7	16·9	10·1
Poor concentration	21·6	24·3	25·2	6·8	20·3	18·7
Temper	32·4	17·5	21·4	13·7	11·8	13·6
Irritable	32·4	40·5	33·0	27·5	32·2	26·4
Not liked	2·7	6·7	4·8	00·0	5·0	4·1
Solitary	37·8	40·5	29·8	31·0	27·1	16·7
Truants	00·0	1·3	0·4	00·0	1·6	00·0
Destructive	5·4	17·5§	6·1	6·8	8·4	0·8
Fights	16·2	28·3§	15·3	24·1	20·3§	5·6
Disobedient	35·1	43·2	31·4	44·8	25·4	19·6
Lies	21·6	32·4§	14·7	10·3*	33·8¶	8·1
Steals	2·7	13·5	4·4	00·0*	10·1	2·4
Bullies	13·5	6·7	5·6	13·7	1·6	4·0
Worried	43·2	35·1	36·4	37·9	42·3	40·7
Miserable	24·3	13·5	10·4	17·2	15·2	10·9
Fearful	35·1	32·4	26·2	31·0	18·6	26·8
Fussy	21·6	17·5	12·9	31·0	38·8†	18·8
Sucks thumb	10·8	9·4	7·2	10·3	18·6	14·3
Bites nails	21·6	17·5	28·0	17·2*	38·9	32·5
Headaches	8·1	10·8	9·4	6·8	6·7	10·1
Stomach aches	10·8	9·4¶	31·4	24·1	10·1‖	33·5
Bilious attacks	5·4	4·0	12·7	16·8‡	00·0‖	11·8
Eating difficulty	10·8	28·3	20·8	27·5	23·7	20·5
Sleeping difficulty	10·8	21·6	17·4	6·8	6·7	19·2
TOTAL NO. OF CHILDREN	37	74	961	29	59	953

G.3. Percentage of children showing deviant behaviour on individual items of the teachers' scale

	Boys			Girls		
Behaviour	PH group	Controls	IOW general population	PH group	Controls	IOW general population
Restless	30·0	33·3‖	15·7	23·0	25·0¶	6·5
Fidgety	35·0	28·8	20·0	16·7	21·7‖	9·8
Poor concentration	65·0*	38·8	35·3	50·0*	31·7	25·3
Irritable	12·5	15·0	8·9	6·7	11·7	5·3
Not liked	30·0	17·8	13·3	16·7	18·3§	9·5
Solitary	35·0	23·0	17·0	37·0	30·0¶	10·1
Truants	00·0	1·1	1·8	00·0	1·7	0·7
Destructive	7·5	3·3	1·5	00·0	6·7	0·4
Fights	25·0	26·3‖	11·0	10·0	16·7¶	3·7
Disobedient	32·6	27·5‖	10·6	6·7	10·0§	3·6
Lies	17·5	12·3	6·9	6·7	15·0¶	2·0
Steals	7·5	2·5	2·3	00·0	3·3	1·4
Bullies	15·0	11·3§	4·2	10·0	11·7¶	1·3
Worried	35·0	18·8	23·5	33·0	33·0	22·2
Miserable	7·5	12·3	8·9	3·3*	15·0§	6·8
Fearful	27·5	23·0	17·6	37·0	27·0¶	6·0
Fussy	15·0	15·0	8·1	00·0†	13·3	7·3
Tears on arrival at school	7·5	2·3	0·4	00·0	5·0	0·8
Aches and pains	10·0	5·0	3·3	6·7	16·7¶	3·4
Absent for trivial reasons	7·5	7·5	6·0	6·7	10·0	5·2
Sucks thumb	2·5	2·5	4·8	10·0	10·0	5·0
Bites nails	17·5	6·3‖	18·8	10·0	11·7	18·8
TOTAL NO. OF CHILDREN	40	80	1080	30	60	1079

KEY TO G.2 AND G.3

* Difference from controls significant at 5 per cent level
† Difference from controls significant at 1 per cent level
‡ Difference from controls significant at 0·1 per cent level
§ Difference from IOW general population significant at 5 per cent level
‖ Difference from IOW general population significant at 1 per cent level
¶ Difference from IOW general population significant at 0·1 per cent level

G.4. Note on the method used for testing the statistical significance of the difference between the percentages

The statistical difference between the percentages was tested by a monograph published by Oppenheim (1966) which was in fact a recalculation and adaptation of the one published in 1939 by Zubin in volume XXXIV of the *Journal of the American Statistical Association* (pp. 539–44). The advantage of the method is that the significance of different proportions can be obtained directly from the percentage figures rather than from the raw frequencies. This is particularly useful for survey data where findings often take the form of large numbers of percentages. The method was selected for use here since (1) an item analysis of behaviour questionnaires requires that a large number of comparisons be made and this device, as Oppenheim points out, is particularly useful in 'focusing attention on the more important differences and sorting the grain from the chaff'; (2) it was also useful here since only percentages and not raw frequencies were available for the I O W study. A similar method was used for investigating differences between groups on selected items of the Manchester scales of social adaptation.

REFERENCE

OPPENHEIM, A. N. (1966). *Questionnaire Design and Attitude Measurement*, Heinemann, London.

G.5. Comparison of children with and without neurological abnormalities on selected items of deviant behaviour: parental scale

Behaviour	Children with neurological abnormalities No. = 24		Children without neurological abnormalities No. = 42		Controls No. = 133	
	No.	%	No.	%	No.	%
Temper tantrums	8	33·3	8	19·0	20	15·0
Restlessness	8	33·3	18	42·8	52	39·0
Fidgety	7	29·1	6	14·2	22	16·5
Often worried	13	54·1*	13	30·9	51	38·3
Rather solitary	11	45·8	12	28·5	46	34·5
Irritable	9	37·5	12	28·5	49	36·8
Disobedient	10	41·6	17	40·4	47	35·3
Fearful	9	37·5	12	28·5	35	26·3

* Difference from children without neurological abnormalities significant at 5 per cent level

G.6. Infant group: raw frequency distributions for selected items on the parent and teacher questionnaires (infant scales)*

Items	Groups % PH infants (mean age 6·8 yrs)	% IOW groups (mean age 5·0 yrs)
Scale A (parent)		
Eating difficulty	32·0	32·6
Restlessness	44·0	52·8
Fidgety	24·0	24·0
Frequently fights	28·0	17·3
Worries	20·0	27·6
Rather solitary	44·0	26·7
Disobedient	20·0*	49·8
Cannot settle to anything for more than a few minutes	32·0	22·4
TOTAL CHILDREN TESTED	25	396
Scale B (teacher)		
Restlessness	32·0	18·6
Fidgety	28·0	18·6
Frequently fights	20·0	11·0
Worries	36·0	25·5
Rather solitary	28·0	21·1
Fearful of meeting new people	24·0	16·0
Disobedient	20·0	12·1
Poor concentration	76·0†	23·4
Fearful of new things/situations	32·0	26·8
Often complains of pains or aches	40·0†	3·4
TOTAL CHILDREN TESTED	25	435

* Significant at 5 per cent level
† Significant at 0·1 per cent level
§ Data from Yule, W. (1972) Personal communication

Appendix H The Manchester scales of social adaptation: findings

H.1. Comparison of mean scores of controls and physically handicapped children on Manchester scales *A* and *F-J*

| | Groups | | | | Significance | |
| | Controls (No. = 148) | | Handicapped (No. = 74) | | | |
Scale	Mean	SD	Mean	SD	t	p
A Social perspective	8·96	4·31	7·71	4·28	2·90	<0·01
F Socialization of play	11·87	3·19	9·51	3·07	7·61	<0·001
G Freedom of movement	3·57	2·15	1·98	2·08	7·57	<0·001
H Self-help	15·95	2·92	11·69	4·67	11·83	<0·001
I Handling of money	5·06	1·77	3·81	1·69	7·35	<0·001
J Responsibility in home	2·54	1·35	1·75	1·32	6·07	<0·001
Total self-direction	38·85	8·47	28·0	9·65	12·19	<0·001

H.2. Comparison of mean scores of PH children with and without neurological abnormalities on Manchester scales *A* and *F-J*

| | Groups | | | | Significance | |
| | PH group without neurological abnormalities (No. = 48) | | PH group with neurological abnormalities (No. = 26) | | | |
Scale	Mean	SD	Mean	SD	t	p
A Social perspective	9·0	4·18	5·34	3·08	4·30	<0·001
F Socialization of play	9·75	2·93	9·07	3·17	1·01	n.s.
G Freedom of movement	2·53	5·71	1·11	1·39	1·36	n.s.
H Self-help	12·85	4·47	9·53	4·13	3·42	<0·01
I Handling of money	3·79	3·44	3·07	1·49	1·12	n.s.
J Responsibility in home	2·12	1·28	1·07	1·11	3·88	<0·001
Total self-direction	31·5	8·87	23·84	8·71	3·90	<0·001

H.3. Comparison of mean scores of mildly, moderately and severely handicapped groups on Manchester scales *A* and *F-J*

Scales	Severity of handicap					
	Mild (No. = 13)		Moderate (No. = 45)		Severe (No. = 16)	
	Mean	SD	Mean	SD	Mean	SD
A Social perspective	8·31	5·01	7·56	3·82	7·69	4·74
F Socialization of play	10·85*	3·56	9·76‡	2·66	7·75	2·89
G Freedom of movement	3·38†	3·20	2·07‖	1·50	0·63	1·36
H Self-help	12·92*	4·63	12·38§	4·18	8·75	4·82
I Handling of money	4·31†	1·70	4·07§	1·53	2·69	1·58
J Responsibility in home	2·00	1·35	1·78	1·31	1·50	1·26
Total self-direction	33·54†	11·59	30·04‖	7·68	21·50	8·81

* Significant difference from severe group at 5 per cent level
† Significant difference from severe group at 1 per cent level
‡ Significant difference from severe group at 5 per cent level
§ Significant difference from severe group at 1 per cent level
‖ Significant difference from severe group at 0·1 per cent level

No significant differences between mild and moderate groups

Appendix I Overall social adjustment

I.1. Overall social adjustment, measure 9 (items relating to child's friendships)

Question	Possible score
Has he many friends at school?	0–2
Has he a special friend there?	0–1
Does he see much of his school friends outside school?	0–1
(If yes) how much time each week does he usually spend with them in the summer?	0–3
Does he have any other friends who live in this area but go to different schools?	0–1
How often does he go to his friends' homes to play?	0–2
How many times did he go last week?	0–2
Does he ever bring his friends here to play?	0–1
How many times last week did he bring a friend here?	0–2

I.2. Overall social adjustment and social class (controls and PH children)

	Social class				
	I and II	III (non-manual)	III (manual)	IV	V
Well adjusted	41	10	59	31	6
Less well adjusted	14	13	22	17	9
TOTAL CHILDREN	55	23	81	48	15

I.3. Early hospitalization (0-3 years) and social adjustment in handicapped group

	Handicapped group (No. = 74)			
	Well adjusted (No. = 40)		Less well adjusted No. = 34)	
Weeks in hospital between 0 and 3 years	No.	%	No.	%
None	14	35·0	16	47·0
1–10	13	33·0	9	26·0
11–50	12	30·0	8	24·0
Over 50	1	2·0	1	3·0

I.4. Characteristics of children with highest social adjustment scores

Handicap	Severity	Sex	IQ	Social class
Congenital abnormalities hands and feet	mild	G	102	III (manual)
Achondroplasia	severe*	G	139	I
Spina bifida	moderate	G	92	III (manual)
Congenital absence left arm	moderate	G	n.a.	III (manual)
Arthrogryposis	severe*	B	101	III (manual)
Vestigial upper limbs	moderate*	G	117	III (manual)
Congenital abnormalities hands and feet	moderate	B	88	III (manual)
Congenital absence upper limbs	moderate*	B	121	I
Thalidomide	mild	G	109	V
Spina bifida	moderate*	G	116	III (manual)
Congenital absence right arm	moderate	G	105	IV
Fragilitas ossium	severe*	G	117	II
Cerebral palsy (diplegia)	mild	B	83	I
Congenital absence right arm	moderate*	G	110	II

* Also included in group with highest academic attainment
n.a. = not available

I.5. Characteristics of children with lowest social adjustment scores

Handicap	Severity	Sex	IQ	Social class
Spina bifida and hydrocephalus	severe*	G	88	IV
Congenital abnormalities hands and feet	moderate*	G	71	III (manual)
Cerebral palsy (right hemiplegia)	severe*	B	74	II
Cerebral palsy (right hemiplegia)	mild*	B	86	III (non-manual)
Right hemiparesis	moderate*	B	below 70	III (manual)
Cerebral palsy (left hemiplegia)	moderate*	G	83	III (manual)
Kyphoscoliosis	mild	B	88	III (non-manual)
Haemophilia	moderate	B	117	I
Cerebral palsy (right hemiplegia)	moderate	B	87	III (non-manual)
Congenital absence left arm	moderate*	B	89	III (manual)
Cerebral palsy (right hemiplegia)	moderate*	G	77	IV
Poliomyelitis	moderate*	G	83	III (non-manual)
Cerebral palsy (left hemiplegia)	mild	B	72	III (manual)
Bilateral talipes	mild	G	70	V
Spina bifida and hydrocephalus	moderate	B	73	IV
Spina bifida	moderate	B	86	III (manual)
Amyotonia congenita	severe	B	82	III (manual)

* Also included in group with lowest academic attainment scores

Appendix J Reading backwardness and related factors

J.1. Social class and reading backwardness

Social class	Backward readers (No. = 29)		Borderline readers (No. = 24)		Others (No. = 169)		Social class in group as a whole (No. = 222)	
	No.	%	No.	%	No.	%	No.	%
I and II	4	13·8	5	20·8	46	27·2	55	24·7
III (non-manual)	4	13·8	1	4·2	18	10·7	23	10·3
III (manual)	10	34·5	9	37·5	62	36·7	81	36·4
IV and V	11	37·9	9	37·5	43	25·4	63	28·3

J.2. Family size and reading backwardness

No. of children in family	Backward readers (No. = 29)		Borderline readers (No. = 24)		Others (No. = 169)		Group as a whole (No. = 222)	
	No.	%	No.	%	No.	%	No.	%
Under 4	17	58·1	10	41·6	110	65·0	137	61·8
4+	11	38·3	13	54·6	54	32·0	78	35·1
Don't know	1	3·6	1	4·8	5	3·0	7	3·1

Appendix K Academic attainment

K.1. Academic attainment and school class in the handicapped juniors

	School class (juniors)		
	I	2	3
High attainment	17	10	11
Low attainment	16	10	10

K.2. Hospitalization after the age of five in high and low attainers in the handicapped juniors

Weeks in hospital	High attainers No. = 38		Low attainers No. = 36	
	No.	%	No.	%
None	24	63	25	69
1–4	4	11	5	14
5–10	9	24	5	14
11–50	I	2	I	3

K.3. Characteristics of children with highest academic attainment scores

Handicap	Severity	Sex	IQ	Social class
Achondroplasia	severe	G	138	I
Vestigial upper limbs	moderate	G	117*	III (manual)
Absence of rectum	moderate	B	119*	IV
Congenital absence upper limbs	moderate	B	121*	I
Spina bifida	moderate	B	113	V
Haemophilia	moderate	B	100	III (manual)
Congenital absence right arm	moderate	G	110*	II
Haemophilia	moderate	B	117	I
Congenital abnormalities hands and feet	mild	G	102*	III (manual)
Haemophilia	moderate	B	132	III (non-manual)
Congenital absence left arm	moderate	B	117	I
Fragilitas ossium	severe	G	117*	II
Thalidomide	severe	B	n.a.	I
Arthrogryposis	severe	B	101*	III (manual)
Thalidomide	severe	B	91	I
Rheumatoid arthritis	moderate	B	116	IV
Spina bifida	moderate	G	116*	III (manual)

* Also included in the group with the best social adjustment
n.a. = not available

K.4. Characteristics of children with the lowest academic attainment scores

Handicap	Severity	Sex	IQ	Social class
Minimal cerebral dysfunction	moderate	B	n.a.	V
Spinal injury and paraplegia	severe	G	n.a.	IV
Spina bifida and hydrocephalus	severe*	G	88	IV
Spina bifida and hydrocephalus	severe	B	86	III (manual)
Poliomyelitis	moderate*	G	83	III (non-manual)
Spina bifida and hydrocephalus	severe	G	below 70	III (non-manual)
Spina bifida	moderate*	B	86	III (manual)
Spina bifida and hydrocephalus	severe	B	78	III (manual)
Cerebral palsy (right hemiplegia)	severe*	B	74	II
Congenital amputation left arm	moderate*	B	89	III (manual)
Cerebral palsy (right hemiplegia)	moderate	B	90	III (manual)
Congenital amputation right leg, abnormal hand	moderate	B	n.a.	III (manual)
Right-sided hemiparesis	moderate*	B	below 70	III (manual)
Cerebral palsy (right hemiplegia)	mild	G	75	V
Spina bifida and hydrocephalus	moderate	G	n.a.	II
Congenital abnormalities hands and feet	moderate*	G	71	III (manual)
Cerebral palsy (right hemiplegia)	moderate*	G	77	IV
Cerebral palsy (right hemiplegia)	mild	B	86	III (non-manual)

* Also included in group with lowest social adjustment scores
n.a. = not available

Appendix L The computer programme

The National Centre for Health Statistics (University of Pennsylvania) automatic interaction detection programme is a Fortran IV version of the Michigan AID programme described by Sonquist and Morgan (1964). Essentially it is a stepwise regression programme where the independent variates ('predictors') need not be quantitative. The programme operates by finding that dichotomy based on any predictor which gives the lowest within-group sum of squared deviations for the dependent variate Y. Essentially this is the dichotomization which 'accounts for' more of the variance of the dependent variate (i.e. has a larger 'correlation' with the dependent variate) than any other dichotomization based on grouping the categories of a simple predictor into two groups. Having made this first dichotomy the programme then takes the 'eligible' group within the largest within-group sum of squared deviations for Y and 'splits' it in a similar manner. A group is 'eligible' for splitting if it has at least the specified number of cases and a within-group sum of squared deviations at least as great as a specified proportion of the original sum of squared deviations. The process of splitting continues until there are no eligible groups which can be split to yield the specified minimum WGSSD reductions or until some specified maximum number of groups has been created.

REFERENCE

National Centre for Health Statistics (University of Pennsylvania) (1964), 'Automatic interaction detection programme', in chapters 2 and 4 in Sonquist, J. A. and Morgan, J. N. (eds.) *The Detection of Interaction Effects*. Monograph 35, Survey Research Centre, Institute for Social Research, University of Michigan, Ann Arbor.

Appendix M Comparative costs of different types of primary school provision for PH pupils

	costs per child per annum (£):
Type of special provision:	
(i) RESIDENTIAL SPECIAL SCHOOLS:	
Spastics Society schools	1 300–1 500
A voluntary society spina bifida school	1 081
A voluntary society PH school	900

(ii) DAY SPECIAL SCHOOLS:	
Day pupils in Spastics Society schools	800–900
LEA day centre (school) for spastic children	934
Day PH school in a large urban authority	571
LEA day SSN school	477
LEA day ESN school	300

(iii) SPECIAL CLASS FOR PH CHILDREN IN ORDINARY SCHOOL:

Basic cost per pupil	115	
Teacher's salary	130	
Ancillary helpers and meals supervisors	119	532
Physiotherapist (sessional basis)	39	
Transport (ten-mile radius)	129	

(iv) ORDINARY CLASS WITH ANCILLARY HELP AND TAXI TRANSPORT: (SHARED BY THREE PH PUPILS)

Basic cost per pupil	120	
Transport (partly rural area)	200	655
Full-time ancillary helper	335	

Appendix N Glossary of medical terms not explained in the text

Achondroplasia A developmental disease which principally affects the bones of the limbs and the base of the skull so that the person is greatly dwarfed by short arms and legs

Amyotonia congenita A congenital muscular disorder characterized by a lack of 'tone' in the muscles

Arthrogryposis A rare congenital disorder characterized by immobility of one or more joints with absence or maldevelopment of the muscles around them. There is wide variation in the distribution of the abnormalities

Bilateral talipes See TALIPES

Cerebellum That part of the brain which among other things has to do with balance

Christmas disease See HAEMOPHILIA

Congenital abnormalities Abnormalities which are present at birth

Diastrophic dwarfism A form of dwarfism characterized by short limbs, curvature of the spine and joint contractures

Dysarthria Imperfect production of the sounds used in speech due to defective neuromuscular control of the organs controlling speech

Epilepsy A condition causing a person to suffer from fits characterized by abnormal and uncontrollable movements. Such fits are described as 'PETIT MAL' when there is only momentary loss of consciousness and no convulsions

Fragilitas ossium Sometimes known as 'brittle bones'. A congenital disorder of variable severity in which the bones are unusually fragile

Haemophilia A bleeding disorder in which the person has a congenital deficiency of one of the necessary blood clotting factors, the antihaemophilic globulin (AHG). CHRISTMAS DISEASE has similar clinical features but here the deficiency is of a different clotting factor, the 'Christmas factor'. Both disorders occur in males but are transmitted by females

Hemiparesis A weakness barely amounting to paralysis affecting one side of the body

Hydronephrosis A chronic disease in which the kidney becomes greatly distended with fluid. It is due to congenital abnormalities resulting in incomplete or intermittent blockage of the ureter connecting the kidney with the bladder

Ileal loop operation The ureters (which lead from the kidney to the bladder) are detached from the bladder and inserted into a section of the small intestine (ileum) one end of which is brought out through the skin of the abdomen to form an opening or 'spout' over which a urine collecting bag can be fitted

Imperforate anus Absence of the anus

Kyphoscoliosis A deformity of the spine in which there is both KYPHO-SIS, a curvature of the spine in which there is a diminution in the concavity of the cervical or lumbar spine and SCOLIOSIS where the spine is curved to one side

Maple syrup urine disease A congenital disorder of metabolism due to a biochemical abnormality. To prevent mental retardation and wide-spread neurological defects the amino-acid composition of the diet must be strictly controlled from an early age

Metabolic disorder A disorder resulting from an enzyme deficiency

Minimal cerebral dysfunction A term generally used to describe children without gross motor disability who have both specific learning disabilities (including weakness in motor co-ordination and deficiencies in visual perception) and often disturbed behaviour

Muscular dystrophy An inherited disease of the muscles which results in degeneration of the muscles and increasing physical weakness. The muscles enabling the child to move are generally affected first; later other muscles are affected including those involved in swallowing and breathing. Most children die in adolescence, frequently of pneumonia

Myelomeningocele A swelling or sac on the back, usually covered only by a thin membrane, containing cerebrospinal fluid (CSF) and the imperfectly formed spinal cord. In MENINGOCELE the sac contains the CSF and covering membranes only

Osteomyelitis An infection of the bone

Peripheral neuritis Also known as polyneuritis. An inflammatory condition of the nerves in various parts of the body in which the nerve fibres in the small nerves degenerate and break down. It may lead to weakness and wasting of the muscles in the limbs and later to loss of voice, difficulty in breathing etc. according to which nerves are affected

Perthe's disease A disease affecting the hip in children, due to fragmentation of the spongy extremity at the head of the femur. The condition settles spontaneously in a few years, but to diminish residual deformity at the head of the femur the hip must be protected from weight bearing

Ptosis A disorder affecting the external muscles of the eyes which results in drooping of the upper eyelids although visual acuity is normal

Rheumatoid arthritis Also known as STILL'S DISEASE. A chronic inflammation of the joints. They become painful and stiff and movement is limited. Disablement may result from joint deformities with pain on movement and weakness and contractures of the muscles and tendons. Some children appear to recover completely but are liable to later relapse

Strabismus Another name for squinting

Talipes The medical word for clubfoot, a congenital deformity of the foot and ankle of varying degrees of severity. In BILATERAL TALIPES both feet are affected

Ventricles   Four cavities within the brain which communicate with each other through narrow channels and through which the cerebrospinal fluid circulates. Any block either within or outside the ventricular system will stop the circulation and will lead to accumulation of fluid in the system behind the block and so to dilation of the ventricles

Name of teacher..............   School.....................
Name of child................   Form....   No. in form......
Date of birth ....   District ....
Nature of handicap...

SECTION A (Extent and effect of physical disability)

I'd like to begin by asking for some details about X's handicap, particularly as it relates to his school activities.

(i) TRANSPORT

How does X get to school – does he require special transport?	NO	0
	YES	1
(IF YES) is this being provided by:	bus	1
	taxi	2
	car	3
	ambulance	4
	other	5
(IF YES) who pays for the transport?		
	voluntary organization	1
	LEA	2
	hospital service	3
	other	5
(IF NO) does anyone usually accompany X to and from school?		
	not accompanied	0
	parent	1
	older sib or adult	2
	peer	3
Are there any problems over getting to school?	NO	0
	YES (specify)	1

(ii) MOBILITY

Is X able to walk and run as well as a normal child of this age?	NO	0
	YES	1

(IF NO) does he have any physiotherapy?

NO	0
YES	1
don't know	9

(IF YES) is this provided:

at school	1
in hospital during school hours	2
in hospital out of school hours	3
elsewhere	4

How often does he get physiotherapy?

once a week	1
more than once a week	2
less than once a week	3
don't know	9

Is his gait abnormal at all?

slightly (e.g. unsteady)	1
moderately	2
very	3

Does he wear or use:

a prosthesis R leg		a prosthesis L leg			calipers		elbow crutches	
YES	NO	YES	NO		YES	NO	YES	NO
0	1	0	1		0	1	0	1

Does he wear or use:

armpit crutches		special boots or shoes			other aid	
YES	NO	YES	NO		YES	NO
0	1	0	1		0	1

(IF YES, to any of above) does he ever need a
wheelchair in school?

NO	0
occasionally	1
sometimes	2
most of the time	3

Does he have any difficulty if he has to walk
a long way?

none	0
a little, but manages distances necessary in school	1
walks moderate distances at a reasonable pace	2
walks only short to moderate distances (20–200 yards) at a slow pace	3
walks only a few steps or not at all	4

Does he have any difficulty with stairs?

none	0
slow, but manages unaided	1
needs assistance	2
can't manage	3
don't know	9

Can you name any particular activities in which he is impeded by poor mobility? (PROBE for team games, PE, music and movement, etc.) LIST

Do the other children make allowances for him or offer to help in any of these activities?

NO	0
occasionally	1
sometimes	2
give too much help	3

Are there any activities from which he is excluded because of poor mobility? LIST

(IF YES, PROBE to see whether this is because he really can't do them or because he isn't allowed to try)

(iii) MANIPULATIVE ABILITY

Does X have any disability or weakness of the upper limbs or hand?

NO	0
YES, R arm	1
YES, R hand	2
YES, L arm	3
YES, L hand	4

(IF NOT OMIT NEXT 3 QUESTIONS)
Does he/she wear a prosthesis?

NO	0
YES, L arm	1
YES, R arm	2

(IF YES) for how much of the time at school does he wear it?

Less than half	1
about half	2
more than half	3

Does he join in group activities as well with or without it?

Better with p.	1
better without p.	2
same	3

I'd like you to tell me now whether X has any difficulty in carrying out the following tasks (with prosthesis if he wears one).
(PROBE FOR EXTENT OF DIFFICULTY)
(Please tick in appropriate box)

0 (none)	1 (slight)	2 (moderate)	3 (severe)

Difficulty in:
(Space was left on the interview schedule for similar details to be obtained for writing, drawing, using a rubber, ruling lines, steadying paper for writing, opening desk and removing book, opening book and turning the pages, using scissors, craft activities, handling other educational equipment, other manipulations: handles, switches etc.)

If X has difficulties of this kind, do the other children offer help spontaneously?

NO	0
occasionally	1
often	2
overhelpful	3

Is there anything on the curriculum from which X is excluded because of difficulties of this kind? (LIST)

What sort of allowances do *you* make for X because of these difficulties? (PROBE for extra time in tests, excuses poor handwriting, modified marking system, etc.) LIST

(iv) SELF-CARE

(a) *Toilet*

Is X sometimes incontinent of the bladder in school?

NO	0
only occasionally	1
YES	2

Is X sometimes incontinent of the bowels in school?

NO	0
only occasionally	1
YES	2

(If NO to both above, go on to (b) feeding)
(If YES to either of above) does X wear a urinal or ileostomy bag?

NO	0
YES	1

How much help does he need in going to the toilet?

no help needed	0
needs a little help	1
needs complete toilet assistance	2

(If he does need help) who gives this?

welfare assistant	1
peer	2
other (specify)	4

(b) *Feeding*

Does X require any special assistance at meals?

NO	0
YES	1
doesn't apply	9

(IF YES) who helps him?

welfare assistant	1
peer	2
teacher	3
other (specify)	4

(c) *Dressing*

Does X require help with dressing?

NO	0
YES	1

(IF YES) does X need help with:

Socks and/ or shoes		Clothes, upper part of body		Clothes, lower part of body		Fastenings		Appliances (calipers etc.)	
YES	NO	YES	NO	YES	NO	YES	NO	YES	NO

(v) HEARING

Do you think X needs a hearing aid?

NO 0
YES 1

(IF YES) is one provided?

NO 0
YES 1

(IF YES) does he wear it?

hardly ever 0
sometimes 1
all or most of the time 2

(IF YES) when he wears his aid, is his hearing:

good 1
moderate 2
poor 3

(IF YES PROBE to see) who checks his aid?
How often?

(vi) SPEECH

Is X's speech normal for a child of this age?

normal, no problem 0
mildly defective 1
considerably defective 2
severely defective 3

If defective at all ask: do you think he requires speech therapy?

NO 0
YES 1

(IF YES) is this provided:

at school 1
in hospital/clinic 2
elsewhere 3
not provided 0

(vii) SIGHT

Does X wear glasses?

NO 0
YES 1

(IF NO) do you think his sight is defective?

NO 0
YES 1

(If he wears glasses) do these correct his vision:

fully 1
only partially 2

(viii) OTHER PHYSICAL DISABILITIES

Has X any other physical difficulties relating to his handicap which we haven't yet discussed? (PROBE for perceptual problems if brain-injured etc.) (LIST)

(ix) SPECIAL AIDS

(a) *Furniture*

Does X require any special furniture, or modifications to existing furniture?

NO	O
YES	I

(IF YES, obtain details)

(b) *Equipment*

Does X have any special equipment? (e.g. pencils, bag, typewriter, feeding utensils etc.)

NO	O
YES	I

(IF YES) obtain details, including who provided this (i.e. school, parents etc.) (LIST)

(c) *Buildings etc.*

Have any other modifications been made in the school for X's benefit? (e.g. ramp, toilet modifications, etc.) LIST

(d) *Suggestions*

Can you think of special equipment or modifications of the kind we've been talking about which you think would be helpful for X to have? (LIST and PROBE to see whether teacher has actually *tried* to get the equipment, from whom and what problems have been met.)

SECTION B (Academic)

I'd now like to ask you a few questions connected with X's schoolwork.

(x) STREAMING

First, I'd like to check on whether this class has been selected by streaming?

NO	O
YES, upper stream	I
YES, lower stream	2
YES, other (specify)	3

(xi) EXTRA HELP

To return to X, do you feel that he would benefit from extra help in:

	Reading		Number work	
	YES	NO	YES	NO

Is X actually getting extra help in:

	Reading		Number work	
	YES	NO	YES	NO

N

If YES, to either of the above, please tell me about the arrangements under which he is getting this help. (PROBE for WHO gives the help, WHERE it is given (ordinary class, special class/group etc.), WHEN and FOR HOW LONG each week) LIST details.

(xii) GENERAL ASSESSMENT

How do you feel X is getting on generally in his schoolwork compared with the others in the class?

Exceptionally well	1
above average	2
average	3
below average	4
very poor	5

(IF BELOW AVERAGE) do you feel that he ever uses his handicap as an excuse to be lazy?

NO	0
occasionally	1
YES	2

SECTION C (Social)

One very important aspect of this study is to find out as much as I can about the social effects of handicapping conditions and I'd like to go on to ask you a few questions related to this.

(xiii) FRIENDS

Do you think that X is a popular child?

very popular	1
average	2
not very popular	3
definitely isolated	4
don't know	9

Does X have a special friend?

NO	0
YES	1
don't know	9

(xiv) TEASING

What about teasing – is there much of that in the school as a whole?

NO	0
a little	1
quite a lot	2

Does X ever get teased?

NO	0
YES	1
don't know	9

(IF YES) how do you get to know about this?

teacher observes	1
child complains	2
other teachers report it	3
other children report it	4

How frequently does X get teased?

only occasionally	1
once or twice a week	2
several times a week	3
daily	4

What does X get teased about? (PROBE to see whether related to handicap, antisocial behaviour) etc. (LIST)

Will you tell me as much as you can remember about the last occasion on which X got teased? (PROBE for WHEN this happened, CIRCUMSTANCES triggering it off, NATURE of teasing, CHILD's response, TEACHER's way of coping)

Does X usually react like this when he is teased? (PROBE FOR X's REACTIONS)

How do you generally cope with teasing? Have you discovered any particularly effective way of dealing with this? (PROBE)

Apart from actual teasing, do the other children show much curiosity about X's handicap?

NO	0
a little at first, but no longer very curious	1
still curious	2

(IF YES) how does X react to their curiosity? (PROBE to see whether X is upset by it etc.)

What about bullying – do you think that X gets bullied more than the other children?

NO	0
YES	1
don't know	9

a) *Informal*

Is the play in the playground generally supervised?

NO	0
sometimes	1
always	2

Does X play much with other children in the playground?

NO	0
sometimes	1
most of the time	2

Does he usually play in a group or with one or two individuals?

in group	1
with individuals	2

b) *Organized*

I'd like to talk a little about more organized group activities – on what occasions are the children in this class divided into groups? (PROBE and LIST – e.g. team games, number work, projects, etc.)

In which of these cases do the children select the groups themselves? (LIST)

When group is selected by the children, is the handicapped child chosen:

more frequently than most	1
average number of times	2
less frequently than most	3
hardly ever	4

(If the answer is 3 or 4) why, in your opinion, is the child seldom chosen?

physical limitation of handicap	1
handicap itself unacceptable	2
child's behaviour unacceptable	3
other	4
don't know	9

What about the groups you select, do you have any special purpose in mind in placing X in a particular group? (PROBE to see whether aim is to assist child's social integration, if necessary, etc.)

Are there any group activities we haven't mentioned already which X's handicap excludes him from? (LIST)

What about class duties? Does X have a particular duty?

NO	0
YES	1
doesn't apply	9

(xvi) GENERAL EFFECT OF DISABILITY

Can you think of any other ways in which X's disability affects his relationship with other children which we haven't touched on yet? (LIST)

(If not mentioned above) do you feel that X makes use of his disability to get more attention or help from other children or from the staff?

hardly ever	0
sometimes	1
frequently	2

What about his attendance at school – does he seem to use his disability as an excuse for poor attendance?

NO	0
occasionally	1
sometimes	2

SECTION D (Teacher's management of the handicapped child)

I'd like now to look at things more from your point of view, and ask you about any difficulties you've encountered in coping with a handicapped child in your class and about ways in which you've coped with these since this information could be of great help to other teachers.

(xvii) INFORMATION AVAILABLE TO THE TEACHER

First of all, did you know you were going to have a handicapped child in your class before X arrived in it?

NO	0
YES	1

(IF YES) how did you know?

child moved up from lower class	1
informed by head	2
other source of information (specify)	3

(IF YES) did you know the nature of his handicap?

NO	0
YES	1

When you found out, did you feel at all worried about having X in your class?

not worried	0
a little worried	1
moderately worried	2

(If teacher was worried) can you remember exactly what you were worried about?
(PROBE – record answer verbatim if possible)

Do you know any other physically handicapped people?

NO	0
YES	1

(IF YES obtain details briefly)

When you were training as a teacher, did your training include anything specifically about handicapped children?

NO	0
YES	1
don't remember	9

IF YES, obtain details about CONTENT AND LENGTH of part of training relating to handicapped children)

Did anyone give you any information about this particular child?

NO	0
YES	1

(IF YES) was the information offered spontaneously or did you have to ask for it?

offered spontaneously	1
asked for	2

From what source, or sources, have you received information which has helped you to understand the child and his problems?

head	1
colleague	2
school medical officer	3
school nurse	4
parent	5
child himself	6
friends	7
reading	8
other	9

Do you feel satisfied with the amount of information you were given about X?

very satisfied	1
satisfied	2
not very satisfied	3
very dissatisfied	4

(IF NOT SATISFIED) what sort of information would have enabled you to understand X's problem better? (LIST)

(IF APPLICABLE) you said you were worried about having X in your class – how do you feel about it now?

not worried	0
only a little worried	1
moderately worried	2
very worried – doesn't really want child there	3

How often do you see the school doctor or another specialist to discuss X's problems?

never	0
less than once a term	1
termly	2
more than once a term	3

(xviii) TEACHER'S MANAGEMENT OF CLASS IN RELATION TO HANDICAPPED CHILD

Have you on any occasion talked to the other children as a group about X's handicap?

NO	0
YES	1

(IF YES) can you give me details of HOW and WHY you did this?

Do you feel that you have to spend too much time helping X at the expense of the other children?

NO	0
occasionally feel this	
often feel this	2

Are there any other problems we haven't talked about which X's presence in the class gives rise to?

NO	
YES	

(IF YES, LIST)

(xix) CONTACTS WITH PARENTS AND CHILD'S HOME

Does this school have a PTA?

NO	
YES	

Have you met either of X's parents, or another close relative?

NO	
parents	
other relative	

How many times in the autumn term of 1970 did you meet either of the
parents (or parent substitute)?

not at all	0
once	1
twice	2
more than twice	3

(If teacher has met parents) can you remember what you discussed with
them? (PROBE if necessary)

school work	1
behaviour	2
physical aspect of disability	3
social aspect of disability	4
school placement	5
other (specify)	6

What impression did you get of the mother's (or mother substitute's)
attitude to the handicap?

very sensible indeed	1
fairly sensible	2
overprotective	3
overdemanding	4
other (specify)	6

SECTION E (Placement)

Do you think this is the best type of school for X to be in at present?

NO	0
YES	1

(IF NO) where do you think X would be better placed?

ordinary school, but smaller classes etc.	1
day PH school	2
special boarding school (specify)	4
ESN school	5
other (specify)	6

Do you think X will manage to cope with an ordinary secondary school?

won't cope	0
might, but unlikely	1
will probably cope	2
will definitely cope	3
don't know	9

Well, that finishes the things I wanted to ask you. Thank you very much
for your help. I'm grateful to you for giving up so much time to discuss
all this.

Appendix P *The parent interview schedule*

Child's name.................................. Date.................... ....
Length of interview .... Who present at interview......

SECTION A (Health)

First of all I'd like to ask you some questions about X's health.

(i) GENERAL HEALTH

First of all, how has his general health been in the past year? Has he had
to see the doctor for anything?   NO   o
                                                         YES   I

(IF YES) can you remember how many times he has seen the doctor, and
why this was? (LIST REASONS)   number of times   ....
                                                       ....

(ii) HOSPITALIZATION

What about hospital – has he had to go to hospital or to a clinic in the
past year either as an in- or out-patient?
(PROBE – for check-up? Special tests? Why was this? How long was he
there? Which hospital?)
What about going to hospital when he was younger? How many times has
he been admitted altogether, not including the last year?
(PROBE – What for? When? For how long? Where?)

(iii) CLINICS

Has he/she ever been to any clinics?
(PROMPT: Such as the speech therapy clinic? child guidance clinic?)
                                                         NO   o
                                                         YES   I
(IF YES, PROBE: What was it for? When?)

(iv) SATISFACTION/DISSATISFACTION WITH MEDICAL SERVICES

Are you satisfied with the medical help you have received or are there
any things about the medical services which you are or were dissatisfied
about?   '   satisfied   o
                                    slightly dissatisfied   I
                                    moderately dissatisfied   2
                                    very dissatisfied   3

(IF DISSATISFIED, PROBE to see whether this related to, e.g. time taken to arrange visits, answer questions, etc., frequency of visits, time spent waiting, attitudes of staff, e.g. doctors and consultants. Specify.)

(v) SEPARATION FROM PARENT(S)

(You mentioned that X was admitted to hospital ....)
Has he/she ever been away from you or your husband for any (other) reason? Such as your going into hospital?

	NO	0
	YES	1

(IF YES obtain details including period of separation)

Or your husband going into hospital?

	NO	0
	YES	1

(IF YES obtain details)

Or X's going away to stay with relatives or friends for a time?

	NO	0
	YES	1

(IF YES obtain details)

Or for any other reasons?

	NO	0
	YES	1

(IF YES, obtain details)

SECTION B (Physical handicap)

(OMIT FOR CONTROLS)

I'd now like to ask you a few questions connected with X's handicap.

(i) MOBILITY

Does X have any difficulty if he has to walk a long way?

none	0
a little, but manages distances necessary for most things	1
walks moderate distances at reasonable pace	2
walks only short to moderate distances (20–200 yards) at a slow pace	3
walks only a few steps, or not at all	4

Does he have any difficulty with stairs?

none	0
slow, but manages unaided	1
needs assistance	2
can't manage	3

Does he ever mention any activities at school which he finds it difficult to take part in because of his (poor mobility)?
(LIST)

Or any he can't take part in at all because of this?
(LIST)

What about at home, or when you go out – what sort of things does his (poor mobility) make it difficult for him to do?
(PROMPT: travel on buses etc.)

When he is at home, does he wear or use:

	NO (0)	YES (1)
prosthesis L leg		
prosthesis R leg		
calipers		
elbow crutches		
armpit crutches		
a stick		
special boots or shoes		
other aid (specify)		

IF YES to any of the above, ask: does he ever use a wheelchair?

NO	0
occasionally	1
quite often	2
most of the time	3

What about physiotherapy – does he have any? NO/YES. If NO, obtain details about whether he ever had physiotherapy and when and why he stopped. If YES, obtain details about where he goes for this, when, how often, how he travels there, if there are any problems.

(ii) HAND CONTROL

What about hand control – does he have any difficulties? (OMIT if obvious difficulties)

NO	0
difficulties R	1
difficulties L	2
difficulties both	3

Would you describe him as a clumsy child for his age?

NO	0
sometimes clumsy	1
definitely clumsy	
definite handicap	

(IF X WEARS A PROSTHESIS, INCLUDE NEXT FOUR QUESTIONS OTHERWISE OMIT)

no prosthesis	0
prosthesis R arm and hand	
prosthesis R hand only	
prosthesis L arm and hand	
prosthesis L hand only	

Can you tell me for how much of the time he wears it when he's at home?

hardly ever	0
less than half	1
about half	2
more than half	3

What do you feel the main value of his prosthesis to be?
(PROBE to see whether functional or cosmetic and also parent's attitude to prosthesis).

no value	0
a little functional value	1
considerable functional value	2
cosmetic value	3

(PROBE to see whether child gets more tired when he wears it etc.)

Are there any tasks which X has difficulty with at school because of his..........?

NO	0
YES	1

(IF YES, LIST)
(IF NO, PROBE – writing? drawing? getting out books? etc.)

Do you think he gets sufficient help at school to cope with these difficulties?

gets no help	0
gets a little but not enough	1
gets sufficient	2
don't know	9

(iii) TOILETING

What about problems of toileting. ... Is X ever incontinent of the bladder? (NO/YES) Bowels? (NO/YES) (IF YES to either obtain details)

Does he have a neurogenic bladder? (NO/YES/POSSIBLY/DON'T KNOW) IF YES, has he had a urine diversion? (NO/YES)

IF NO diversion, does he wear any sort of appliance such as a bag, nappies etc. (NO/YES; IF YES, specify)

IF YES, can he cope with this himself when he's at school or does he need some help? (obtain details)
Also obtain details about accidents at school (wetting and/or soiling, their frequency, who helps child, frequency of urine infections, if any).

Does he have any problems at all at school connected with toileting? (obtain details).
IF YES, can you think of any ways in which the school could help with these difficulties?

(iv) DECOMPRESSION VALVE

What about a valve ... does he have one? (NO/YES) IF YES, have you had any problems over the last year with it?

(v) FEEDING

Does he require any special help at meals? (NO/YES)
(IF YES, what sort of things does he have difficulty with?)

Does he have dinner at school? (NO/YES)
(IF YES) who helps him when he's at school? (Specify)

(vi) DRESSING

Does he require help in dressing? (NO/YES)
(IF YES) does he need extra help with:
socks and shoes (NO/YES), clothes, upper part of body (NO/YES), clothes, lower part of body (NO/YES), fastenings (NO/YES), appliances (NO/YES)

(vii) HEARING

Do you think X needs a hearing aid? (NO/YES)
(IF YES) is one provided? (NO/YES)
(IF YES) does he wear it? (HARDLY EVER/SOMETIMES/ALL OR MOST OF THE TIME)
(IF YES) when he wears his aid, is his hearing: (GOOD/MODERATE/POOR)
(IF YES PROBE to see) who checks his aid? How often?

(viii) SIGHT

Does X wear glasses? (NO/YES)
(IF NO) do you think his sight is defective ? (NO/YES)
(IF HE WEARS GLASSES) do these correct his vision: (FULLY/ONLY PARTIALLY)

Does he have a squint? (NO/YES)

(ix) MISCELLANEOUS

Has he any other difficulties connected with his handicap which we haven't talked about yet?
(PROBE – perceptual problems, epilepsy, etc.)

Does he have any special equipment or furniture at school to help him? (PROMPT: such as..............who suggested this? Who provided it?)

Can you think of any (other) things of this kind which it would help him to have at school?

How does he feel about his handicap? How much does he worry about it? Or talk about it? How often?

[OBTAIN DETAILS IF POSSIBLE ABOUT CHILD'S ATTITUDE TO HANDICAP, later rate on four-point scale from 1 (very well adjusted) to 4 (very poorly adjusted)]

SECTION C (Pre-school and school experiences)

I'd like to ask you some (more) questions about X's schooling now. Did X ever go to a nursery school or class? (NO/YES)

(IF YES) was it run privately or by the local authority?

local authority	1
privately	2

(NOTE name of school and local authority)

Was it in his present school?

NO	0
YES	1

Has X attended a local authority day nursery?

NO	0
YES	1

Apart from this, has he had any other pre-school experience, such as a play group, private day nursery or anything like that?

NO	0
YES	1

(IF YES) what was the nature of the group?

How old was X when he first started school part-time (where appropriate) or full-time? (Specify. Include nursery school, but not day nursery.)

Since the age of five, how many schools has X attended? (count present school as one) . . . .
. . . .

When did he enter his present school? (MONTH . . . . . . YEAR . . . . . .).

When X first went to school, how soon did he settle down?

within month	1
within 1–3 months	2
still unsettled after 3	3

Is X happy at his present school?

not happy	0
not entirely happy	1
happy	2
very happy	3

How do you think X is getting on with his school work compared with other boys and girls of his age?

exceptionally well	1
above average	2
average	3
below average	4
poorly	5

Have you or your husband seen anyone at the school over the past year about X?

NO	0
YES	1

If YES, how many times?

once	1
2 or 3 times	2
more than 3 times	3

Whom did you see? [HEAD/CLASS TEACHER/OTHER (SPECIFY)]

Did you ask if you could see them, or did they ask to see you?

contact initiated by parent	1
contact initiated by school	2
don't know	3

Are you satisfied with the progress X is making at school?

not satisfied	0
fairly satisfied	1
satisfied	2

(OMIT NEXT THREE QUESTIONS FOR CONTROLS) Has the class teacher of anyone else at school been particularly helpful and understanding about X's handicap?

NO	0
YES	1

(IF YES) in what ways?

Do you feel dissatisfied with the school in any way at all? Whatever you say will be of course entirely confidential.

satisfied	0
slightly dissatisfied	1
moderately dissatisfied	2
very dissatisfied	3

(IF DISSATISFIED, PROBE if necessary for reasons, and specify these below)

(Apart from the particular points we've discussed) are you generally satisfied with his placement at this school, or do you think he'd benefit more from being somewhere else?

satisfied	0
elsewhere	1

(IF ELSEWHERE, specify)
(Record reasons, if alternative placement desired)
Have you decided yet where you'd like X to go when he leaves his present school? (NO/YES – IF YES, specify)

I'm quite interested in learning what parents feel about boarding schools – how would you have felt if X had had to go to a boarding school instead of to his present one?

agreeable	1
neutral	2
not very pleased	3
strongly against	4
don't know	9

What about special schools – in particular schools for physically handicapped children. There are several questions I'd like to ask you about these. First of all, has it at any time been suggested by anyone from the health or education services that X should go to a special school?

NO	0
YES	1

(IF YES) when was this? Was it before he went to school or was it a question of transferring him?

suggested initial placement	1
suggested transfer from os	2

Who suggested this?
(SPECIFY, as accurately as possible)

How did you (and your husband) feel about this?

in favour	0
uncommitted	1
slightly against	2
moderately against	3
strongly against	4

(Record answer VERBATIM. Also PROBE to see if parents agreed in feelings)

(IF AGAINST) why did you not want X to go to a special school? (Record VERBATIM, and PROBE to find out why these attitudes are held – e.g. Who told you this? Do you know anyone with a child at a special school? etc.)

denial that child handicapped enough to go there	0
lower educational standards, fear child would fall behind	1
association of special schools with 'backward children'	2
feeling that stigma of mental handicap is attached to special school	3
didn't want boarding education and no day special school available	4
wants child to attend same school as sibs	5
positive social advantages in mixing with non-handicapped children	6
fear that behaviour or emotional difficulties might arise (specify)	7
Other (specify)	8
very vague answer	9

Did you take any action when it was suggested that X should go to a special school?

NO	0
YES	1

(IF YES) what did you do?
(PROBE to find out WHO parents contacted, how long the uncertainty went on, the extent of their anxiety, who supported their decision to send X to an OS etc.)

(IF IT WAS NEVER suggested that X should go to a special school, ask) what would your feelings have been if someone had suggested X should go to a special school?

(Record VERBATIM)

in favour	0
uncommitted	1
slightly against	2
moderately against	3
strongly against	4

(IF AGAINST) why would you not have liked X to have gone to a special school? (On the actual interview schedule the same response categories were listed as previously.)

SECTION D (Social adjustment)

I'd like to ask you a few questions about X's friends now – who he plays with and so on. Has he got many friends at school?

NO	0
a few	1
several	2
don't know	9

(If 1 or 2 ask: do you know the names of any of them?)

What about a special friend – does he have one at school?

NO	0
YES	1
don't know	9

Does he see much of his school friends outside school hours? (If interview is in the winter, add 'during the spring or summer')

NO	0
YES	1
don't know	9

(IF YES) how much time each week does he usually spend with them? Does he just see them once or twice a week, or more often?

once or twice weekly	1
3 or 4 times weekly	2
daily	3

What sort of things do they do together?
(OBTAIN DETAILS)

What about other friends – does he have any friends who live near here but who go to different schools?

NO	0
YES	1

(OBTAIN DETAILS – how many? A special friend? How old are they? How often does he see them?)

Where do they usually play?
Does he go round to any of his friends' homes to play? How often?

never	0
once or twice weekly	1
more than once or twice weekly	2
don't know	9

How many times last week did he go to a friend's house?

not at all	0
once or twice	1
more than once or twice	2
don't know	9

When he goes out, do you always know where he's going?

NO	0
YES	1

How long do you let him stay away from the house during the holidays without an adult or older child without worrying about what he's up to?

don't allow him to be out alone	0
up to 1 hour	1
1–4 hours	2
over 4 hours	3

Does he ever bring his friends here?

NO	0
YES	1

How many times last week did he bring a friend here?

none	0
once or twice	1
more than twice	2
don't know	9

(IF APPLICABLE)
What about his brother(s) and/or sister(s)? Does he spend much time playing with them?

NO	0
YES	1

How does he get on with them? Do they squabble much? (obtain details if unusual behaviour)

Is he jealous at all of the others?

NO	0
YES	1

(IF YES, obtain details – how does he show it? When did he start to be jealous?)

How does he get on with you?

What about your husband?

Do you ever all go out together as a family?

NO	0
YES	1

(IF YES) where do you go? What sort of things do you do?
(PROBE – Trips? Sport? Cinema? etc.)

Does X have any special time for going to bed in the evening? At what time does he usually go?

Do you let him stay up later sometimes? To watch a special TV programme for instance?

NO	0
YES	1

Can we go back to talk about the other children at school for a moment – what about *teasing* – does he ever get teased?

NO	0
YES	1
don't know	9

(IF YES) how do you get to know about this?

parent observes	1
child complains	2
sibs report it	3
others report it	4

How often does he get teased?

only occasionally	0
once or twice a week	1
several times a week	2
daily	3

Do you think this is more than most children get teased?

not more	0
more	1

What does he get teased about?
(PROBE to see whether related to handicap, antisocial behaviour, etc.)
(LIST)

Will you tell me as much as you can remember about the last occasion on which he got teased?
(PROBE for WHEN this happened, CIRCUMSTANCES triggering it off, NATURE of teasing)

How did he react on that occasion? How does he usually react?

What about you? – how do you feel when you hear that X has been teased?
(Record VERBATIM if possible)

Apart from actual teasing, do the other children show much curiosity about X's handicap?

NO	0
at first, but no longer	1
still curious	2
excessively curious	3

(IF YES) how does X react to their curiosity?
(PROBE to see whether X is upset by it, etc.)

What about bullying – has X ever been bullied? (NO/YES) (IF YES obtain details)

Can you think of any (other) ways in which X's handicap affects his relationship with other children which we haven't talked about?
(LIST)

SECTION E (Behaviour)

Perhaps I could ask you now in a little more detail about X's behaviour and feelings. Do you think that he has any behaviour or emotional difficulties?

NO	0
YES	1

(IF YES) do you think that the difficulties are more than most boys/girls of X's age have?

not more	1
vague or indefinite	2
more	3
not known	9

What sort of difficulties has he got?
(At this stage get a listing only. Do not probe for details. After parent stops, ask 'Does he have any other difficulties?' until parent says 'No'.)
(LIST)

What do you think these difficulties might be due to?
(Write down the informant's answer VERBATIM as far as possible. Encourage informant to offer opinion. But do *not* give specific probe.)

Have you gone to anyone for help or advice about these difficulties?

NO	0
YES	1

(IF YES) who did you see? Where did you go?
(SPECIFY WHERE, SINCE WHEN, ON WHOSE SUGGESTION, WHETHER STILL ATTENDING)

(IF NO) do you feel you need or would like help from anyone about X's difficulties?

not wanted	0
wanted	1
vague or uncertain	2
not known	9

THE INTERVIEWER SHOULD NOW OBTAIN A DETAILED ACCOUNT OF ALL THE BEHAVIOURAL OR EMOTIONAL DIFFICULTIES MENTIONED EARLIER BY THE INFORMANT. QUESTION FOR DESCRIPTION OF ACTUAL BEHAVIOUR. THE INTERVIEWER SHOULD ALSO ASK ABOUT:
Where the behaviour is shown:
SEVERITY of the behaviour, FREQUENCY, DATE OF ONSET, PRECIPITANTS, COURSE of behaviour over last year.

Now may I ask you in a bit more detail about the (behaviour or difficulties) you mentioned earlier.

What exactly does he do? Could you please describe it for me?

(Suggested possible PROBE)
Is he like this when he's at school? ... or staying with friends and relations? When was he first like this? How often does he show this behaviour now? What seems to bring it on? What makes it better? Has it been getting better or worse over the last year? In what way?

FOR INFERENTIAL ITEMS LIKE 'WORRIES' ASK: what is it about his behaviour that makes you think he's (worrying etc.)?

I would like to check now whether X has shown a number of other difficulties which many boys and girls have.

(IF NO BEHAVIOURAL OR EMOTIONAL DIFFICULTIES HAVE BEEN REPORTED BY THE INFORMANT, ASK:)
Perhaps I could just check now whether he has had any of the number of other health or behaviour problems often shown by boys and girls?
(Proceed with list of items but do not ask items already covered, and do not probe on behaviour which was present more than a year ago. On others obtain as detailed as possible an account of the behaviour in question. Probe about where shown, severity, frequency, onset dates, precipitants.)
Probe on: where shown, severity, frequency, onset date, precipitants.

Does he ever have severe headaches?	NO	O
(IF YES) is he sick with them?	YES	I

What about stomach aches?	NO	O
(IF YES) does he vomit?	YES	I

(PROBES) what time of day does he get them? Does he get them more at weekends or during the week? What about during school holidays?

Does he ever wet his bed?	NO	O
	YES	I

(IF YES) how often does he wet the bed? Has he always done so ... or when did he start?

Does he ever wet his pants, or are there ever any accidents?

NO	O
YES	I

(IF YES) how often. Is there any difficulty with sleeping? Always ask:

Does he have any difficulty getting off to sleep?	NO	O
	YES	I

(PROBES) does he ever wake in the night? Or scream ... or come to your bed? Or have nightmares?

How active is X? Would you say that he is an unusually overactive or restless child?

(IF YES) how does he show it?
(PROBES) will he stay still if expected to? Can he stay still for as long as an hour if he is doing something he is interested in?

If child is unable to stay still, ask: does he get upset if he is forced to be still even for a little while?	NO	O
	YES	I

Does he stutter or stammer or have any other difficulty with speech?

NO	O
YES	I

(IF YES) what is it like? How often? When is it worst? When did it start? Is he having speech therapy? Where? How often?

Does X suck his thumb – or anything else, pencils, clothing, things like that?

NO	O
YES	I

(IF YES) what does he suck? How often? Does he tend to do it at any particular time? When did he start doing it?

Does X bite his nails . . . or pencils, or anything else?

NO	O
YES	I

What about fits . . . has X ever had a fit or convulsions after the first year – or any blank spells?

NO	O
YES	I

(IF YES) obtain details e.g. When? How often? What happened? Does X get treatment? etc

Is he usually happy or miserable?

happy	O
miserable	I
other (specify)	5

(IF UNHAPPY) how does he show it? What does he do? How often is he like that? Does anything special seem to make him unhappy?

Does he get worried easily?

NO	O
YES	I

(IF YES) how does he show it? What sort of things does he worry about? How often does he get worried?

How easily does he get cross or irritable? Does he tend to sulk?

NO	O
YES	I

(IF YES) how does he show that he's cross? What sort of things makes him cross or sulky? How often is he like that?

Does he ever have temper tantrums?

NO	O
YES	I

(IF YES) what are they like? Does he scream? . . . or lie on the floor . . . or break things? How long do they last? What seems to bring them on?

Does he have tantrums when at school . . . or when with relatives and friends? How do you deal with them?

Does he tend to be overfussy about things? Like having clean hands or a clean plate? or about the way he puts on his clothes? or about anything else? In what way?

NO	O
YES	I

Does he get worried or frightened in certain situations? or are there special things that frighten him? (PROBE for fears such as fear of the dark, going to school, meeting new people, dogs, etc. Obtain details about whether specific anxiety, panic attack, avoid situation because anxious, etc.)

SECTION F (Social background)

This section of the interview schedule covered the usual questions asked in surveys of this kind, including the composition of the household and family, parental occupations, housing and contacts and satisfaction with the social and welfare services.

Author Index

General Index

absence from school, 15, 58, 184, 192–4, 225
achondroplasia, 8, 35, 133, 313, 339
adaptations to schools, *see* school design
adolescence, 17, 303
advisers for special education, 222, 238–9, 258, 263, 266–7, 275, 298–9, 302
age, 27, 169, 200, 296, 315
aids, special, 217–20, 239, 246, 250, 265–6, 274, 298–9, 302
amyotonia congenita, 35, 52, 339
ancillary help, *see* personal assistance
architecture, *see* school design
arithmetic, 181–5, 208, 226–7, 295–6
Arnold-Chiari malformation, 26
arthrogryposis, 35, 241–2, 339
ascertainment, 5, 49, 62
assessment, 5, 48–50, 62, 66, 235, 302
Association for Special Education, 300
Association for Spina Bifida and Hydrocephalus, 233, 241
ataxia, 24, *see also* cerebral palsy
athetosis, 24, *see also* cerebral palsy
attitudes: of child to handicap, *see* self-concept
of peers, *see* peer relationships
of parents, *see* parental attitudes
of the public, 12–15, 89–95, 98
of teachers, 65–6, 72, 228–31, 236, 247, 275, 280–2, 297–8

behavioural disorders:
antisocial disorders, 141–5, 195, 293–4, 323

assessment of, 31, 141
and attainment, 184, 194–5
definition of, 140–1
individual items of deviant behaviour, 145–9, 324–7
in infants, 71, 148–50, 327
neurotic disorders, 141–5, 195, 293–4, 323
and neurological abnormalities, 136–40, 144–5, 147–8, 326
and peer relationships, 111–12, 146
reported by parents, 165
see also emotional problems
Bender Visual Motor Gestalt Test, 27
blindness, 6, 13, 15, 93
brain disorder, *see* neurological abnormalities
broken homes, 42–3
bullying, 116

categories of handicapped children, 5, 11, 297
cerebral palsy, 8–11, 23–5, 35, 39–40, 48, 62, 93, 96, 106, 110–11, 137, 139, 168, 171–3, 176, 180, 183–4, 191, 193, 200–1, 205, 239–40, 243, 246, 257, 278, 283–6, 291, 294, 311, 313, 319–20, *see also* neurological abnormalities
class size, 45, 171, 202–3, 296, 315
clumsiness, 25
computer programme, 199–203, 337
concentration, poor, 71, 77, 139–40, 147–50, 184–5, 204, 225, 227, 294, 324–5, 327
congenital abnormalities, 9–10, 35, 102, 106, 120, 168, 193, 201–2,